★ ✦ ★

# Britain's Greatest TV Comedy Moments

★ ✦ ★

# Britain's Greatest TV Comedy Moments

### Edited by

## LOUIS BARFE

Atlantic Books

London

✷ ✦ ✷

First published in hardback in Great Britain in 2012 by Atlantic Books,
an imprint of Atlantic Books Ltd.

Copyright © Louis Barfe, 2012

Further copyright information can be found on p. 403.

1 2 3 4 5 6 7 8 9

A CIP catalogue record for this book is available from the British Library.

ISBN: 978 085789 123 5

Text design and layout: carrdesignstudio.com
Printed in Great Britain by the MPG Books Group

Atlantic Books
An imprint of Atlantic Books Ltd
Ormond House
26–27 Boswell Street
London
WC1N 3JZ
www.atlantic-books.co.uk

✷ ✦ ✷

# Contents

# Introduction

If you're looking at this book in the shop, it's safe to assume you like comedy. If you are the owner of this book, it is even safer to assume that you like comedy. For the purposes of this introduction, I shall assume that you're not a humourless masochist, and that you weren't bought the book as a present by someone who hates you as much as you hate humour.

Comedy has been a feature of television from the days of John Logie Baird's experiments, but the forms we know – primarily the sketch show and the situation comedy – both emerged after the Second World War, as BBC Television was re-establishing itself at Alexandra Palace. The first situation comedy on British television was *Family Affairs*, which ran for one series in late 1949 and early 1950. It was written by Eric Maschwitz – who also penned the lyrics of 'These Foolish Things' and 'A Nightingale Sang in Berkeley Square'. While *Family Affairs* can claim to be the first, many would argue that the sitcom as we know it was pioneered by Galton and Simpson. Certainly, Ray and Alan made great strides in taking television comedy away from the staginess that had pervaded it in its earliest years, towards a greater naturalism. Meanwhile, British television's first real sketch show, as opposed to a variety bill, was Terry-Thomas's own series *How Do You View?* It ran for five series and a special between 1949 and 1953, and reports suggest that it was a clever series, pushing the limited technology to its boundaries, as well as sending up the medium on which it appeared. Sadly, not a single second of it survives, only scripts and production stills.

Anyone assembling a book with the title *Britain's Greatest TV Comedy Moments* is setting themselves up for a fall. Everyone reading this book will be able to name favourite sketches or scenes that have been omitted. This is inevitable for a number of reasons. Firstly, humour is subjective. Something that makes you or me roar with laughter might leave other people scratching their heads. Secondly, being a caring sort of outfit, Atlantic Books didn't want to be responsible for anyone developing a hernia from lifting this book. Thirdly, maybe some of the greatest TV comedy moments are lost to posterity. How do we know that *How Do You View?* wouldn't be worthy of inclusion? In fact, I am convinced that the 1960 BBC one-off *Fred Emney Picks a Pop* could be one of the greatest TV comedy moments of all. Fred Emney satirizing the popular music business? It can only be pure gold. Unfortunately, the videotape on which it was recorded was re-used shortly after its single transmission, so I'll never know for certain. Finally, some agents either came back to our ever-so polite requests and offers of money with a flat 'no' or pretended to be a Chinese takeaway in the hope that we'd leave them alone. If you notice any surprising absences, blame them, whether they were responsible or not. That'll teach the blighters.

What this is, then, is a representative spread of the highlights of television comedy over the last fifty or so years. If some of the choices seem slightly eccentric, that's because this book is a trade-off between the nice people at Atlantic Books' understandable desire to highlight the most popular scenes of a particular show and my own anorakish inclination to avoid the obvious at all costs. For example, I wanted to illustrate the primacy of *Python* with 'Ethel the Frog', a spoof of a current affairs programme based loosely on the saga of the Kray twins, but the publishers made a convincing case for the 'Dead Parrot' sketch . I let that one pass in exchange for being allowed to include a scene from *Chance in a Million*, a series that, in the days before DVD, I used as a litmus test of comedy fandom. If you remembered it fondly, we could be friends. Viewed again, it still stands up superbly and reads well on the page. And while I have never once found Ricky Gervais funny, clearly *The Office* has to be in here somewhere.

Another obstacle is the fact that some of the most memorable moments in TV comedy are visual. I would have been failing in my duty if I had chosen to represent *Only Fools and Horses* with a blank page save for the words 'Del Boy falls through the bar' – and yet really nothing more is required. Many of Marty Feldman's set-piece sketches contain little or no dialogue. They're brilliant, but they don't really work on the page. Feeling very strongly that Feldman had to be represented within these pages, I plumped for a more verbal example.

Just in case you're wondering about my credentials for compiling a book like this – I've been obsessed with comedy ever since I first laid eyes on a TV set as a child. One of my earliest memories is of a Thames Television sketch show called *What's On Next?* It starred the great Barry Cryer and Anna Dawson, the less-great Jim Davidson and the unflappable William Franklyn. Soon after that, with guidance from my *Goons* fanatic of a grandfather, I discovered Spike Milligan and begged to be allowed to stay up for *Q8* and *Q9*. Since those formative years, I've remained a voracious viewer of comedy – I've seen a lot and forgotten very little of it – and have ended up writing about my obsession for a living ...

This will account for some of the more obscure choices in the following pages. *End of Part One* is the missing link between *Monty Python* and alternative comedy. It tackled the mild racism of situation comedies like *Mind Your Language* mercilessly, while remaining joyously surreal. For some unknown reason, it was shown on Sunday teatime, rather than later in the evening where it might have stood a chance of becoming a cult. It's a fine series, as you'd expect from Andrew Marshall and David Renwick, and one fully deserving of a DVD release, as I hope the extract included here will prove.

Right. I think it's time to let the comedy moments commence.

# Hancock (1961)

## 'The Blood Donor'

### Ray Galton and Alan Simpson

*Hancock's Half Hour* wasn't television's first situation comedy, but it was the one that set the tone for the genre in Britain. Having begun on BBC Radio in 1954, the television series first aired in 1956, and after six successful series at 23 Railway Cuttings, East Cheam, with shifty lodger and criminal mastermind Sid James, Tony Hancock moved alone to an Earl's Court bedsit for his final BBC Television run. With each show now running to twenty-five minutes, the title was changed from *Hancock's Half Hour* to *Hancock*, and the penultimate show, 'The Blood Donor', remains the best known of all Ray Galton and Alan Simpson's scripts. Justifiably, as it encapsulates the Anthony Aloysius St John Hancock character perfectly. The pomposity, insecurity, ignorance, arrogance and dishonesty are all present and correct. In the days before commercial video releases, it achieved greater longevity and memorability than most other Hancock shows thanks to being recorded for an LP by Pye Records shortly after the original TV transmission.

However, the show was one of the most problematic in Hancock's TV career. The comedian had been involved in a car accident driving home from the previous week's recording (for 'The Bowmans') and a concussion meant that he was unable to learn his lines properly. The recording went ahead with cue cards and teleprompters, as becomes clear from a close study of Hancock's eyeline. Previously a diligent learner of scripts, Hancock came to rely on such devices for the rest of his career, until his sad demise in Australia in 1968.

**Series:** *Hancock* (BBC TV, six shows, 1961; preceded by six series of *Hancock's Half Hour*, fifty-eight shows, 1956–60), show 5.

**Original transmission:** BBC TV, Friday 23 June 1961, 8 p.m.

**Cast in excerpt:** Tony Hancock (Hancock), June Whitfield (Nurse), Patrick Cargill (Dr McTaggart)

**Producer/director:** Duncan Wood

## INT. BLOOD DONOR DEPARTMENT, LONDON HOSPITAL - DAY

Several patients sit reading magazines, awaiting attention. At the end of the room are some screens, behind which the blood donations take place. TONY enters and approaches the NURSE at the reception desk.

> NURSE
>
> Good afternoon sir.

> TONY
>
> Good afternoon. I have come in answer to your advert on the wall next to the Eagle Laundry in Pelham Road.

> NURSE
>
> An advert? Pelham Road?

> TONY
>
> Yes. Your poster. You must have seen it. There's a nurse pointing at you, a Red Cross Lady I believe, with a moustache and a beard.

> [NURSE looks offended]

> TONY
>
> Pencilled in of course. You must know it. You must know it, it's one of yours, next to 'Hands Off Cuba', just above the cricket stumps. It says 'Your blood can save a life.'

> NURSE
>
> Oh I see, you wish to become a blood donor.

> TONY
>
> I certainly do. I've been thinking about this for a long time. Something for the benefit of the country as a whole. 'What should it be?' I thought. 'Become a blood donor or join the Young Conservatives?' But as I'm not looking for a wife and I can't play table tennis, here I am. A body full of good British blood and raring to go.

> NURSE
>
> Yes quite. Well now, if you'd take a seat, I'll just take a few particulars.

TONY sits down opposite her and rolls his sleeve down. She takes a form and a pen.

> NURSE
>
> Can I have your name?

> TONY
>
> Hancock, Anthony Hancock. Twice candidate for the County Council elections, defeated, Hon Sec. British Legion, Earl's Court branch, treasurer of the darts team and the outings committee.

> NURSE
>
> I only want the name …

> TONY
>
> We're going to Margate this year by boat. If there are any young nurses like yourself who would care to join us, we would be more than happy to accommodate you.

> NURSE
>
> Thank you, I'll bear it in mind. Date of birth?

> TONY
>
> Er, yes. Shall we say the 12th of May 19— or … I always remember the 12th of May, it was Coronation Day you know, 1936.

> NURSE
>
> You're only twenty-five?

> TONY
>
> No, no, the Coronation was in 1936, I was born a little before that in, er, 19—, er …

Hancock's previous BBC Television series had all come from the BBC's Lime Grove or Riverside Studios, but this final run was made at the newly opened BBC Television Centre. Galton and Simpson made reference to this by setting one of the shows in a stuck lift at the showpiece complex.

[Makes a quick mental calculation]

Is all this really necessary?

NURSE

I'm afraid so. The 12th of May …

TONY

Yes. I always remember that, the Coronation, we all got a day off school, did you? And we got a cup and saucer in a box and a bar of soap. Very good, I've still got that, and a spoon for the Silver Jubilee, and a biscuit tin with their pictures on …

NURSE

How old are you?

TONY
[Disgruntled]

Thirty-five.

NURSE

Thank you. Nationality?

TONY

You've got nothing to worry about there. It's the blood you're thinking about isn't it? British. Undiluted for twelve generations. One hundred per cent Anglo Saxon with perhaps just a dash of the Viking, but nothing else has crept in. No, anybody who gets any of this will have nothing to complain about, there's aristocracy in there you know, you want to watch who you're giving it to. It's like motor oil. It doesn't mix, if you get my meaning.

NURSE

Mr Hancock, when a blood transfusion is being given, the family background is of no consequence.

TONY

Oh come now, surely you don't expect me to believe that. I mean after all East is East, really …

NURSE

And blood is blood, Mr Hancock. It is classified by groups not by accidents of birth.

TONY

I did not come here for a lecture on Communism
young lady.

NURSE

I happen to be a Conservative.

TONY

Then kindly behave like one, madame.

NURSE

Have you had any of these diseases?

She hands him a printed list. TONY reads it. He tries to
remember a couple of the diseases. Looks uncomfortable at
another one. Looks completely puzzled at another one. Hands
the list back.

TONY

No I haven't. Especially that one. I told you
before, you have nothing to fear from me, I am
perfectly healthy. Fit? Fit? If we'd had our own
rocket, I could have been the first one up there,
I had my name down for the Blue Streak, but no,
we missed our chance again. It's not right having
those foreigners hurtling round up there, you mark
my words—

NURSE

Mr Hancock.

TONY

Eh? Oh I beg your pardon, I get carried away over
things like that, it's a sore point with me. We
ready now then?

[Rolls up his sleeve again]

NURSE

Just one more thing. Have you given any blood
before?

TONY

Given? No. Spilt? Yes. Yes, there's a good few
drops lying about on the battlefields of Europe.
Are you familiar with the Ardennes? I well
remember Von Runstedt's last push. Tiger Harrison

and myself being in a forward position were cut
off behind the enemy lines. 'Captain Harrison,' I
said, 'Yes sir?' he said. 'Jerry's overlooked us,'
I said. 'Where shall we head for?' 'Berlin,' he
said. 'Right,' I said. 'Last one in the Reichstag
is a sissy.' So we set off, got there three days
before the Russians.

                    NURSE
You've never been a blood donor before?

                    TONY
No. So there we were, surrounded by stormtroopers.
'Kamerad! Kamerad!' they said.

                    NURSE
             [Hands him a card]

If you'll just sit over there with the others,
doctor will call you when he's ready.

                    TONY
Thank you. So we started rounding them up and—

[She gets up, puts some papers under her arm and leaves him]

     Oh.

TONY goes and sits down between two of the other donors. He
looks at them.

Hancock's next TV series was made for commercial television company ATV,
without the aid of Galton and Simpson's scripts. Unfortunately, the standard of
the series was patchy, and represented Hancock's last foray into proper situation
comedy until the Australian series he was making at the time of his death. The
1967 series *Hancock's* was a slightly dressed-up variety show, with Hancock as
the proprietor of a down-at-heel nightclub.

TONY

Well, I think it's a grand job we're all doing …
Yes, I think we can all be very proud of ourselves
… Some people, all they do is take, take, take out
of life, never put anything back. Well, that's
not my way of living. Never has been. You're only
entitled to take out of life what you are prepared
to put into it. Do you get a badge for doing this?

MAN

No, I don't think so.

TONY

Pity. We should have something for people to pick
us out by.

MAN

It's not really important, is it? As long as we
give the blood and help someone, that's the main
thing.

TONY

Oh well, quite, quite. As long as they get their
corpuscles, quite. That's reward in itself I
agree. No names, no pack drill, quite. I just
think we ought to get a badge as well. I mean,
nothing grand, a little enamelled thing. A little
motto, that's all. Nothing pretentions. 'He gaveth
for others so that others may live.' I mean, we
are do-gooders. We should get something for it.

MAN

What do you want? Money?

TONY

Don't be vulgar. I'm a great believer in charity.
Help others, that's my motto. I contribute to
every flag day going. The lapels of my suits are
always the first things to go. Covered in holes
they are. Yes, I always give what I can.

[Brings out his diary]

Here, you look at this. It's all in my diary.
Congo relief, two and six. Self-denial week, one
and eight. Lifeboat day, sixpence. Arab refugees,

one and two. It's all down here, yes. I do what
I can. My conscience is clear. Finally, when I'm
called by the great architect, and they say 'What
did you do?' I'll just bring my book out, I'll
say, 'Here you are, mate. Add that lot up.' I've
got nothing to fear. I could go tomorrow. Oh yes.

He takes out a pencil from the spine of the diary and makes
an entry.

> TONY
> June 1961, gave blood for the needy. How much do
> you reckon that's worth? Three quid? Just to keep
> the book straight. Just for my own benefit. I'm
> not trying to put a price on it.

The MAN reacts in disgust. TONY puts the diary back and
relaxes, very pleased with himself.

> TONY
> Do you come here often?

> MAN
> This is my twelfth time.

> TONY
> Well, there's no need to boast about it, old man.
> How much did you give to the Arab refugees?

> MAN
> Oh, really.

> TONY
> No, come on. How much? You're shouting about how
> much blood you've given. How much did you give to
> the Arab refugees?

> MAN
> If you must know, I gave five pounds.

> TONY
> Oh. Well, some people are better placed than
> others. I would have given more, but I have
> commitments. I can't afford to go around chucking
> fivers all over the place. I have to send my
> mother thirty bob a week.

MAN

Well, let's forget about it, shall we?

TONY

Well yes, alright.

MAN

I find the whole thing most distasteful.

TONY

Alright, alright.

NURSE

Mr Johnson, we're ready for you now.

MAN

Yes, thank you.

The MAN gets up and leaves. TONY turns to a large WOMAN sitting on his other side.

TONY

A bit of a bighead, isn't he? If you can't give to charity without shouting about it from the rooftops. Is this your first time?

WOMAN

I come here every six months, for the last twelve years.

TONY

Oh well, you've got a bit to spare, haven't you? Too much blood is as bad as too little, I always say.

WOMAN

Are you trying to be offensive?

TONY

No, nothing personal. Just an observation. I think it's very laudable to give so much. Of course, some people make it up quicker than others. I mean, I expect you're a big eater. It doesn't take you long to recoup the, er … that is to say … they've certainly brightened up these hospitals, haven't they? Of course, it's the health service that's done that. They spend more money on paint.

Out of every thirteen and sixpence paid in,
sixpence ha'penny goes up on the wall. Well, it's
worth it, I mean.

> NURSE
> Mrs Forsythe? We're ready for you. Would you come
> this way?

The WOMAN gets up and follows the NURSE. TONY calls after her.

> TONY
> Best of luck. Just think Cliff Richard might get
> yours. That'd slow him down a bit.

TONY settles back in his chair and looks for something to do.
He starts humming, crosses his legs, bangs his knee with the
side of his hand to make his leg jump in reflex. It doesn't
work. He bangs it harder. It still doesn't work. He bangs
it quickly, hurting his knee and the side of his hand, but
his knee still doesn't jump up. He looks puzzled at this.
He takes his pulse. He can't find it. He feels all round his
wrist and on the side of his temple. He still can't find it.
He puts his hand over his heart and smiles in relief as he
feels it beating. He looks at the posters around the room.

> TONY
> Drink-a-pint-a-milk-a-day. Drink-a-pint-a-milk-a-
> day. Drink-a-pint-a-milk-a-day.

The NURSE comes back and sits at her desk, a few yards away
from TONY. He hasn't noticed her.

> TONY
> Coughs and sneezes spread diseases.
>
> [Sings to the tune of *Deutschland Über Alles*]
>
> Coughs and sneezes spread diseases, trap the germs
> in your handkerchief, coughs and sneezes spread—

He catches sight of the NURSE who is looking at him coldly.
He smiles in embarrassment.

> TONY
> I, er, felt rather lonely sitting here by myself.
> It's funny what you do when you're on your own,
> isn't it?

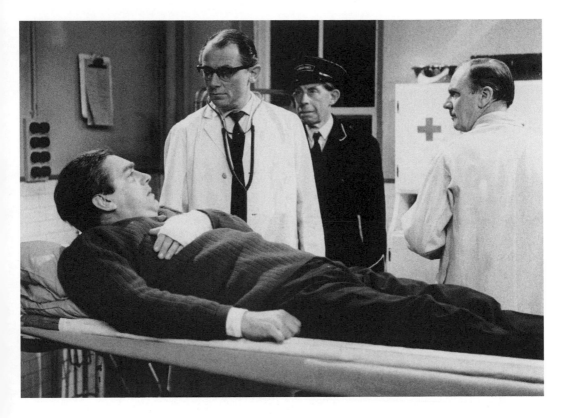

[Laughs in embarrassment]

Is, er, is this a normal sort of day for you then?
Do you get many people in normally, or is this,
er, er, normal?

NURSE
[Without looking up from her work]

It's about average.

TONY
Yes, yes, quite. Yes indeed. My word, yes. Of
course, it's a vocation, nursing, I've always
said that. One of the highest callings a woman
can aspire to. It's not the money, is it? Strange,
isn't it? The different values we place on society.
I mean, you take modelling. You get some skinny
bird, up in the West End, all bones and salt
cellars, dragging a piece of fur along a platform,
fifty quid a week. And then there's you lot,

dedicated, three years training, humping great trolley loads of mince about all day long. It's not right. There's Adam Faith earning ten times as much as the prime minister. Is that right? Is that right? Mind you, I suppose it depends on whether you like Adam Faith and what your politics are.

The NURSE has ignored TONY all through his speech, concentrating on her work.

> TONY
>
> I understand you get a cup of tea and a biscuit afterwards?

> NURSE
>
> Yes.

> TONY
>
> But no badge.

> NURSE
>
> No.

> TONY
>
> They're taking their time in there, aren't they? Everything's all right, I suppose?

> NURSE
>
> Yes.

> TONY
>
> Oh, I just wondered. I just though some of the poor devils might pass out at the sight of a needle. I've seen it before. Men built like oak trees, keeling over like saplings in a hurricane. It was quite nasty.

> NURSE
>
> Needles don't bother you, then?

> TONY
>
> Me? No. I've had too many of them, my dear. I've had the lot. I've got arms like pin cushions. Yes, I reckon I've had a syringeful of everything that's going, in my time. Needles the size of drainpipes some of them. You name it, I've had it.

A SECOND NURSE comes out of the door.

> SECOND NURSE
> Mr Hancock, Doctor is ready for you now.

> TONY
> Who? Me? Um, now. Yes, well. There's nobody else
> before me? I'm in no hurry.

> [Looks round]

> Does anybody want to go first?

> SECOND NURSE
> There isn't anybody else. You're the last one.

> TONY
> Oh, well, this is it then.

> [To the first NURSE]

> Here we go, then. Over the top.

The NURSE makes a Churchillian V-sign at TONY.

> TONY
> [Confidentially to SECOND NURSE]

> What's he like on the needle, this bloke, is he
> steady handed?

> SECOND NURSE
> There's nothing to worry about.

> TONY
> Is he in a good mood?

> SECOND NURSE
> You'll be quite alright. Doctor MacTaggart is an
> excellent doctor.

> TONY
> MacTaggart, he's a Scotsman. Ah well, that's
> alright. Marvellous doctors, the Scots. Like
> their engineers, you know. First rate. It's the
> porridge, you know. Lead on MacDuff.

# *That Was The Week That Was* (1963)

## 'But, my dear ...'

## Peter Shaffer

**Series:** *That Was The Week That Was* (BBC TV, thirty-seven shows over two series , 1962–3), series 1, show 12.

**Original transmission:** BBC TV, Saturday 9 February 1963, 10.35 p.m.

**Transmitted live:** Studio TC2, BBC Television Centre, 9 February 1963.

**Cast in excerpt:** Lance Percival (Senior Official), David Kernan (Junior Official).

**Producer/director:** Ned Sherrin.

*That Was The Week That Was*, or *TW3* as it was almost universally known, represented British television's first successful attempt at satire. Until the late 1950s, even news bulletins were hamstrung by the so-called fourteen-day rule, which prevented broadcasts about anything that had been debated in Parliament in the previous fortnight. Even after the rule was relaxed, topical comedy was a no-no, until the satire movement got underway with the opening of The Establishment, Peter Cook's club in Soho, and the founding of the magazine *Private Eye*. BBC director-general Hugh Carleton Greene gave the go ahead for satire on television, and in November 1962 the first *TW3* was aired. Although scheduled at fifty minutes, being the last programme of the evening meant that it was open-ended, a freedom used gleefully by producer Ned Sherrin and the cast.

Although conventional comedy writers contributed items, the writing team was composed mainly of journalists and dramatists, one of whom was Peter Shaffer, already a successful West End playwright. In 1962, John Vassall, a civil servant working in the Admiralty, was arrested and charged with spying for the Russians. He confessed fully, explaining that he had been blackmailed into doing so, his homosexuality having made him a target. In Vassall's possession were non-contentious letters from his old Admiralty boss, Conservative MP Tam Galbraith, addressed warmly to 'Dear Vassall' and

'My dear Vassall'. These led briefly to false concerns that the
relationship between the hapless, blameless Galbraith and
his civil servant had been inappropriate. In future, politicians
would have to be more careful in their modes of address, and
Shaffer mapped out the minefield, with Lance Percival as the
senior civil servant and David Kernan as his junior.

★ ❋ ★

INT. OFFICE - DAY

A senior official sits at his desk; a junior official quakes
nervously as he hands a letter he has just composed to his
senior.

> SENIOR OFFICER
> [Taking the letter]

Give it here.

[Reading] 'To Mr Jenkins.'

Good. None of that 'dear' nonsense.

'Pursuant to your letter …' Pursuant?

> JUNIOR OFFICER
It's the usual phrase, sir.

> SENIOR OFFICER
I don't like it. The word has an erotic penumbra.
Take it out.

> JUNIOR OFFICER
Yes, sir.

> SENIOR OFFICER
> [Reading]

'I am hoping for the favour of an early
reply.'Favour?

> JUNIOR OFFICER
The Oxford Dictionary defines the verb favour as
'to look kindly upon'.

> SENIOR OFFICER
>
> Exactly. I am amazed you can be so naive. Looking kindly upon anyone who earns less than you do is a deeply treacherous procedure.

> JUNIOR OFFICER
>
> I'm very sorry, sir.

> SENIOR OFFICER
>
> You need some basic training in modern manners, I can see that. If a man comes 300 miles to see you with papers, keep him waiting in the hall – or better still the drive, if you have one. If you offer him so much as a sandwich you will be suspected of improper relations; and a three-course lunch spells treason.

> JUNIOR OFFICER
>
> Yes, sir.

> SENIOR OFFICER
>
> You really are an innocent, aren't you?

> JUNIOR OFFICER
>
> I'm afraid I am, sir.

> SENIOR OFFICER
>
> Well we must change all that.

> [Continuing to read]

> 'Hoping for the favour of an early reply … Thanking you in anticipation.'

> Are you doing this on purpose?

*TW3* was produced under the auspices of BBC Television's current affairs department. Hugh Carleton Greene had seen a one-off special starring Canadian satirist Mort Sahl and decided that the light entertainment department couldn't be trusted.

                    JUNIOR OFFICER
What, sir?

                    SENIOR OFFICER
*Thanking you in anticipation.*

                    JUNIOR OFFICER
Is that wrong, sir?

                    SENIOR OFFICER
Wrong? It's just about the most sexually
provocative sentence I've ever read. It whinnies
with suggestiveness.

                    JUNIOR OFFICER
I hadn't intended it like that, sir.

                    SENIOR OFFICER
We're not concerned with your intentions, man
- merely with the effect you create. And I can
tell you that it's nauseating. You have the
correspondence style of a lovesick au pair girl.
In more honest days one would have said kitchen-
maid.

                    JUNIOR OFFICER
But, sir—

                    SENIOR OFFICER
Don't interrupt, or I may lose control. Now
understand this: in the civil service you will
never thank anybody for anything, especially in
anticipation. You will simply end your letter
without innuendo of any kind. Now let's see what
you've done. [Reading] 'Yours faithfully'… I don't
believe it.

                    JUNIOR OFFICER
That's normal, sir.

                    SENIOR OFFICER
Normal? In the context of a man writing to a man
it's nothing less than disgusting. It implies you
can be unfaithful!

                    JUNIOR OFFICER
I never thought of that, sir.

When BBC schedulers decided to place a filmed series after *TW3*, Sherrin and
Frost sabotaged the venture by giving away the plot. *TW3* soon reverted to
being the last show of the evening.

                         SENIOR OFFICER
You think of very little, don't you? Even the word
'Yours' at the end of a letter is dangerous. It
suggests a willingness for surrender.

                         JUNIOR OFFICER
Then what can I say, sir?

                         SENIOR OFFICER
What do the pensions department use? They're about
as unemotional as you can get, without actually
being dead.

                         JUNIOR OFFICER
'Your obedient servant', I think.

                         SENIOR OFFICER
Are you mad?

                         JUNIOR OFFICER
Sir?

                         SENIOR OFFICER
Your obedient servant … That's just plain
perverted. People who want to be other people's
obedient servants are the sort who answer those
advertisements: Miss Lash, ex-Governess of
striking appearance. To sign yourself an obedient
servant is an ipso facto confession of sexual
deviation. And that, as we all know, is an ipso
facto confession of treason.

                         JUNIOR OFFICER
Oh, I say, sir!

                         SENIOR OFFICER
What do you say?

[Looking at him narrowly]

I believe you are one of those cranks who believe
that there are loyal homosexuals! I think you
secretly believe that the way to stop homosexuals
being blackmailed into subversive acts is to
change the law so they can't be.

JUNIOR OFFICER
Well, it had crossed my mind, sir. Amend the law
and the possibility of Vassalls is lessened.

SENIOR OFFICER
Sloppy, left-wing sentimentality. The only way
to stop a homosexual being blackmailed is to
stop him being a homosexual. And the only way
you can do that is to lock him up in a building
with five hundred other men. That way he can see
how unattractive they really are. Now take this
pornographic muck out of here and bring it back in
an hour, clean enough to be read by a six-year-
old girl, or John Gordon. And leave out everything
at the end except your name: a bare signature,
brusque and masculine. What is your name, by the
way?

JUNIOR OFFICER
Fairy, sir.

SENIOR OFFICER
I don't think somehow you are going to go very far
in Her Majesty's Service. Good morning.

# *Not Only... But Also...* (1965)

## 'A Spot of the Usual Trouble'

### Peter Cook and Dudley Moore

When the revue *Beyond the Fringe* – combining the Footlights alumni Jonathan Miller and Peter Cook with Dudley Moore and Alan Bennett from the Oxford revue world – first took to the stage in Edinburgh, nobody could have had any idea of the lasting effect that the show would have. Not only did it re-establish satire as a genre of comedy, it also created – in Cook and Moore – one of the most important comedy partnerships of all time. Four years after that Edinburgh debut, Moore was offered his own BBC Television spectacular, and insisted on Cook being involved. The result was *Not Only... But Also...*

Much TV comedy at the time was in the spirit of variety, while *Not Only... But Also...* was more like a sophisticated cabaret. Sketches nestled alongside jazz from the Dudley Moore Trio and guest singers. Many of the comic items were one-offs, like the famous 'One Leg Too Few' sketch about the monoped actor auditioning for the role of Tarzan. Others, however, featured recurring characters, like Cook's buffer par excellence, Sir Arthur Streeb-Greebling, and a pair of cloth-capped idiots called Pete and Dud. In the years since, Cook has come to be viewed as the dominant figure in the partnership, but the scripts were fully collaborative, often being edited down from tape-recorded improvisations. Moore said less, but had many of the killer lines. What follows is perhaps the best remembered and most loved of all of the Pete and Dud conversations.

**Series:** *Not Only... But Also...* (BBC2, twenty-two shows over three series and one special, 1965–70), series 1, show 2.

**Original transmission:** BBC2, Saturday 23 January 1965, 9.15 p.m.

**Producer/director:** Joe McGrath

INT. PUB - NIGHT

DUD and PETE, are sitting at a round pub table.

                        DUD
     Alright, Pete, then, are you?

                        PETE
     Not too bad, you know, not too bad. Cheers.

                        DUD
     What you been doing lately, then?

                        PETE
     Well quiet, pretty quiet, not been up to much - I
     had a spot of the usual trouble the other day.

                        DUD
     Oh, did you? What happened, then?

                        PETE
     A spot of the usual trouble - well, I come home
     about half-past eleven - we'd been having a couple
     of drinks, remember? - I come home about half-past
     eleven, and, you know, I was feeling a bit tired,
     so, you know, I thought I'd go to bed, you know,
     take me clothes off, and so on, you know.

                        DUD
     'Sright - well, don't you take your clothes off
     before you go to bed?

                        PETE
     Er - no, I made that mistake this time, got it the
     wrong way round - anyway, I got into bed, settled
     down, I was just about, you know, reading *The
     Swiss Family Robinson*.

                        DUD
     Good, ain't it.

                        PETE
     It's a lovely book, Dud, a lovely book - an' I
     got up to about page 483, second paragraph, when
     suddenly -'bring, bring - bring, bring'.

> DUD
>
> What's that?

> PETE
>
> That's the phone, going 'bring, bring'. So I picked up the phone, and - you know who it was?

> DUD
>
> Who?

> PETE
>
> Bloody Betty Grable. Calling transatlantic, bloody Betty Grable. I said, 'Look, Betty, what do you think you're doing, calling me up half-past eleven at night?' She said, 'It's half-past two in the afternoon over here.' I said, 'I don't care what bloody time it is, there's no need to wake me up'. She said, 'Peter, Peter - get on a plane, come dance with me, be mine tonight.'

> DUD
>
> I thought it was the middle of the afternoon?

PETE

Yes, what she probably meant was 'be mine tonight tomorrow afternoon our time'.

DUD

No – didn't she mean tomorrow afternoon – er.

PETE

Anyway,'Be mine tonight,' she said – I said,'Look, Betty – we've had our laughs, we've had our fun, but it's all over'. I said,'Stop pestering me, get back to Harry James and his trumpet – stop pesterin me,' I said. I slammed the phone down and said, 'Stop pestering me.'

DUD

Shouldn't you have said 'Stop pestering me' before you put the phone down?

PETE

I should have, yes.

DUD

It's funny you should say that,'cos a couple of nights ago, you remember, we had a couple of drinks

PETE

I remember that, yes.

DUD

And I come home, you know, I was going to bed, felt a bit tired – I was having a nightcap.

BBC Television's then head of light entertainment Tom Sloan is reputed to have greeted the pilot for *Not Only... But Also...* with the declaration that if it was entertainment then he must be in the wrong business. BBC2 controller Michael Peacock told him, gleefully, that he was in the wrong business, and that he wanted a series.

PETE

Course you were.

DUD

And I was just dropping off nicely, and all of a
sudden I heard this hollering in the kitchen.

PETE

Hollerin'?

DUD

Screaming and banging on the door, you know, and
I thought I must have left the gas on – so I go
down there – I fling open the door – you'll never
guess – it's bloody Anna Magnani, up to her knees
in rice, screaming at me – 'Lesse more entrate –
amore me per favore!'

PETE

Italian.

DUD

Italian, yes – she was covered in mud, she grabbed
hold of me, she pulled me all over the floor – she
had one of them see-through blouse—

PETE

All damp, showing everything through it.

DUD

Yes, and we rolled all over the floor – I picked
her up, I said, 'Get out of here! Get out of here,
you Italian, thing,' I said. 'Get out of here,' I
said.

PETE

'You Italian thing' – a good thing to call her.

DUD

Yes … I said, 'Don't you come here, messing up my
rice again, mate.'

PETE

I should hope not. I had the same bloody trouble
about three nights ago – I come in, about half-
past eleven at night, we'd been having a couple of
drinks I remember – and I come in, I get into bed,

you see, feeling quite sleepy, I could feel the
lids of me eyes beginning to droop - a bit of the
droop in the eyes - I was just about to drop off,
when suddenly,'tap, tap, tap' at the bloody window
pane - I looked out - you know who it was?

                    DUD
Who?

                    PETE
Bloody Greta Garbo! Bloody Greta Garbo - stark
naked save for a shortie nightie. She was hanging
on to the window sill, and I could see her
knuckles all white … saying 'Pieter, Pieter …'.
You know how these bloody Swedes go on - I said,
'Get out of it' - bloody Greta Garbo. She wouldn't
go - she wouldn't go, I had to smash her down with
a broomstick, poke her off the window sill, she
fell down on the pavement with a great crash.

                    DUD
She just had a nightie on, is that all?

                    PETE
That's all she had on, Dud, just a—

                    DUD
See-through?

                    PETE
A see-through, shortie nightie. Nothing else -
except for her dark glasses of course. Dreadful
business.

                    DUD
Well, it's funny you should say that.

                    PETE
Yes, it's funny I should say that.

                    DUD
Four nights ago, I come home, you know, we'd been
having a couple of drinks.

                    PETE
Couple of drinks, yes.

DUD

I come home, I come through the door, and – sniff
– sniff, sniff, I went – you know – funny smell, I
thought, smells like wood burning.

PETE

Probably burning wood, Dud.

DUD

What's that?

PETE

'Burning Wood' – that's a perfume worn by sensual,
earthy women.

DUD

Funny you should say that, because I come in the
bathroom, you know, I thought, 'bit stronger here',
you know, funny. I come in the bedroom – it's
getting ridiculous, this smell, you know, so I get
into bed, you know, turn the covers back – it's
a bit warm in bed. I thought, 'funny', you know,
being warm like that, and, I get into bed, I put
out the light – and, I was just going off to kip –
and suddenly I feel a hand on my cheek.

PETE

Which cheek was that, Dud. Come on – which cheek
was it?

DUD

It was the left upper. I said, I thought, you
know, 'funny'. I turned on the light – bloody hand
here, scarlet fingernails.

PETE

Who was it?

DUD

You'll never guess – bloody Jane Russell.

PETE

Jane Russell?

DUD

Jane Russell, in bed with me, stark naked – I
said, 'Jane'…

PETE

With the huge …

DUD

With the big … I said, 'Jane,' I said, 'get out of here.'

PETE

Get out?

DUD

'Get out of here,' I said, 'you may be mean, moody and magnificent, but as far as I'm concerned, it's all over.' So I threw her down; I took her out of bed, threw her down the stairs; I threw her bra and her - er - gauze panties after her, I threw them down there and the green silk scarf … I said, 'Get out of here! Get out of here, you hussy!' I threw her lighter, her fag-holder. I threw a bucket of water over her, I said, 'Get out of here, you hussy!' - I said, 'Don't come in my bed again, mate, it's disgusting!' Terrible … I was shocked to the quick.

PETE

You're quite right, you got to do something about these bloody women who pester you.

DUD

What you doing tonight, then?

PETE

Well … I thought we might go to the pictures.

Sadly, many of the *Not Only… But Also…* recordings were junked after transmission. The studio material for the final colour series, transmitted in 1970, has gone completely, leaving only a handful of filmed inserts. There is hope, however. A missing show from the first series, featuring a guest appearance from Peter Sellers, turned up in the USA recently.

# Till Death Us Do Part (1967)

## 'Alf's Dilemma' (or 'Cleaning Up TV')

## Johnny Speight

**Series:** *Till Death Us Do Part* (BBC1, fifty-six shows over one broadcast pilot, seven series, three specials and two *Christmas Night with the Stars* segments, 1965–75), series 2, show 10.

**Original transmission:** BBC1, 27 February 1967, 7.30 p.m.

**Cast in excerpt:** Warren Mitchell (Alf Garnett), Dandy Nichols (Else Garnett), Una Stubbs (Rita), Anthony Booth (Mike).

**Producer/director:** Dennis Main Wilson.

Years before the Murdoch papers took up residence in Wapping, another media phenomenon occupied this district of east London, namely Alf Garnett. A bigoted, deferential working-class Tory, Garnett was intended to be an unsympathetic character, through whom writer Johnny Speight could broach taboo subjects. Speight – who had created a similarly belligerent, if leftish, tramp character for the comedian Arthur Haynes – leavened the Garnett effect by putting him in opposition to his more liberal daughter Rita, her lefty Liverpudlian other half Mike and his own wife Else, who had no strong political convictions, but who could deflate Alf's pomposity, often unwittingly.

The plan backfired slightly. Alf the ogre became Alf the hero for many viewers, for saying the things that they were really thinking. Nonetheless, *Till Death Us Do Part*, at its peak, stands up as a progressive, challenging, funny situation comedy. In tandem with Galton and Simpson's *Steptoe and Son*, it presented an unsentimental, unpatronizing view of the working classes at a time when television was still relatively expensive and exclusive. Speight fought endless battles with producers and executives to use realistic, mildly profane language. When successful, he became a target for Midlands schoolteacher Mary Whitehouse and her 'Clean Up TV' campaign. Speight's solution was to make Garnett one of Mrs Whitehouse's most ardent fans and supporters.

INT. THE GARNETT'S LIVING ROOM – DAY

ALF is reading and nodding occasionally at his book. His son-in-law, MIKE, is also reading. ELSE is biting her nails. RITA is painting her nails. RITA finally breaks the silence.

> RITA
> [To MIKE]

Must be interesting. I'm talking to you. Oi. [Nudges him] Eh?

> MIKE

What?

> RITA

I'm talking to you. I said that must be interesting.

> MIKE

What?

> RITA

That book. I said it must be interesting.

> MIKE

You what?

> RITA

Oh. I said that book must be interesting.

> MIKE

Oh yeah, it's great.

MIKE turns away from RITA.

> RITA

Unlike you to get your head stuck in a book. What is it? Eh?

RITA leans over MIKE.

> MIKE

Get off.

> ALF

Some rubbish, I suppose.

MIKE
It's Ian St John's *Boom at the Kop*.

ALF looks round disdainfully.

ALF
*Boom at the Kop*? Ha ha. They ought to put a bomb
under that Liverpool football ground. The only
boom they need. Blimey. Load of rubbish. Ian St
John? I didn't think he'd be able to read, let
alone write.

MIKE

Shut up. It's a great book by a great player about
a great football team.

ALF

Great team? Get off. At least West Ham play
attractive football.

MIKE

And lose every week.

ALF

Well, at least they know how to lose, don't they?
I mean, not like your team. Obsessed with winning,
they are. Do anything to win, they would. And that
little monkey St John, he's the worst of the lot.

MIKE

Alf, look, you don't know anything about the game.

ALF

Suppose you do?

MIKE
[Pointing to cover]

Look, that's the Saint scoring the winning goal in
the Cup Final at Wembley. Great picture.

ALF

Fluke.

MIKE

And here's what they said about it. Alan Obie in
the *Express* said about that fluke: 'Like a human
battering ram, chunky St John runs forward and
the ball sped from his head into the net. This
was it. All that settled this grim, relentless,
but absorbing test of character. The goal that
destroyed the last-ditch, no-surrender Leeds
defence.'

ALF

Sounds like a bloody schoolboy's comic, don't it?
Load of piffle. Sounds like Dead Shot Dick of
Carson's Green. Piffle.

MIKE

Well, the sports writers were satisfied, eh, and
so was the prime minister, Mr Harold Wilson, who
commented, 'As a Yorkshireman who is MP for a
Liverpool constituency, I had divided loyalties,
but I think the right team got it.'

ALF

What? That bloody turncoat? Old Wilson would say
anything to suit his self, he would. Gorblimey,
if Leeds had won, he'd have said exactly the same
about them. Load of schoolboy codswallop, that's
what that is. Look, you want to read something
sonny, you want to read something a bit edifying.
Something a bit educative.

MIKE

Educative? What are you reading, anyway? Mickey
Spillane?

ALF

No. Not Mickey Spillane. Mrs Whitehouse, innit?
Mrs Mary Whitehouse.

MIKE

Mary Whitehouse?

RITA

The 'clean up TV' woman?

MIKE

That old …

ALF

Yes, and that woman, that woman is concerned for
the moral welfare of this country. The moral fibre
is being rotted away by the corrupt television.

MIKE

Blimey. If she had her way, all you'd get on
television is Pinky and Perky and bloody Noddy.

RITA
[To ELSE]

And Mrs Thursday, eh?

In the original *Comedy Playhouse* pilot, the family was called Ramsey, not Garnett. Johnny Speight changed the name to avoid confusion with the England football team's then manager, Alf Ramsey.

In that pilot, Else was not played by Dandy Nichols. Instead, the role was taken by Gretchen Franklin, later better known as Ethel in *EastEnders*.

                    ELSE
     I like Mrs Thursday.

ALF seems to be in pain.

                    ELSE
     What's the matter with you?

                    ALF
     I got that bug, ain't I? I've been on and off all
     day at work, I have. Blimey, I've got to go.

ALF runs to the lavatory.

                    ELSE
     You're not off out the back, are you?

                    ALF
                [From outside]

     Where do you think I'm going?

                    ELSE
     You can't use that, it's blocked up.

ALF returns.

                    ALF
     Eh?

                    ELSE
     It's blocked up. Been blocked up all day it has.

Despite Warren Mitchell being Jewish, in the seventies, he was happy to reprise a character not unlike Alf Garnett for a series of commercials for Wall's pork sausages.

ALF
Blimey, that's all your bloody tea leaves, isn't it? I've told you about bunging them down there, ain't I?

ELSE
It's nothing to do with tea leaves.

ALF
Of course it's to do with tea leaves.

ELSE
I've been putting them down there for years.

ALF
Yeah? Well now look what's happened. Cumulative, ain't it? What am I supposed to … I mean, ain't you got the plumber in?

ELSE
He can't come round until tomorrow.

ALF
Well, what am I supposed to do until then?

MIKE
Hang on.

ALF
Shut up.

ELSE
If it's urgent, Mrs Carey said that we could use hers next door.

ALF
Why didn't you say so in the first place, then?

ALF runs out and then comes back.

                ELSE
Why have you come back?

                ALF
I want something to read out there, don't I?

                ELSE
Wait a minute.

                ALF
I can't.

                ELSE
    [Running into the kitchen]

Wait a minute.

                ALF
What is it?

ELSE returns with toilet paper.

                ALF
Well, blimey, she's got some in there, ain't she?

                ELSE
Yeah, I suppose she has, but we don't want to
impose. If she's kind enough to let us use her
toilet, at least we can provide our own paper.

                ALF
Blimey.

        [To MIKE]

Shut up you.

        [To ELSE]

I'm going to look a right Charlie, aren't I,
walking in with that?

ELSE reels off several sheets. ALF puts them in his Mary
Whitehouse book, then runs off.

# *Marty* (1968)

## 'Vet's Waiting Room'

### Barry Took and Marty Feldman

Think of Marty Feldman and the first thing that comes to mind will probably be his bulging eyes – the product of an overactive thyroid. His appearance aided his comedy immeasurably. He looked funny, whatever he did, and much of the best material in his own shows was very visual – not least one particular sketch about a game of golf that moves far from the links, on the backs of trucks, through domestic gardens and down drainpipes. However, Feldman was also a highly skilled creator of verbal comedy, working as a scriptwriter for hire with his long-time collaborator Barry Took on TV shows like *The Army Game* and *Round the Horne* on radio .

He made his name as a comedy performer on commercial television in *At Last the 1948 Show*, with John Cleese, Graham Chapman, Tim Brooke-Taylor and Aimi MacDonald, before moving to BBC2 for his own series in new-fangled colour in 1968. For this he was paired with producer Dennis Main Wilson, a manic, energetic genius who had put the *Goon Show* on the radio and brought Alf Garnett to television. Barry Took later described the three main themes of the *Marty* show as 'soccer, time and human beings who were misfits'.

Very much under the last heading came one of Feldman's stock characters, a very irritating, disruptive man with a constricted throaty voice, sometimes referred to as Mr Globb, who was sent to try figures of authority, often played by John Junkin with what Took called 'an air of puzzled despair'.

**Series:** *Marty* (BBC2, six shows, 1968), show 1.

**Original transmission:** BBC2, Monday 29 April 1968, 8 p.m.

**Cast in excerpt:** Marty Feldman (man with thing in basket), Tim Brooke-Taylor (cat lover), Roland MacLeod (vet), John Junkin (man with second thing in basket).

**Producer/director:** Dennis Main Wilson.

INT. VET SURGERY - DAY

MARTY enters, pushing a large prop basket, from which
whinnies, moos, snarls and plumes of smoke are emerging.
MARTY sits down next to a man with a cat in a box.

> CAT LOVER
> How many animals have you got in there, then?

> MARTY
> Just the one. It's a thing.

> CAT LOVER
> Oh.

> MARTY
> Yes, it followed me home, you know. I didn't have
> the heart to send it away. You know how attached
> you get to them.

> CAT LOVER
> Is it tame?

> MARTY
> Er, up to a point.

Producer Dennis Main Wilson had been responsible, in his radio days, for putting 'The Goon Show' on air. In another show from Feldman's first series, following a sketch in which the character 'the annoying man' disrupts a choral recital of 'The Whiffenpoof Song' by ordering numerous convoluted changes to the lyrics, Main Wilson's producer credit was sung.

More squawking from the basket. MARTY reaches in and attempts to discipline the creature with his cap.

> CAT LOVER
> What is it?

> MARTY
> What?

> CAT LOVER
> What is it?

> MARTY
> Well, to be frank, I'm not quite sure. I looked him up in the *Cattle-breeders' Guide*. He wasn't in there. I looked him up in the *Standard Book of British Birds*, and he wasn't in there either. I finally found him in the Book of Revelations.

An anguished howl issues from the basket. MARTY reaches in with his cap again.

> MARTY
> Yes, Book of Revelations. They venerated him in ancient times, you know. They worshipped him as a god. I'm very fond of him, but I don't worship him.

MARTY stands up and addresses the basket again.

> MARTY
> Dirty thing. Dirty thing. You'll go deaf. I think he's getting a bit restless in the basket, you know? I think he wants to go out and have a little scamper about, go walkies. Do you think I ought to let him out?

                          CAT LOVER
No, I don't think so.

                           MARTY
No, probably not a good idea. Might disgrace
himself. Besides, there's all the palaver of
unchaining him, ain't there?

                          CAT LOVER
Why did you bring him to see the vet?

                           MARTY
Well, he's got a touch of the beak and hoof.

                          CAT LOVER
Beak and hoof?

                           MARTY
Yes, he's been off his food lately. He won't touch
his din-dins.

                          CAT LOVER
What do you feed him on?

                           MARTY
He's not particular. He likes owls.

                          CAT LOVER
Owls?

                           MARTY
Yes, look at him ruffle up his scales when I say
owls. Look at his little red eye glisten. Oh he's
lovely. Who's going to have his owls when he gets
home? That's it, you see. I'd like a litter from
him. Or a clutch. I've put him out to stud, but
none of the animals I've introduced him to seem
that keen.

An ear-piercing screech comes from the basket.

                           MARTY
See, that's it. He wants his din-dins, and I've
come out without an owl about me. You don't happen
to have an owl you don't want, do you?

CAT LOVER
I don't seem to have one about me, no.

MARTY eyes up the caged budgie on the lap of the woman next to him.

MARTY
Do you want that budgie? No, no, no. It's not a good idea for him to have snacks between meals.

More shrieking. MARTY begins beating the hidden beast with an umbrella, which gets shorter and shorter, as the animal eats it. Finally, only the handle remains, and a burp comes from the basket. Then MARTY is pulled into the basket too. Eventually, he escapes.

MARTY
He always gets a bit playful at this time of year.

The VET emerges, with a bloodied nose and clothes all askew.

VET
[Wearily]

Next.

MARTY
Do you mind if I went next? He might turn nasty, you see?

CAT LOVER
No, please, you go on ahead.

A man is exiting the examining room with a basket like Marty's.

BASKET MAN
Don't take it to him, he don't know nothing about 'em. Come with me.

Feldman appeared on the first ever TV edition of the *Billy Cotton Band Show* in 1956, as part of the variety act Morris, Marty and Mitch.

# Monty Python's Flying Circus (1969)

## 'Dead Parrot'

### John Cleese and Graham Chapman

*Monty Python's Flying Circus* is perhaps the best example of old-school BBC Television commissioning policy at work. The policy was simply to find good people and trust them to turn in some good shows. The *Python* team had been assembled by Barry Took, then working as an adviser to the BBC Television comedy department. John Cleese and Graham Chapman, both ex-Cambridge Footlights, had been working on *At Last the 1948 Show* for Rediffusion, while Oxford-educated Michael Palin and Terry Jones had been part of the creative force behind the children's show *Do Not Adjust Your Set*, along with Eric Idle (also ex-Footlights) and Terry Gilliam. Barry Took thought that the six, while talented enough apart, could produce something really special together, and engineered a meeting. Head of comedy Michael Mills justified Took's faith by giving them thirteen weeks on BBC1 without the need for a pilot.

The result was a literate, surreal sketch show that played with the genre more than any previous show had, although influences from the *Goons* and the later TV work of Spike Milligan and Michael Bentine were noticeable. In particular, Bentine's use of animation in *It's a Square World* (BBC, 1960–64) presaged Terry Gilliam's work on *Python*, which was often used to seamlessly link a sketch that had no obvious ending to another with no obvious starting point. The principals benefited from the presence of Scottish director

**Series:** *Monty Python's Flying Circus* (BBC1/2, forty-six shows over four series, 1969–74), series 1, show 8.

**Original transmission:** BBC1, Sunday 7 December 1969, 11 p.m.

**Cast in excerpt:** John Cleese (Mr Praline), Michael Palin (Shopkeeper), Eric Idle (Announcer), Terry Jones (Porter), Graham Chapman (Colonel).

**Producer/director:** Ian Macnaughton

Ian Macnaughton, a former actor with a chaotic manner at odds with conventional BBC light entertainment discipline, but with just enough steel to get the shows made on time. Like the best pop music, *Python* bemused the old and enthused the young, who noted with gratitude that TV comedy was changing before their very eyes.

★ ☆ ★

INT. PET SHOP - DAY

MR PRALINE enters the shop carrying a dead parrot in a cage. He walks to the counter where the SHOPKEEPER tries to hide below cash register.

> PRALINE
> Hello, I wish to register a complaint … Hello? Miss?

> SHOPKEEPER
> What do you mean, miss?

> PRALINE
> Oh, I'm sorry, I have a cold. I wish to make a complaint.

> SHOPKEEPER
> Sorry, we're closing for lunch.

> PRALINE
> Never mind that, my lad, I wish to complain about this parrot what I purchased not half an hour ago from this very boutique.

> SHOPKEEPER
> Oh yes, the Norwegian Blue. What's wrong with it?

> PRALINE
> I'll tell you what's wrong with it. It's dead, that's what's wrong with it.

> SHOPKEEPER
> No, no it's resting, look!

PRALINE

Look, my lad, I know a dead parrot when I see one
and I'm looking at one right now.

SHOPKEEPER

No, no, sir, it's not dead. It's resting.

PRALINE

Resting?

SHOPKEEPER

Yeah, remarkable bird the Norwegian Blue,
beautiful plumage, innit?

PRALINE

The plumage don't enter into it - it's stone dead.

SHOPKEEPER

No, no - it's just resting.

PRALINE

Alright then, if it's resting I'll wake it up.

[Shouts into cage]

Hello Polly! I've got a nice cuttlefish for you when you wake up, Polly Parrot!

SHOPKEEPER
[Jogging cage]

There, it moved.

PRALINE
No he didn't. That was you pushing the cage.

SHOPKEEPER
I did not.

PRALINE
Yes, you did.

[Takes parrot out of cage, shouts]

Hello Polly, Poll.

[Bangs it against counter]

Polly Parrot, wake up. Polly.

[Throws it in the air and lets it fall to the floor]

Now that's what I call a dead parrot.

SHOPKEEPER
No, no it's stunned.

PRALINE
Look, my lad, I've had just about enough of this. That parrot is definitely deceased. And when I bought it not half an hour ago, you assured me that its lack of movement was due to it being tired and shagged out after a long squawk.

SHOPKEEPER
It's probably pining for the fjords.

PRALINE
Pining for the fjords, what kind of talk is that? Look, why did it fall flat on its back the moment I got it home?

SHOPKEEPER
The Norwegian Blue prefers kipping on its back.
Beautiful bird, lovely plumage.

PRALINE
Look, I took the liberty of examining that parrot,
and I discovered that the only reason that it had
been sitting on its perch in the first place was
that it had been nailed there.

SHOPKEEPER
Well of course it was nailed there. Otherwise it
would muscle up to those bars and voom.

PRALINE
Look matey, [picks up parrot] this parrot wouldn't
voom if I put four thousand volts through it. It's
bleeding demised.

SHOPKEEPER
It's not, it's pining.

PRALINE
It's not pining, it's passed on. This parrot is no
more. It has ceased to be. It's expired and gone
to meet its maker. This is a late parrot. It's a
stiff. Bereft of life, it rests in peace. If you
hadn't nailed it to the perch, it would be pushing
up the daisies. It's rung down the curtain and
joined the choir invisible. This is an ex-parrot.

This item had its origins in a sketch performed in *How to Irritate People*, a
one-off special made for the American market by David Frost's company David
Paradine Productions. The original version of the sketch was about a broken-
down car, which the garage owner refused to acknowledge as non-functioning.
Graham Chapman, very often the source of the twist that turned a funny idea
into a surreal masterpiece, suggested that a Norwegian Blue parrot would be
better. Incidentally, there is no such breed of animal.

SHOPKEEPER
Well, I'd better replace it then.

PRALINE
[To camera]

If you want to get anything done in this country you've got to complain till you're blue in the mouth.

SHOPKEEPER
Sorry, guy, we're right out of parrots.

PRALINE
I see. I see. I get the picture.

SHOPKEEPER
I've got a slug.

PRALINE
Does it talk?

SHOPKEEPER
Not really, no.

PRALINE
Well, it's scarcely a replacement then, is it?

SHOPKEEPER
Listen, I'll tell you what.

[Handing over a card]

Tell you what, if you go to my brother's pet shop in Bolton he'll replace your parrot for you.

PRALINE
Bolton, eh?

SHOPKEEPER
Yeah.

PRALINE
Alright.

PRALINE leaves, holding the parrot.

Caption: 'A SIMILAR PET SHOP IN BOLTON, LANCS'.

CUT to close-up of sign on door: 'Similar Pet Shops Ltd'.

PULL OUT reveals identical pet shop. SHOPKEEPER now has a moustache. PRALINE walks into the shop. He looks around with interest, noticing the empty parrot cage still on the floor.

> PRALINE
> Er, excuse me. This is Bolton, is it?

> SHOPKEEPER
> No, no it's, er, Ipswich.

> PRALINE
> [To camera]

That's Inter-City Rail for you.

PRALINE leaves.


## INT. RAILWAY COMPLAINTS DEPARTMENT - DAY

CLOSE-UP of sign on desk: 'Complaints'. PORTER stands at the desk. PRALINE approaches.

> PRALINE
> I wish to make a complaint.

> PORTER
> I don't have to do this, you know.

> PRALINE
> I beg your pardon?

> PORTER
> I'm a qualified brain surgeon. I only do this because I like being my own boss.

> PRALINE
> Er, excuse me, this is irrelevant, isn't it?

> PORTER
> Oh yeah, it's not easy to pad these out to thirty minutes.

PRALINE

Well, I wish to make a complaint. I got on the
Bolton train and found myself deposited here in
Ipswich.

PORTER

No, this is Bolton.

PRALINE
[To camera]

The pet shop owner's brother was lying.

PORTER
Well, you can't blame British Rail for that.

PRALINE
If this is Bolton, I shall return to the pet shop.

INT. PET SHOP - DAY

Caption: 'A LITTLE LATER LIMITED'.

PRALINE enters.

PRALINE
I understand that this is Bolton.

SHOPKEEPER
Yes.

PRALINE
Well, you told me it was Ipswich.

SHOPKEEPER
It was a pun.

PRALINE
A pun?

SHOPKEEPER
No, no, not a pun, no. What's the other thing
which reads the same backwards as forwards?

PRALINE
A palindrome?

SHOPKEEPER

Yes, yes.

PRALINE

It's not a palindrome. The palindrome of Bolton
would be Notlob. It don't work.

SHOPKEEPER

Look, what do you want?

PRALINE

No, I'm sorry, I'm not prepared to pursue my line
of enquiry any further as I think this is getting
too silly.

COLONEL
[Coming in]

Quite agree. Quite agree. Silly. Silly. Silly.
Right get on with it. Get on with it.

CUT to ANNOUNCER eating a yoghurt.

ANNOUNCER
[Seeing camera]

Oh … er … oh … um! Oh! er …

[Shuffles papers]

I'm sorry … and now frontal nudity.

CUT to outside street. A shabby man in a long overcoat, his
back to the camera, passes two pepperpots and a girl. As
he passes each one he opens his coat, wide. They react with
shocked horror. Then he turns to camera and opens his coat.
A big sign hangs around his neck: 'BOO'. CUT to ANNOUNCER
eating yoghurt. The COLONEL comes in and nudges him.

ANNOUNCER

Oh, oh, I'm sorry. I thought the film was longer.

[Shuffling papers]

Ah. Now Notlob, er, Bolton.

# *Up Pompeii!* (1970)

## 'Britannicus'

## Talbot Rothwell

In the late 1950s and early 1960s, Frankie Howerd's career was in the doldrums. Ten years earlier, he had been a top-of-the-bill variety and radio comedian, but his style fell out of favour until he was booked by Peter Cook for a season at The Establishment, Cook's nightclub. Far from being a fish out of water, Howerd cleverly played on being old and out of touch to lull audiences into a false sense of security. Once he had them there, he hit them with superbly satirical material. A one-off appearance on *That Was The Week That Was* consolidated this success, and Howerd was back.

**Series:** *Up Pompeii!* (BBC1, fourteen shows, 1969–70), series 1, show 4.

**Original transmission:** BBC1, 20 April 1970, 9.10 p.m.

**Cast in excerpt:** Frankie Howerd (Lurcio), Jeanne Mockford (Senna), Max Adrian (Ludicrus Sextus), Elizabeth Larner (Ammonia).

**Producer/director:** David Croft.

One of the bookings that came his way following the revival of his fortunes was the part of Pseudolus in the West End production of *A Funny Thing Happened on the Way to the Forum* in 1963. Six years later, when *Carry On* film scriptwriter Talbot Rothwell wrote a one-off *Comedy Playhouse* set in Ancient Roman times, Howerd was the natural choice to play Lurcio, the slave narrator, who was attempting to tell a story ('The Prologue') amid constant interruptions. Rothwell's terrible puns and innuendo were much in evidence, and Howerd delivered them all with relish, chiding the audience for seeing filth in the material. The one-off was a hit, and was followed by two series of Roman ribaldry.

EXT. ROMAN SQUARE – DAY

LURCIO enters, passing two ladies who are leaving.

>           LURCIO
> Greetings, citizens. Greetings. Now, the prologue,
> the prologue. Our story today is taken from the
> book, *The Odyssey*. *The Odyssey*. Now, this is a
> book full of odds and … ends.

A shattering noise, followed by a couple arguing (Out of view).

>           LURCIO
> It's my master and mistress having a row.

LURCIO approaches the door and blows a whistle.

>           LURCIO
> Half-time!

LURCIO closes the door.

>           LURCIO
> Oh dear, what a to-do. It's my master and mistress
> having a row. They always have a row on this day
> in the year. I don't know why they don't forget
> their wedding anniversary, it's so stupid. And of
> course it'll all come back on me, you know, the
> slave of the household. She'll be saying 'Lurcio,
> pick up those bits and stick 'em'.
>
> [To audience, who are laughing at the innuendo]
>
> Together, together. [Disapprovingly] To-gether.
> No, well I mean, you've been to all those museums
> and seen those ancient vases with cracks all over
> them? Well, this is how it happens, you see?
>
> [Sits down, with a squeak]
>
> Oooh, draughty. Quiet now please. The prologue.
>
> [High-pitched] Now, today [splutters]… now,
> today, ladies and gentlemen, we have *The Odyssey*.
> Now we're going to give you a story. This is
> Odysseus and the Sirens. Odysseus and the Sirens.
> Now, one day, the sirens went off, but the air
> raid shelter was a long way from …

A woman enters, wailing.

                    SENNA
    Woe, woe and thrice woe.

                    LURCIO
    Oh, here she is. Misery. Oh dear. This is the
    soothsayer, Senna. Oh, she is a silly old pod.

                    SENNA
    I have just returned from a visit to Mars.

                    LURCIO
    To where?

                    SENNA
    Mars.

                    LURCIO
    Oh, how is your poor old mother, dear? Is she
    still in the Darby and Jonas club?

              [To camera]

    Because she was always in the club, you know.

                    SENNA
    Mars, the great god of war.

                    LURCIO
    Oh, that Mars. Yes.

                    SENNA
    Beware a great battle will be fought in a far-off
    land across the sea.

All but two of the original *Up Pompeii!* master tapes – the *Comedy Playhouse*
pilot and this episode, series 1, show 4 – were wiped soon after transmission.
Fortunately, copies of the missing shows were later located in the archive of
the Canadian Broadcasting Corporation, and returned to the BBC.

LURCIO
A battle in a far-off land across the sea? You're
warmongering now. Go on, do your mongering
somewhere else, please.

SENNA
Cry havoc and let slip the dogs of war.

LURCIO
Let slip the dogs of war?

SENNA
Only the blessed will escape their bloody fangs.

LURCIO
Well, it'll be no bloody fangs to you, mate.

SENNA walks off, still wailing.

LURCIO
All right, love, we'll do our best.

[To camera]

Oh, what a funny woman. She's a misery. She really is a misery.

[Sits down]

Now, the prologue. Odysseus and the Sirens. These sirens were strange creatures. Strange creatures, the sirens. They were half-women and half-fish, you see. Yes, half-fish. And their measurements, or for those with their own teeth, their vital statistics, were thirty-eight, thirty-eight and three drachmas a pound. Filleted. Mind you, they're very nice, some of them. Yes. Most attractive, especially those with the soft roes. They had lovely long fair hair, and they had lovely shoulders, and slim waists, and thereby hangs a tail. What do you expect? Wit? You won't get it in this show.

There is a commotion from the house. Sextus emerges from the front door.

LURCIO

Oh gawd, second half.

[Picks up fragment of ceramics]

Is there a potter in the house?

SEXTUS

Oh Lurcio, I am so sorry about all this, but I'm afraid my wife has no artistic appreciation.

LURCIO

I'm sorry.

SEXTUS

All I was doing was admiring the bust of a wood nymph.

A woman runs screaming from the villa.

LURCIO

The wood nymph?

Talbot Rothwell is credited with writing the line 'Infamy, infamy, they've all got it in for me', delivered by Kenneth Williams as Julius Caesar in *Carry On Cleo*. However, Rothwell had been given the joke by Frank Muir and Denis Norden, who had coined it for the radio comedy series *Take It From Here*.

SEXTUS nods.

                    LURCIO
Would she would or would she wouldn't?

                    SEXTUS
I didn't get time to find out.

AMMONIA appears at an upper-storey window holding a chamber pot.

                    AMMONIA
And keep out of my sight, rapist libertine.

                    LURCIO
Oh, no, mistress, don't throw that, please. Don't.
I was just going to use it.

                [To audience]

For the crocuses.

                    AMMONIA
Oh, wretched, wretched man. How could you do this
to me after twenty years of marriage?

                    SEXTUS
Well, my dear, that's exactly what I said to
myself. How could I do it to you after twenty
years of marriage?

AMMONIA throws the pot at SEXTUS. LURCIO picks up a large fragment.

                    LURCIO
Is there a chamberlain in the house?

# The Morecambe and Wise Show (1971)

## 'Grieg's Piano Concerto'

### Eddie Braben

**Series:** *The Morecambe and Wise Show* (BBC1 and BBC2, sixty-nine shows, over nine series and nine specials, 1968–77), 1971 Christmas special.

**Original transmission:** BBC1, Saturday 25 December 1971, 8 p.m.

**Cast:** Eric Morecambe, Ernie Wise, Andre Previn (themselves).

**Producer/Director:** John Ammonds.

When John Eric Bartholomew first met Ernest Wiseman in 1940, television was out of service for the duration of the Second World War. Beginning their careers on the variety stage, they had no idea of the medium that they would eventually dominate. After seven successful years at Lew Grade's ATV, they transferred to the BBC, where they were paired with producer John Ammonds and, after their previous writers Sid Green and Dick Hills returned to ITV, Liverpudlian writer Eddie Braben. Braben redefined the pair's dynamic, taking it away from the conventional funny man/straight man set-up. Instead, Eric became a worldly idiot, with Ernie his vulnerable, slightly pretentious friend, writing utterly useless plays. One important aspect of the new dynamic was that Eric was allowed to belittle his chum, with jibes about his (non-existent) wig or his 'short fat hairy legs', but woe betide anyone else who tried it.

The most memorable items from Eric and Ernie's BBC years can be found in the run of Christmas specials they made between 1969 and 1977. This sketch, from the 1971 Christmas show, had its origins in a strange party piece played on the piano by Morecambe that he claimed to be Grieg's Piano Concerto. For one of the ATV shows, Sid Green and Dick Hills wrote a sketch around it, including both the suggestion that Morecambe should ring Grieg for advice on how to play it and the assertion that he was playing all the right notes, but not necessarily in the right order. When André Previn agreed to guest on Eric and Ernie's 1971 Christmas special, Eddie Braben rebuilt the sketch from the ground up to create the version that everybody knows. The reference to 'Aye aye, that's your lot' was the catchphrase of violin-playing variety comedian Jimmy Wheeler, who died in October 1970. Also, the mention of the Argyle Theatre, Birkenhead, is made even funnier when you know that it was destroyed by Luftwaffe bombs in 1940.

★ ☆ ★

ERNIE
And now, the highlight of the evening. A truly great international star.

[Grins]

Good evening. And now we have another famous person here from the world of music. Let's give another warm welcome to the principal conductor of the London Symphony Orchestra, Mr André Previn. Thank you for bringing your many musical talents to our humble little show.

PREVIN
Well, thank you for that tremendous introduction. It doesn't come out of my fee, does it?

ERNIE
Fee? What fee? Oh.

[Laughs awkwardly]

Joke. I suppose you're looking forward to the night are you?

PREVIN
Oh, well now, who wouldn't?

ERNIE
Yes, exciting, isn't it?

                              PREVIN
I've come a long way to conduct the Mendelssohn
Violin Concerto. Especially with Yehudi Menuhin as
my soloist.

                              ERNIE
Er, yes.

                              PREVIN
I'll tell you the truth. I'll be honest with you.
I wasn't going to come on your show at all until
you told me that Mr Menuhin had agreed to play.

                              ERNIE
I did say that, did I?

                              PREVIN
Oh yes. By the way, has Yehudi arrived?

                              ERNIE
Who?

                              PREVIN
Yehudi Menuhin.

                              ERNIE
Well, I'm glad you mentioned that. As a matter of
fact, I mean I can explain the whole situation.

A hand comes through the curtains with a piece of paper.

                              ERNIE
Well, what do you know, a telegram. A telegram
from out of …

Hand stays a little too long, as if expecting a tip. ERNIE
slaps it, and it disappears.

                              ERNIE
Oh dearie me, yes, yes, it's from Yehudi.

                              PREVIN
Who?

                              ERNIE
Yehudi Menuhin.

PREVIN

Oh yes, of course, what does he say?

ERNIE

[Reading telegram]

He says, oh, he can't come. Isn't that a shame?
'Dear boys, can't make it tonight on your show.
Opening at the Argyle Theatre, Birkenhead, in Old
King Cole.' What a shame.

[Hands telegram to Previn]

PREVIN

Yes. Yes. Yes.

[Hands telegram back]

Goodnight.

[Turns to leave]

ERNIE

No, no, please, don't go. There are other great
musicians, other great works.

PREVIN

Such as?

ERNIE

Such as …

[Pauses and plays for time]

Grieg's Piano Concerto.

PREVIN

That's a great work, you're right. Great work, but
I mean do you have someone of the calibre of Mr
Menuhin?

ERNIE

Who?

PREVIN

Yehudi.

ERNIE

Oh, Yehudi Menuhin. Better.

PREVIN

Better than Yehudi Menuhin?

ERNIE

Can knock spots off him. I think you're in for the
thrill of a lifetime. Here to play Grieg's Piano
Concerto is Mr Eric Morecambe.

Someone is behind the curtain, punching it to find the gap.
Eventually ERIC emerges in a concert pianist's tails.

ERIC
[Bowing to the audience]

Thank you, thank you.

[Looks at PREVIN]

It's the fixer.

ERNIE

It's the fixer. Eric, say hello to Mr Preview.

ERIC turns to shake PREVIN's hand.

ERIC

Ah, Mr Preview, how are you? A pleasure to be with
you, and ready when you are. A-one-two-a-one-two-
three-four.

PREVIN

Wait a minute. You got me here under false
pretences.

ERIC & ERNIE

False pretences?

ERIC

What's he mean, what's he mean?

ERNIE

I told you it wouldn't work. He's expecting Yehudi
Menuhin.

                    PREVIN

He's a comedian.

                     ERIC

And a very funny one too. I must be honest, he
makes me laugh when he puts the violin under his
chin, gets the last note, and shouts 'Aye aye,
that's your lot' and goes straight to the bar. I
like that. I'm very keen on him.

                    PREVIN

Eric Morecambe is a comic. He can't play the
piano.

                     ERIC
        [Putting hand on PREVIN's shoulder]

Just a moment, sir. You seem to doubt my musical
prowess.

                    PREVIN
        [Putting hand on ERIC's shoulder]

I certainly do.

                     ERIC

Let me put your mind at rest, sir, because you
are now looking at one of the few men who have
actually fished off the end of Sir Henry Wood's
promenade. Now follow that with the sea lions.

                    ERNIE

I was there when he did it.

                     ERIC

Of course you were.

For their television shows, Morecambe and Wise performed on a wooden
rostrum built up from the studio floor. This gave them the sound of a real
stage, and gave them a better eye-line to the studio audience, looking
slightly over the cameras.

                    [To PREVIN]

He put the bait on.

                    PREVIN
Look, I don't dispute for one moment that Mr
Morecambe is a great comic, I just find it
difficult to believe that he can play the Grieg
Piano Concerto.

                    ERNIE
I do assure you that he knows all the classics. I
do assure you, Mr Preview.

                    ERIC
Privet.

                    PREVIN
Er, Previn.

                    ERNIE
All the masterpieces, he knows them. The Planets
Suite by Gustav Holst.

                    ERIC
Not forgetting the three-piece suite by Arthur
Negus. Who was it do you think … look at me when
I'm talking to you … oh, you are. Who was it
do you think that introduced Glenda Jackson to
Tchaikovsky?

                    PREVIN
I don't know.

                    ERIC
               [Pointing at chest]

Me.

                    ERNIE
               [Pointing at ERIC]

Him.

                    ERIC
Was it?

Yes.

ERIC

And if you don't believe me, you can get in touch with the other world-famous conductor, Sir Ivy Benson. He'll tell you all about me, won't he?

ERNIE

He will.

PREVIN

Goodnight.

ERIC & ERNIE

No, please don't go.

ERNIE

Don't go Mr Preview.

ERIC

Privet.

PREVIN

Previn.

ERNIE

I can assure you that Eric is more than capable.

PREVIN

Well, all right, I'll go and get my baton … Yes. It's in Chicago.

ERIC

It's in Chicago. Pow! He's in! I like him. I like him.

ERNIE

We've got one here. Believe me, you're in for a surprise, Mr Preview.

ERIC

Previn.

PREVIN

Privet.

[Shakes head and turns away]

                    ERNIE
        Open the curtains, please.

Curtains swish open to reveal an orchestra and a grand piano.

                    ERIC
        This is the band?

                    ERNIE
        This is the band, yes.

                    ERIC
        I've seen better bands on a cigar.

            [Turns to musicians]

        Which one's the fixer?

Orchestra laughs uproariously and spontaneously.

                    ERNIE
        Which one? The one in the gold lamé suit.

                    ERIC
        They usually are. Right, I'll go and get the
        music. Incidentally, where's the piano?

            [Points at grand piano]

        Never mind, this'll do.

            [Turns to PREVIN]

        Now I do hope, sir, that you understand all these
        squiggly lines?

                    PREVIN
        I think so, yes.

                    ERIC
        The reason I ask is that the second movement is
        very important to me, you see, in the second
        movement, not too heavy on the banjos. Keep it
        down, because wunga-changa, wunga-changa, vulgar,
        vulgar.

                    PREVIN
        We'll keep it way down.

ERIC

That's the word I was looking for. Way down. Yes,
that's very good. Because that is me there, you
see? Playing the Grieg Piano Concerto

ERIC holds up sheet music with the words 'GRIEG'S PIANO
CONCERTO AS PLAYED BY ERIC MORECAMBE' and his picture on the
front, then turns to show the orchestra.

ERIC

A signed autograph later on, boys.

ERNIE

If I could just explain to Mr Preview. You see
I want you to notice that Eric does play the
original version of Grieg's Piano Concerto.

ERIC

Yes, the one we played before we went decimal.

PREVIN

Look here. Wait, though. This is not the original
version.

ERNIE

No?

PREVIN

I'll explain, it's very simple. After the opening
timpani roll, in the original version, the piano
takes over. Here you have that piece played by the
full orchestra.

ERIC

Ah yes, but this is a special arrangement.

PREVIN

A special arrangement of the Grieg Piano Concerto?
I've never heard of that before.

ERIC

That's the idea. I mean everybody plays it this
way. I thought we'd do something different.

PREVIN

Look, whatever you say, whatever you say.

                              ERNIE
          I'll announce it, shall I?

                              PREVIN
          Yes, do that.

                              ERIC
                           [To PREVIN]

          You're doing well. You're doing well.

                              PREVIN
          Thank you.

ERIC stands behind ERNIE, posturing.

                              ERNIE
          Ladies and gentlemen, tonight, Grieg's Piano
          Concerto by Grieg. Soloist Mr Eric Morecambe,
          conducted by André Previn.

ERNIE vacates the stage. PREVIN signals to the orchestra
to start the introduction. ERIC messes about on the steps,
walking down then up again then sauntering towards the piano
keyboard. By the time his cue to start playing comes, he
has not quite made it to the stool. PREVIN looks at ERIC,
baffled.

                              PREVIN
          What's the matter? What happened?

                              ERIC
          The introduction.

                              PREVIN
          The introduction's wrong?

                              ERIC
          It's too short.

                              PREVIN
          It's too short?

                              ERIC
          Oh, you noticed?

                              PREVIN
          By how much is it too short?

ERIC

Well you see, I went down here like that and came
back.

ERIC weaves up and down the stairs.

PREVIN

You wasted some time there.

ERIC

I wasted some time, yes.

ERIC strides back from the piano towards PREVIN in Groucho
Marx style, and stops with his feet about three feet apart.

ERIC

I would say about that much.

ERNIE

About a yard?

ERIC

About a yard. If you can lengthen it by about a
yard, we'll be in.

PREVIN

What do you think we can do about that?

ERIC

Well, that's nothing to do with me. My musical
manager [indicates ERNIE], he does all this.

ERNIE

Could we get in touch with Grieg?

ERIC

That's a good idea.

PREVIN

You mean call him on the phone?

ERNIE

Call him on the phone? Why not?

PREVIN

Well, I didn't bring his phone number.

ERIC

Well, it's Norway something or other, isn't it?

ERNIE

What's the code?

ERIC

Fingal's Cave or something?

ERNIE

I think it's Fingal's Cave.

ERIC

Mind you, you might not get him. He could be out skiing.

PREVIN

Could we just try it again? Try it again.

ERIC

I'll tell you what. This time I'll sit down there waiting.

PREVIN

What a good thought. You'd be ready.

ERIC

He's in, isn't he?

ERNIE

Ladies and gentlemen, Grieg's Piano Concerto, soloist Mr Eric Morecambe, conductor Mr Andrew Preview.

PREVIN begins the intro, but ERIC misses his cue.

PREVIN

Any time.

ERIC

Could I have a word with you, please?

PREVIN steps down to the piano, and looks under the lid, while ERIC looks over it. PREVIN then looks over the lid, while ERIC looks under.

ERIC

Has he gone?

ERNIE

No, he's here.

ERIC

Ah, he's there. You see, I hope you don't mind me
saying this, but when you got to the part that
was my cue, I couldn't see you for the lid of the
piano.

PREVIN

The lid of the piano was in the way?

ERIC

Was it?

ERNIE

Was it?

PREVIN

Yes.

ERIC

Yes, it was, in the way, the lid of the piano.

PREVIN

I don't know what we can do about that.

ERNIE

He wants to be taller, does he?

[To PREVIN]

Could you wear high heels?

PREVIN

Again?

ERIC

You don't have to.

PREVIN

I don't know what we can do.

ERIC

Would you jump up in the air so I can see you over
the lid of the piano?

                    PREVIN
You want me to actually jump in the air on the
rostrum so you can see my cue?

                    ERIC
Yes, if you'll do that for me.

                    PREVIN
            [Resigned and baffled]

Yes, I'll do that for you.

                    ERNIE
I'll announce that for you.

                    ERIC
He's a nice man.

                    ERNIE
Isn't he charming?

                    ERIC
I like him.

                    ERNIE
            [Runs onto the rostrum]

Grieg by … with him and him.

            [Runs off]

PREVIN starts the intro again, and, on cue, jumps in the air.
ERIC stands up and gives PREVIN a thumbs up over the lid.

                    ERIC
        Great!

ERIC starts playing a piano piece loosely based on Grieg's
Piano Concerto, in the manner of someone attempting *Chopsticks*
on an out of tune upright piano in a backstreet pub. ERNIE
is dancing joyfully. PREVIN walks over and fixes ERIC with a
glare. ERIC stops.

                    ERIC
Something wrong with the violins?

                    PREVIN
No, there's nothing wrong with the violins.

                    ERIC
    That's only your opinion.

                   PREVIN
    Wh-what were you playing just then?

ERIC starts playing it again, briefly, then stops.

                    ERIC
    You're playing all the wrong notes.

ERIC looks away from PREVIN, and bares his teeth at the
audience. He stands up, walks over to PREVIN and grabs him by
the lapels, until they are nose-to-nose.

                    ERIC
    I am playing all the right notes, but not
    necessarily in the right order. I'll give you that.
    I'll give you that, sunshine.

ERIC lets go of PREVIN and gives him the famous two-handed slap.

> ERNIE
> That sounded quite reasonable to me. Are you satisfied, Mr Preview?

> PREVIN
> No!

> ERIC
> No? What do you mean no?

> PREVIN
> I'm not satisfied.

> ERIC
> Why not?

> PREVIN
> Look here, I mean, with all due deference, would you mind?

PREVIN moves to take over the piano stool from ERIC to show him how to play the piece.

> ERIC
> Don't forget, for another four pounds we could have got Edward Heath.

PREVIN plays the piano perfectly. ERIC and ERNIE look dumbstruck. ERIC looks at ERNIE, then at PREVIN and shrugs.

> ERIC
> Rubbish.

> [Eric and Ernie walk off]

PREVIN begins to play ERIC's version of the concerto. ERIC and ERNIE return.

> ERIC
> That's it!

PREVIN plays a jaunty tune while ERIC and ERNIE dance gleefully around the piano.

# Steptoe and Son (1972)

## 'The Desperate Hours'

### Ray Galton and Alan Simpson

When Tony Hancock left the BBC in 1961, he decided not to take the writers who had provided his finest half-hours over to commercial television with him. Staying at Television Centre, Ray Galton and Alan Simpson turned their attention to a series of their own, entitled *Comedy Playhouse*, thirteen one-off situation comedies that would allow them to show off their considerable range. It was the fourth of the run that elicited the greatest interest. A bleak, almost Pinteresque study of a young rag and bone man trying to escape his manipulative, seedy old father, and make his own way in the world, *The Offer* was the birth of *Steptoe and Son*.

Whereas Hancock had been a comic, the stars of *Steptoe and Son* were serious actors. Harry H. Corbett, playing the frustrated younger man, Harold, had been a protégé of Joan Littlewood at her Theatre Workshop in Stratford, east London; while Wilfrid Brambell, who played Harold's father Albert, had learned his trade at the Abbey and Gate theatres in his native Dublin. Their performances brought out the full depth of Galton and Simpson's writing, and the series could be, by turns, both hilarious and moving, as it dealt with Harold's abortive attempts to find happiness or better himself, all of which were thwarted due to his inability to cut himself free from his aged parent.

In this scene from one of the later series, Harold and Albert are held hostage by a pair of escaped prisoners. The four men find they have more in common than they perhaps first realized.

**Series:** *Steptoe and Son* (BBC TV, then BBC1, fifty-nine shows over one *Comedy Playhouse* pilot, eight series, two specials and two *Christmas Night with the Stars* segments, 1962–74), series 7, show 6.

**Original transmission:** BBC1, Monday 3 April 1972, 9.35 p.m.

**Cast in excerpt:** Harry H. Corbett (Harold Steptoe), Wilfrid Brambell (Albert Steptoe), Leonard Rossiter (Spooner), J.G. Devlin (Ferris).

**Producer/director:** John Howard Davies.

INT. LIVING ROOM - NIGHT

Harold and Albert are wrapped up warmly to defeat the bitter cold. A harsh wind blows outside.

> HAROLD
> I wish I'd stayed out in Malaya when I was in the army. I had it made there, and I didn't know it.

> [Sits down next to ALBERT at the table]

> There was this Chinese bird fancied me. Chin-Lo.

> [ALBERT grimaces]

> Her father owned a steamship line or something. Was rolling in it. All I could think about was getting back home. To this. I must have been off my chump. We were all the same, all the lads. All from the ratholes of England. They couldn't wait to get back home.

> ALBERT
> Best country in the world.

> HAROLD
> Don't give me that. It's cold, miserable, damp, it's expensive, it's overcrowded, the pubs shut early …

The lights fail.

> HAROLD
> … and the bleeding lights keep going out.

> ALBERT
> The meter's run out, have you got a shilling?

> HAROLD
> I told you, I'm skint. I've only got about three and a half pence.

> ALBERT
> We'll just have to put another of those foreign coins in, won't we?

HAROLD

That meter holds more stocks of foreign coins than the Bank of England.

ALBERT

Them French francs fits nice. Where are they?

HAROLD

On the sideboard.

ALBERT goes to get the foreign coins. HAROLD walks over to the radio and lights a candle.

HAROLD
[Pretending to be an announcer]

BBC Radio 2, and here is the news. Last month, Britain's international currency reserves shot to astronomical heights, when the electricity meter at 24 Oildrum Lane, Shepherd's Bush, was emptied. Our political correspondent said …

The radio springs into life.

ANNOUNCER
[On radio]

… an up-to-the-minute newsflash. Earlier this evening, two prisoners made a daring escape from Wormwood Scrubs in west London. The men are John Edward Spooner, aged thirty-eight, and Frank Arthur Ferris, aged sixty-four. Both men were serving seven years for armed robbery. The two men are considered to be dangerous, and should not be approached by the general public. If sighted, you should immediately contact your local police station.

Jingle plays.

DJ

And now back to Harold Macmillan, his electric guitar and the Hawaiian Five. Take it away, Harold.

HAROLD bangs the radio on the table.

ALBERT

I don't know why they don't leave the gate open
down at the Scrubs. They're always getting out.
We should have a reduction on the rates. It's
dangerous living round here.

HAROLD

Come on, hurry up and find them coins. I'm
freezing.

ALBERT

There's no francs left.

HAROLD

Oh gawd, I'll have a look.

[Gets up, hits leg on chair]

Oh gawd, my bleeding shin. Oooh.

ALBERT

There's a Yugoslavian one here with a hole in the
middle.

HAROLD

I think I've got a leg here with a dent in the
middle. Well, that'll do.

ALBERT

No, it won't. It's too small.

There is a knock at the door.

ALBERT

Who the hell's that at this time of night?

HAROLD

I clean forgot, it's Prince Philip. I invited him
round for supper. He's always on the earhole. How
the hell do I know who it is? You go look and I'll
sort this out.

[Sorting through coins]

Escudos? That's no good. Five kroner? That's too
big. Pfennigs? That looks the right size.

[Lights come on]

Ha ha hey. Good news. Pfennigs fits in perfectly.
All we've got to do is lay our hands on tons of
pfennigs, Meredith. Now we—

HAROLD turns round to see ALBERT at the door with the two
escaped convicts. SPOONER has one hand over ALBERT's mouth
and an iron bar in the other.

SPOONER
One move and the old man gets it.

HAROLD
Who are you? What are you doing here?

FERRIS
Do as you're told and nobody'll get hurt.

SPOONER
Is anybody else here?

HAROLD
No, just only me and my dad.

[Steps forward]

Let him go. No, don't hit him. He's an old man.

SPOONER
Well, don't try anything then. Alright Frank, go
and have a look around.

FERRIS
Yeah, yeah.

HAROLD
You're the two blokes who's escaped from the
Scrubs?

When choosing his stage name, Pinner-born pianist Reg Dwight dubbed
himself Elton Hercules John, and has always claimed the middle name to be
inspired by that of the Steptoes' horse.

SPOONER

Clever boy. You heard it on the radio, did you?

HAROLD

About five minutes ago.

SPOONER

Did they say we were dangerous?

ALBERT

[Frightened]

Yeah.

SPOONER

Well, they're right. We are. Very. So watch it.
Play your cards right, and nothing will happen to
you, alright? Now that we understand each other,
we can behave like civilized human beings.

HAROLD

What do you want from us?

SPOONER

Well, I'll tell you. First of all, we want some
grub. We're starving.

HAROLD

So are we.

SPOONER

Look sonny, don't try and be funny. Grandad, out
in the kitchen and bring us some grub. Don't try
anything funny, or else Pretty Boy here will have
a slight indentation in his nut. And hurry up.

ALBERT scuttles off to the kitchen.

SPOONER

Right, now give me the keys to your car.

HAROLD

The car? What car? We haven't got a car.

SPOONER

Come off it, everybody's got a car.

> HAROLD

We haven't.

> SPOONER

You've got a garage out there.

> HAROLD

That's not a garage, that's stables out there.

> SPOONER

What, you mean an 'orse?

> HAROLD

We're rag and bone men. She's the only transport we've got.

> FERRIS

We can't make a get-away on a horse, Johnny.

> HAROLD

Dick Turpin did.

SPOONER turns and glares at HAROLD.

> SPOONER

Look sonny, you're beginning to aggravate me. I've had just about enough of you already.

> FERRIS

What are we going to do, Johnny, if they haven't got a car?

> SPOONER

Oh shut up, will you?

> [To HAROLD]

Have you got a telephone?

                    HAROLD
Yes, it's over there.

                   SPOONER
                  [To FERRIS]

Right, ring Margie, tell her where we are and tell
her to get a car over here.

                    HAROLD
You can't do that.

                   SPOONER
Why not?

                    HAROLD
'Cos we haven't paid the bill. It's been cut off.

                   SPOONER
I know something else that's going to be cut off
in a minute if you're not careful.

                    HAROLD
There's a public call box down the bottom of the
road.

                   SPOONER
I can't very well go down there, can I? The place
will be crawling with old bill.

FERRIS sits at the table.

                   SPOONER
Right, how much money have you got in the house?

                    HAROLD
Not much. We've had a very bad week. Trade's been
very slack lately.

SPOONER raises the iron bar to HAROLD's face.

                   SPOONER
How much? Come on, empty your pockets.

HAROLD empties his pockets.

                   SPOONER
Three and a half pence?

HAROLD

The old man might have a bit tucked away
somewhere.

SPOONER

I don't believe him.

[Grabs HAROLD by the collar of his coat]

If you're lying, I don't fancy your chances of
waking up in the morning.

HAROLD

Nobody's lying. I told you. We're skint. There's
some foreign coins in the electric meter. If
you're thinking of getting out of the country,
they might come in handy. I mean there's francs.
You might be able to change them if you take them
to a bank somewhere.

SPOONER

Gor blimey. Of all the houses around here to break
into, we have to pick this one. No money, no car,
no telephone. Nothing.

[Sits down next to FERRIS and adopts Irish accent]

'Oh there's a likely looking house there, Johnny.
Let's break in there, we'll be alright there.' You
berk.

FERRIS

Wasn't my fault.

SPOONER

Wasn't my fault. Shouldn't have brought you with
me. Should have gone on my own. I could have been
miles away by now.

[Takes heater on chair away from HAROLD]

Course, he gets his bleeding trousers caught on
the barbed wire, and I have to go up the wall to
get him down again. He's been holding me back ever
since he got away. He's too old. You see, he can't
keep up with me. He can't run, he's got bad legs.
He's a right liability.

HAROLD

Tha-that's the same for me.

SPOONER

We wouldn't have got caught doing the job in the
first place if it hadn't been for him.

HAROLD

Really?

SPOONER

Yeah. We got into the vaults like good 'uns. Could
have had it away on our toes. Course, he goes
potty. Stuffs all his pockets with gold bullion.
Couldn't move. Rooted to the spot, he was. He's
too weak. He's too old. He's gone.

HAROLD

It's just like him out there. He's held me back
all my life, he has.

SPOONER

You're better off on your own, I reckon.

HAROLD

You can say that again.

ALBERT enters with food.

ALBERT

Here we are. It's all we have, I'm afraid, sir.

SPOONER

What's this?

ALBERT

That's cold porridge from this morning. No milk
I'm afraid. And that's bread and that's cheese.
You can scrape the green bits off.

SPOONER

We can't eat this. That's disgusting. There'd be a
riot if you served that in prison.

ALBERT

It's all we've got.

SPOONER

[To HAROLD]

You don't have to eat this, do you?

HAROLD

Lately, yes.

SPOONER

Poor bastard. You'd be better off inside.

FERRIS takes the porridge.

FERRIS

I'll eat it, thanks very much.

SPOONER

Gawd, you'd eat anything, wouldn't you? He's got no taste, no finesse. Do you know when I look at you, I go …

[To ALBERT]

Oi! Where are you off to?

ALBERT

The karzi.

SPOONER

Tie a knot in it.

ALBERT grimaces.

SPOONER

[To FERRIS]

I don't know how I got tied up with you in the first place. We've got nothing in common at all.

FERRIS

The trouble with you is that you've got it too easy. I was brought up during the Depression. You ate what you could get.

ALBERT

That's right, I remember them days. They don't know nothing about it, these kids.

# *The Goodies* (1975)

## 'The End'

## Graeme Garden and Bill Oddie

The Cambridge Footlights of the early 1960s was a particularly rich breeding ground for TV comedians. They helped to provide principal members of both the *Monty Python* team and *The Goodies*: John Cleese, Graham Chapman, Graeme Garden, Tim Brooke-Taylor and Bill Oddie were all involved in the 1962 Footlights production *Double Take*. Garden and Oddie wrote and performed with Cleese in BBC Radio's *I'm Sorry, I'll Read That Again*, while Brooke-Taylor worked with the same tall future Python on *At Last the 1948 Show*. Garden, Oddie and Brooke-Taylor came together as a team on BBC2's *Twice a Fortnight* and *Broaden Your Mind*, neither of which took off as hoped, but which gave BBC bosses enough confidence in the trio to try a show of their own.

The idea they came up with was for a show somewhere between sitcom and sketch, about three malcontents available for hire to do 'anything, anytime'. In the show, Graeme would be a sort of mad scientist, Tim would be an effete vain patriotic idiot, while Bill would be a bearded troublemaker. Very often, one of the three would have a mad idea, sometimes bordering on an attempt at world domination, while the other two would try to thwart him or, at the very least, calm him down. It became a winning formula and one that kept BBC2 viewers happy for ten years, followed by another series for LWT in 1982. Although dismissed sometimes as *Python* for kids, *The Goodies* was usually, on first transmission, a staple of the 9 p.m. BBC2 comedy slot, and some of the shows tackled serious subjects, including apartheid in South Africa

**Series:** *The Goodies* (seventy-seven shows over nine series, six specials and one *Christmas Night with the Stars* segment, 1970–82), series 5, show 13.

**Original transmission:** BBC2, Monday 5 May 1975, 9 p.m.

**Cast in excerpt:** Tim Brooke-Taylor (Tim), Graeme Garden (Graeme), Bill Oddie (Bill), Corbet Woodall (newsreader), Sheila Steafel (the Queen).

**Producer/director:** Jim Franklin.

and, in the case of this excerpt, the menace of urban renewal and redevelopment.

★ ☆ ★

INT. LIVING ROOM - DAY

BILL is standing by an open window. A bird sings. GRAEME is busy in the corner.

>                    BILL
>      Look at that. Kew Gardens. A verdant oasis amidst
>      the concrete jungle of the metropolis, wherein
>      carefree birds do blithely flit and sing their
>      winsome songs.

BILL picks up airgun and fires out of the window. Birdsong stops.

>                  GRAEME
>      Please, do you mind? This is a very delicate job.

GRAEME picks up a big mallet and thumps mightily on an unseen project.

>                  GRAEME
>      There, finished.

>                    BILL
>      Eh?

>                  GRAEME
>      I have been commissioned by none other than the
>      well-known property magnate Harry Highrise to
>      design the New Kew Gardens redevelopment scheme.

Puts a new model on top of the model of Kew.

>                    BILL
>      Oh lovely, a wonder of modern architecture. Well,
>      at least there's one bit of greenery left.

>                  GRAEME
>      Where? Where?

>          [Plonks a great big block in the gap]

                              BILL
          What's that?

                            GRAEME
          A 350-foot-high block of offices.

                              BILL
          It looks more like a 350-foot-high block of concrete.

                            GRAEME
          Exactly.

                              BILL
          Yes, but Graeme, as an architect, doesn't it strike
          you … No windows and no doors …

                            GRAEME
          Right. Clever, eh? I mean do you realize what the
          rent'll be on this place? four thousand pounds a
          square foot, per minute.

                              BILL
          Nobody could afford that.

                            GRAEME
          No. So there's no point in wasting money on windows
          and doors, is there? In fact there's no rooms in
          there either, so squatters can't move in. Clever, eh?

                              BILL
          Well, all I can say is you wait till Tim finds out. I
          bet he'll be cross.

      TIM enters with a newspaper.

                              TIM
          I'm cross. Look at this. Redevelopment scheme for Kew
          Gardens. Rape. Sacrilege. I'm going to write to the
          Queen.

                              BILL
          Now you're for it.

      GRAEME looks sheepish.

                              TIM
          Right. Here goes. What's the address?

[Looks in *Yellow Pages*]

Queens. Queens. Grayson. La Rue. Regina. Here we are. Oh yes, of course.

[Addresses envelope]

Buckingham Pal … Gra, take a letter. Dear Liz. Elizabeth. Mrs Marm. Oh, Queen. I wish to complain about the wicked plans of Mr Harry Highrise and his evil so-called architect. What's his name? Mr …

[Looks at newspaper]

Graeme Garden. Graeme Garden. May I suggest that they be locked up. No, have their botties smacked. No, be beheaded. Twice. Slowly. Love, Tim. PS Any chance of three OBEs?

[Looking at newspaper]

GRAEME GARDEN? What on earth did you do a thing like this for?

GRAEME

Fifty thousand quid.

TIM

Oh, fair enough. Can I have a look at the cheque? I like cheques.

GRAEME

Ah, well, Mr Highrise is going to send it on when the work's finished.

BILL

You gullible fool! And where is he going to send this cheque?

GRAEME

To this office.

BILL

Oh yes, and where is this office going to be? Right in the middle of the Kew Gardens Redevelopment scheme.

BILL picks up the concrete office block. A model of the office is inside. GRAEME gasps.

> GRAEME
>
> I didn't put that there. Oh, he wouldn't. Oh, I'm sorry.

> TIM
>
> Right, I'm going to have a word with Mr Highrise. I'm going to …
>
> [Opens the door, walks into a concrete wall]

> BILL
>
> Wait a minute, this wasn't here when you came in. It's solid concrete.

> TIM
>
> Agh, the window!

Concrete rises up the window.

> BILL
> [Reading newspaper]
>
> It is hoped that the scheme will be completed by October 7th …

BILL looks at calendar – it is 7th October. Panic ensues.

> TIM
>
> He won't beat us. Sing up, lads. We shall not be moved, we shall not be moved, we shall not be … Let us out!

Concrete fills up the window.

Bill Oddie and Graeme Garden wrote many scripts for LWT's *Doctor* ... series of situation comedies, drawing on Garden's medical training. John Cleese and Graham Chapman – the latter, like Garden, a qualified doctor – also worked extensively on the series.

Caption: 'Sixteen days later'.

The Goodies are watching TV.

> NEWSREADER
>
> The Goodies continue their protest against the Kew Gardens redevelopment scheme, encased in a 350-foot block of solid concrete. Earlier today, a special personal message of congratulations was recorded by Her Majesty [turns page] the Queen.

Fuzzy photo of crowd in front of Buckingham Palace with arrow to the royal balcony.

> QUEEN
> [Voice-over]
>
> Testing, two, three. If I ruled the … testing, one, two. Get off my dress. Am I on yet? Two, three. Oh, dear Tim, Bill and the other one. We have been most impressed by your gallant protest, and we have pleasure in making the following posthumous awards. An OBE to Tim. An OBE to Bill. And [blows raspberry] to the other one. We must say we are most pleased that in this day and age, Englishmen are still prepared to sacrifice their lives for their principles. Goodbye.

> BILL
>
> Au revoir.

> QUEEN
> [Voice-over]
>
> No, goodbye.

> TIM
>
> Sacrifice our lives? What's she mean by that? I thought she'd get us out. We're trapped.

> GRAEME
> [Holding phone]
>
> Don't fret. I'm calling the Ministry of Works.
>
> [Puts phone down]

They're on strike.

                    TIM AND BILL
Yelp!

                    GRAEME
But as soon as they've settled it they're going to
call us right back.

CAPTION: 'Six months later'. Phone rings.

                    GRAEME
See? What did I tell you? Hello. Yes, yes, oh.
Yes, all right. I'll tell them.

                    TIM AND BILL
Yes?

                    GRAEME
Now, the Ministry of Works have promised to get us
out.

                    TIM AND BILL
Oh, what a relief.

                    GRAEME
But …

                    TIM AND BILL
But what?

                    GRAEME
But first they have to finish the Bridgend to
Cromer motorway.

                    BILL
What?

                    TIM
Don't panic.

                    BILL
Sorry.

GRAEME moves to map of Britain.

                    GRAEME
Which has only 200 yards left to go.

                            BILL
        Well, that won't take long.

                            TIM
        No.

                            GRAEME
        No, except that …

                            TIM
        Except what?

                            BILL
        Don't panic.

                            TIM
        Sorry.

                            GRAEME
        Except that, before they finish, they have to
        complete the Aberystwyth to Yarmouth freeway, the
        Swansea to Southend through route, the Bolton to
        Dorchester motorway, the South Wales ringway, the
        Goole to Guildford scenic drive, the Stockport
        flyover, the Bolton bypass and the King's Lynn
        circular.

GRAEME has been drawing on the map. All of these routes form
a game of Noughts and Crosses.

                            GRAEME
        Then they'll finish the Bridgend to Cromer
        motorway. I win.

                            BILL
        And how long's that going to take?

The 'Harry Highrise' mentioned in the script is a thinly veiled reference to
property developer Harry Hyams, who built the Centre Point development
in London's Oxford Street, then left it unoccupied for nearly a decade after
nobody was willing to meet the exorbitant rent he was demanding.

GRAEME

Once the Ministry start drilling into our block we
will be freed in just ten point three seconds.

BILL

Very good.

GRAEME

Mind you, they won't finish the work on the
motorway for one year, seven months, four days,
three hours and five minutes.

BILL

Uhuh.

TIM

So, as I understand it, we shall be stuck in here,
the three of us, together, with no one else, for
another one year…

BILL

… seven months …

TIM

… four days …

GRAEME

… three hours …

TIM

… five minutes …

BILL

… and 10.3 seconds.

GRAEME

Correct.

TIM

Shall we panic?

GRAEME

Certainly.

All panic.

# *Porridge* (1975)

## 'Happy Release'

### Dick Clement and Ian La Frenais

*Porridge* had its origins in *Seven of One*, a series of stand-alone situation comedies all starring the versatile Ronnie Barker, transmitted on BBC2 in 1973. *Prisoner and Escort*, the second show of the run, concerned the northward journey of veteran jailbird Norman Stanley Fletcher to begin a sentence at Slade Prison in the wilds of Cumbria. The escort of the title was Mr Barrowclough, a kindly prison officer played by Brian Wilde, and a marked contrast to the chief prison officer at Slade, the brusque, vindictive Mr Mackay. When the show moved to a series, Fletcher was given a cellmate, a first-time offender from Birmingham called Lennie Godber. For all his cynicism, Fletcher took Godber under his wing and tried to ensure that the lad's first visit to chokey would also be his last, and that he survived his stretch with his dignity intact.

**Series:** *Porridge* (BBC2 then BBC1, twenty-one shows in total over one stand-alone pilot, three series and two specials, 1973–7), series 2, episode 5.

**Original transmission:** BBC1, 21 November 1975. 8.30 p.m.

**Cast in excerpt:** Ronnie Barker (Fletcher), Fulton Mackay (Mr Mackay), Richard Beckinsale (Godber), David Jason (Blanco), Colin Farrell (Norris).

**Producer/director:** Sydney Lotterby.

Although the emphasis was on laughs, Dick Clement and Ian La Frenais managed to capture some essential truths about prison life. Producer Sydney Lotterby was informed by one prison governor that if anyone asked what life was really like inside, he told them that *Porridge* was an accurate a portrayal as any. In Fletcher, Clement and La Frenais created a perfect anti-hero, a criminal with whom the viewers could sympathize, particularly in his (usually successful) attempts to stay one step ahead of Mr Mackay, whose mission was to make the prisoners' lives hell. Barker brought Fletcher to life brilliantly – so much so that it was easy to forget that under the dyed hair was one of the 'Two Ronnies' – but that's not to detract from the other principal cast members.

In this excerpt from an episode in the second series, Fletcher is in the prison hospital with an old man, called Blanco, and Norris, a sleazy, cheating sort of criminal the other prisoners despised, or, in prison slang, a 'charmless nurk'. Naturally, the hidden treasure is a fabrication, and the map leads the released Norris to the pitch at Leeds United FC.

★ ☆ ★

INT. PRISON HOSPITAL - DAY

An orderly opens curtains to reveal FLETCHER with his foot in traction.

> FLETCHER
>
> Thank you, Charlie. I'll do the same for you some day. Oh, hello, Mr Mackay. How kind. I don't think it's official visiting hours. You know?

> MACKAY
>
> You're a lucky man, Fletcher.

> FLETCHER
>
> No grapes, then?

> MACKAY
>
> I just wanted to verify with my own eyes that you weren't malingering.

> FLETCHER
>
> No. No. I have broken my foot. There it is, look. In the plaster. The evidence is irrefootable.
>
> [Laughs and looks at BLANCO]
>
> Oh, he's asleep.

> MACKAY
>
> I won't pretend your indisposition isn't very frustrating, Fletcher.

> FLETCHER
>
> Oh, not for me, it isn't, no. Better grub in here. Better beds. Got me own little cushion, see.

MACKAY

Since you lost your soft number in the library, I
was all set to make your life a misery.

FLETCHER

Yeah, I gathered that when you sent me up that
twenty-foot ladder, yeah, to clean the pigeon
droppings out of the guttering.

MACKAY

Wouldn't surprise me if you fell off intentionally.

FLETCHER

Ha ha, come on! No, no, it's just poetic justice,
that's all. You see, you was out to victimize me,
weren't you? All you did was give me the passport
to comfort and seclusion, see? Mind you, I have
got to put up with that scrote Norris over there
for the next few days.

NORRIS

Yeah, that cuts both ways, don't it?

FLETCHER

You shut your head, Norris or I'll hit you with my
frying pan, mate.

NORRIS

Violence, violence.

MACKAY

Quiet, the pair of you.

BLANCO

What's the matter?

MACKAY

And you, don't want any trouble from you.

NORRIS

It's not me. He's been on at me all afternoon, Mr
Mackay.

MACKAY

That's one thing I can't blame Fletcher for,
Norris. You are not the pleasantest of men. In
fact, you're a horrible creature.

NORRIS

I've had surgery. Ingrowing toenail. Look.

MACKAY

l know the surgery I'd give you had I my way.

FLETCHER

Couldn't wait 'til you got out, could you? Had
to burden our already overworked prison medical
service.

MACKAY

Which is exactly what you're doing, Fletcher.

FLETCHER

Well, we know whose fault that is.

MACKAY

Only four weeks, maximum. I can bide my time. I'll
soon have you up on your foot.

FLETCHER

Not before it's mended.

MACKAY

You're in discomfort, are you?

FLETCHER

No, not to speak of.

MACKAY

Come on, Fletcher. Admit it, it's giving you hell,
isn't it?

FLETCHER

No.

MACKAY

Not even a twinge?

FLETCHER

Not now the plaster's on, no.

MACKAY

There's no justice.

MACKAY lets FLETCHER's leg down from traction, suddenly.

FLETCHER
[Turns to BLANCO]

And the next object is … a thwarted screw.

[Speaks into pee bottle]

A thwarted screw.

NORRIS
[Groans]

Oooh, gawd, I'm in pain.

FLETCHER

Pardon?

NORRIS

I'm in pain.

FLETCHER

Good.

GODBER enters pushing food trolley.

GODBER

Meals on wheels!

FLETCHER

Here she comes! Here, Blanco, look at this. What's
on the menu, Len, apart from yesterday's gravy
stains?

GODBER

Braised steak. Carrots. Mashed potatoes. Bananas
and custard.

FLETCHER

Oh, what's for afters?

GODBER

Tomato soup.

FLETCHER

Hear that. Blanco? Bananas and custard.

BLANCO
[Weakly]

I've got no appetite.

FLETCHER

Oh, you must eat. You must eat. Keep your strength
up. If you don't eat, you'll be ill, won't you?
Oh, you are ill, ain't you?

NORRIS

'Ere, if he don't want his. I'll have it.

FLETCHER

No, you will not. Put it by his bed. He can have
it later … or I will.

GODBER

How are you, Fletch?

FLETCHER

Mustn't grumble. How's yourself?

GODBER

Not as comfy as you. Look at them nice clean
sheets.

FLETCHER

Yeah. Well. Give us some more carrots, will you?

NORRIS

'Ere, don't let me go short.

FLETCHER

Shut up, Norris.

GODBER

Here you are, Fletch.

FLETCHER

Ta. That looks good.

GODBER

There you are, Blanco. I'll just leave it there.
He don't look too chipper.

FLETCHER

Nah, he's alright. He's just a bit depressed,
that's all.

GODBER

Looks at death's door to me.

FLETCHER

'Ere, shut up! Don't talk about being at death's
door when you're in hospital. Especially when
you're at death's door like him.

GODBER

That's a good one, Fletch.

FLETCHER

You've got to laugh, ain't ya?

GODBER

You're cheery, Fletch.

FLETCHER

Well, life of Riley in here, innit, eh? Had a
day out yesterday. Went down to Carlisle General
and got plastered. Lovely nurses down there, you
know, all poking their heads around the door… and
things, you know. 'Cause there I was, the villain,
see? *Convict 99*, manacled to a wheelchair.

GODBER

Like *Ironside*. Only bent.

FLETCHER

Yeah. That's right. Course, it was my air of
villainy what titillated them. Some had bigger
titillations than others. There was one ravishing
West Indian sister in there. Cor—

A prison officer puts his head around the door.

PRISON OFFICER

Come on, lad, you've had long enough to fiddle
around with that.

FLETCHER

That's exactly what she said.

GODBER

Can I just hear the end of this?

PRISON OFFICER

No, you can't. Now come on.

GODBER

Oh well, tell me later, then.

FLETCHER

It'll keep. Look after yourself.

GODBER

Sleep well. Hey, it's ever so nice having the cell
to myself now. It don't half smell fresh in there
without your feet.

While the smaller scale scenes, such as in Fletcher and Godber's cell, were
shot on video tape at BBC Television Centre, the halls and stairways of HMP
Slade were constructed on a larger scale at the BBC Television Film Studios in
Ealing, and shot on 16mm film. Designer Tim Gleeson and producer Sydney
Lotterby took great pains to ensure that footsteps on the metal steps and
gantries sounded completely authentic.

NORRIS

What do you think we feel?

GODBER

Shut up, Norris.

FLETCHER

I should think you'll be glad to get out of here,
won't you, Norris, eh? It'll give you a better
opportunity to be more revolting to a larger
number of people, won't it?

BLANCO

I'll certainly be glad to see the back of him. I
never had much, you know, possessions, like, but
three days before you come in here, he had 'em
all.

FLETCHER

Is this true?

BLANCO

He had me wireless and me silver snuffbox. Real
silver, Fletch. Antique. I kept me snout in it. He
had me snout an 'all.

FLETCHER

Is this true, you?

NORRIS

Yeah. Fair and square.

BLANCO

And my musical box what played 'Waltzing Matilda'
when you opened the lid.

FLETCHER

He just took 'em? Well, make no mistake, Blanco,
he's going to give them back. Don't worry.

NORRIS

Fair and square. It was cards, wasn't it?

FLETCHER

Oh dear. You never played cards with him, did you,
Blanco?

                    BLANCO
     Brag, it were. Nine-card brag.

NORRIS gets up out of bed and puts on dressing gown, then
approaches FLETCHER's bed.

                    NORRIS
     Fair and square.

                    FLETCHER
     You give them back, Norris.

                    NORRIS
     Oooh, like heck.

FLETCHER throws empty urine bottle at NORRIS as he's leaving.
NORRIS yelps.

                    FLETCHER
     Next time, it'll be a full one! Don't you worry,
     Blanco, I'll get them back for you, mate.

                    BLANCO
     It doesn't matter, Fletch. What do I want with a
     'Waltzing Matilda' music box where I'm going?

                    FLETCHER
     You're not going anywhere. You've got another two
     years.

                    BLANCO
     I'm going sooner than that.

                    FLETCHER
     You can't escape, Blanco. You're too old to get
     over the wall. You been watching too much of that
     *Colditz*.

                    BLANCO
     I'm going out of here in a wooden overcoat.

                    FLETCHER
     Oh, now, come on. What kind of talk is that?

                    BLANCO
     My time's up. I won't stay the distance. Tired
     heart, the doctor said. Tired everything, more
     like. I come in here to die.

FLETCHER

You talk rubbish, don't you? You're not ready for celestial porridge yet a while, mate. You're not old. You look old, but then, that's porridge.

BLANCO

Eh?

FLETCHER

Porridge puts years on a man's physical appearance. It's well known. Actually, you're only twenty-nine.

BLANCO

Sixty-three.

FLETCHER

You're not past it at sixty-three. The government's older than that - and what a state the country's in.

BLANCO

Mind you. It weren't much better when I were a lad. Depression. No work. Took to stealing. Such a waste. I spent nigh on half my life in one nick or another. Lost all my family. Mostly through negligence. Mine. That's why I'm resigned to passing on. Well, more than that. Relieved.

FLETCHER

Listen. There's years of mileage left in you yet, mate. Look at Charlie Chaplin. He was over eighty when he became a father for the umpteenth time. Winston Churchill was older than you when he had his finest hour. As was my uncle Wilfred.

BLANCO

Oh? What did he do?

FLETCHER

When he was seventy-two, he married this gorgeous young dental assistant. Of course, it killed him … You should have seen the smile on his face in the coffin, though.

BLANCO

Died with his boots on, did he?

*Porridge* was the basis for one of the few entirely successful and satisfying feature films developed from a British TV sitcom. It concerned a football match between the old lags and a team of Z-list celebrities, and an escape attempt involving the visitors' coach.

> FLETCHER
>
> Yeah, and his teeth out. Couldn't get the coffin lid down for three days. It's all a question of how you feel. For instance, this old man goes to the doctor and says, 'My wife and I aren't getting pleasure out of sex any more.' The doctor was taken aback. He says, 'How old are you?' 'Eighty-one.' 'How old's your wife?' 'Seventy-nine.' 'Seventy-nine and Eighty-one? When did you first notice this?' He says, 'Twice last night. Then again this morning.'

FADE TO NIGHT

The inmates are sleeping.

> BLANCO
>
> Fletch? Fletch!

FLETCHER mumbles.

> BLANCO
>
> I want to talk to you.

> FLETCHER
>
> Oh … What's the matter?

> BLANCO
>
> I want to tell you something while he's asleep. He is asleep, isn't he?

NORRIS snores.

> FLETCHER
>
> Yeah, unless he snores while he's awake, yeah.

BLANCO

You see, I've got something of value. You see, you
know I've got no family. I told you that. The few
things I've got, well, Norris has got them now.
But I've still got one thing of value. And I want
to bequeath it.

FLETCHER

You're getting morbid again.

BLANCO

No. No. I'm not being morbid. I'm being practical,
'cause if anything happened to me, no one would
know about my legacy.

FLETCHER

Look if you want to make a will, Blanco, it's no
good talking to me. You need a solicitor, ain't
you? We got one on our landing. He'll see you
right. Straight as a die, he is. He'll be all
right.

BLANCO

Oh aye? What's his name?

FLETCHER

Corkscrew Carter. Nice bloke.

BLANCO

Thing is, you see. My legacy's not the sort you
can legalize.

FLETCHER

Why? What is it?

BLANCO

Ill-gotten gains. Buried in Leeds.

Another of the one-offs in *Seven of One* was also the basis for a highly
successful series, namely Roy Clarke's *Open All Hours*, featuring Barker as the
tight-fisted shopkeeper Arkwright and David Jason as his nephew Granville.

FLETCHER

Oh. Ill-gotten gains. Say no more.

BLANCO

Shall I tell you about it?

FLETCHER

Not now, Blanco, no.

BLANCO

Well, it were like this. There were three of
us, we'd done a wages van on its way to a fridge
factory near Otley. Do you remember reading about
it?

FLETCHER

No.

BLANCO

It were all in the *Yorkshire Post*.

FLETCHER

Yeah, well, unless it made the *Muswell Hill
Standard* or *Titbits*, I'd have missed it.

BLANCO

I suppose so. Anyway. It was an untidy job. A lot
of things went wrong.

FLETCHER

Yeah, well, you wouldn't be here if they hadn't.

BLANCO

The other two lads were brothers. There was Jack
Barrett and Harry, erm …

FLETCHER

Barrett, was it?

BLANCO

That's right. Did you know him?

FLETCHER

No. Only through his brother, like.

BLANCO

Their escape were in the *Yorkshire Post* and all.
They got away in a fishing boat from Bridlington.

FLETCHER

Yeah, is this going to take long, Blanco? Only my
foot's gone to sleep and I'd like to catch it up.

BLANCO

Not that the Barretts knew where I'd put the loot.

FLETCHER

Yeah, well, much as I'd like to stroll down felony
lane with you …

BLANCO

'Cos I was the one with the map, to show where
it's buried.

FLETCHER

Oh gawd, it's bleeding Treasure Island now!

BLANCO

Eight thousand pounds.

FLETCHER

How much?

BLANCO

Eight thousand pounds.

FLETCHER

Eight big 'uns?

NORRIS is clearly earwigging while pretending to sleep.

BLANCO

Aye, maybe nine. All in used notes. Didn't have
time to count it. Of course, *Yorkshire Post*
said it were  nearer fifteen, but that would be
the thieving company, trying to diddle Lloyd's,
wouldn't it?

FLETCHER

Well, I'm sorry old son, but I never realized the
magnitude of your legacy.

BLANCO

The map's yours, Fletch.

FLETCHER

I don't know what to say. Words fail me, Blanco.
I tell you something, old lad. The money will be
wisely spent, rest assured. There's one question
I'd like to ask you, presuming you don't snuff it,
like … Which, of course, we all hope and pray for.
That you won't, I mean. On your release, you'll
want your map back, I suppose, will you?

BLANCO

Well, if I do stay the distance, I suppose so, yes.

FLETCHER

And you'd trust me to give it to you back?

BLANCO

Of course I would, Fletch.

FLETCHER

Do you know, in all my life, I don't think
anybody's shown me that sort of trust? Probation
officers. Borstal principals. Judges. And yet
here's you. A man who ain't known me long, or with
any great intimacy, you're willing to trust me
with all you've got in the world.

BLANCO

I am that, Fletch.

FLETCHER

You must be bleeding barmy.

FLETCHER turns over with the map in his hand under the
bedclothes and goes to sleep.

# *Q6* (1975)

## 'Jehovah's Burglars'
## Spike Milligan and Neil Shand

**Series:** *Q6* (six shows, 1976, preceded by *Q5*, and *Oh! In Colour,* followed by *Q7, Q8, Q9* and *There's a lot of it About*), show 3

**Original transmission:** BBC2, Thursday 20 November 1975. 9 p.m.

**Cast in excerpt:** Spike Milligan (Burglar 1/Police Sergeant/Grotty Thing), David Lodge (Burglar 2), Peter Jones (Man in house), Robert Dorning (Old man), Chris Langham (Police cadet), John Bluthal (Fang the police dog).

**Producer/director:** Ian Macnaughton.

When *The Goon Show* hit the radio airwaves in 1951, it signalled the beginning of a revolution in British comedy. Music hall had its surrealists and iconoclasts, and Spike Milligan, with the help of writers Eric Sykes, Larry Stephens and John Antrobus, wedded that tradition to his own disdain for authority and the willingness of American comics and cartoons (the 'Goon' name comes from *Popeye*) to blow things up and kill characters repeatedly for comic effect – think of Wile E. Coyote hurtling over any number of precipices in his pursuit of the Road Runner. In Goonland, our lords and masters were cowards or worse, and most people were idiots. The result was dynamite, and perfect for an austere post-war Britain.

Even in the Goon days, attempts were made to transfer Milligan's genius to television, most notably in *A Show Called Fred* and *Son of Fred*, but there was one crucial snag. For radio, Milligan could write about characters crossing the Sahara on a Wurlitzer theatre organ, and, by the grace of the BBC's resourceful sound effects staff, it would happen. On television, even if visual effects could convey Milligan's ideas, they tended to be expensive. When Milligan buckled down for his first full solo television series, *Q5*, in 1969, he picked up on an idea from the *Fred* shows, which was to make a virtue of the limitations, make the production deliberately grotty and to draw attention to the shortcomings at every opportunity.

Nowhere is this attitude more gloriously visible than in this sketch from Milligan's 1976 *Q6* series, which features

several of the members of his television repertory company –
Australian Jewish actor John Bluthal, the always delightful
Peter Jones, David 'I was in *Cockleshell Heroes*' Lodge and
a young Chris Langham – all together in one place, where a
very unconventional robbery is taking place ...

★ ☆ ★

INT. STUDIO

A painted backdrop of an ocean scene, with a mountainous
island in the background. SPIKE MILLIGAN and DAVID LODGE
rip through the paper and emerge dressed as clergymen in
snorkels.

>                    SPIKE
>     By Jove, I enjoyed that swim, Jim.

>                    DAVID
>     So did I, Eric.

>                    SPIKE
>     It's not real water, you know, it's only a piece
>     of paper with the water painted on it. That's why
>     we're not wet, you know.

>                    DAVID
>     Well, as we're dry, why don't we do a sketch on
>     land together?

>                    SPIKE
>     Spiffing idea. Let's do it over here where we
>     marked for the rehearsal this evening. Ah yes.

Caption: 'BBC TV ECONOMY SKETCH'.

>                    SPIKE
>     Knock, knock, knock on the invisible door.

Studio is bare, apart from a prop staircase. PETER JONES is
walking from the back of the studio, dressed as a French
waiter.

>                    PETER
>     Come, come, coming down the invisible hall. Walk,
>     walk, walk. Click, squeak, crunch, open.

SPIKE
Good evening, we have reason to believe that you
are a man standing in an invisible hall.

PETER
Yes, but he's out. Can I help?

SPIKE
We are Jehovah burglars.

PETER
But I'm not Jewish.

SPIKE
I'll come to that later. Me and my friend here are
being persecuted for our beliefs by the police.

PETER
What are your beliefs?

SPIKE
We believe that you've got a lot of good
silverware and stuff like that in the house.

PETER
[To camera]

Good heavens, that's absolutely true.

>               SPIKE
>           [To camera]

We only believe in the absolutely true.

SPIKE and DAVID have now entered the invisible house. DAVID
is placing invisible valuables in a sack. Next to him is a
notice on a stand, reading 'VERY VALUABLE SILVERWARE SHOULD
BE KEPT IN A SAFE AND IT'S YOURS'.

>               PETER
> What are you doing?

>               DAVID
> You.

>               PETER
> But why are you removing that very valuable
> silverware that should be kept in a safe, and it's
> mine.

>               SPIKE
> We have a disbeliever here, brother. We must
> convert him.

PETER kneels down.

>               SPIKE
> Close your eyes and say after me: 'Oh my bleedin'
> 'ead'.

SPIKE thuds PETER with a soft cosh.

>               PETER
>           [Toppling over]

Oh my bleedin' 'ead. Here come de ground.


CUT TO INT. POLICE STATION - DAY

CHRIS LANGHAM is a pimply police cadet with chequered
constable's helmet. SPIKE rushes in and puts on a policeman's
helmet with a revolving blue light on top. Also present is
JOHN BLUTHAL, dressed in a dog suit, smoking a cigar. A map
of London is on the wall behind them.

> CHRIS
> Sergeant, there's just been a distinct thud on the head at 365 Hagley Road, Birmingham.

> SPIKE
> [Looking at camera]

> This is a job for the police.

SPIKE picks up telephone and coshes it.

<u>CUT TO EXT. STREET - DAY</u>

SPIKE and CHRIS perched on the same bicycle, singing 'I'll Be Seeing You', leading a barking JOHN along on a lead.

<u>CUT TO INT. PRISON CELL - DAY</u>

SPIKE and Robert Dorning sit inside a prison cell.

> SPIKE
> 'Ere, they're playing our song.

<u>CUT TO STUDIO. HALLWAY IN INVISIBLE HOUSE</u>

PETER is face down on the ground. He now has a lump on his head, a red lump, which is held on by a piece of elastic under the chin. SPIKE, CHRIS and JOHN enter as the police, and address PETER.

> SPIKE
> Pardon me, sir, we have reason to believe that a lump on the head has been committed at this address. Heel, Fang, heel.

> JOHN
> [In W.C. Fields voice]

> Heel, Fang, he says.

SPIKE turns to DAVID, holding his swag bag.

> SPIKE
> I'm sorry, sir, but I shall have to arrest your wrists with handcuffs.

> DAVID
> In connection with what?

                    SPIKE
With the rest of your arms.

                    DAVID
You can't arrest me, I'm a distant cousin of the
Queen.

SPIKE immediately contorts himself on the floor.

                    SPIKE
This puts me in a very difficult position.

                    JOHN
Lend him a quid until he's straight.

                    SPIKE
Heel, Fang.

                    JOHN
Heel, Fang, he says.

                    CHRIS
Sergeant, I think I can hear someone coming down
the stairs.

                    JOHN
Quick, let's run out of shot.

                    SPIKE
Where's agent …

                [Checks name]

This could mean promotion for you.

An OLD MAN (Robert Dorning) appears on the stair landing,
holding a po and a poker.

> Throughout *Q6*, large luggage labels can be seen hanging from the clothes
> of all of the participants. These were BBC wardrobe department tags,
> and Milligan had decided that they should be left on the costumes as an
> obscure running joke.

Oh, I'm sorry, burglar. My wife thought she heard
policemen down the stairs. Oh dear, I'll be better
soon.

There's a terrific explosion from where the OLD MAN was just
standing. SPIKE, CHRIS and JOHN return with huge handcuffs,
and put the handcuffs on the burglar. They fall to the
ground. During all of this the dog  is barking. They put
handcuffs on DAVID again and they crash to the floor again.

SPIKE

So, trying to escape, eh? I arrest you for being
Houdini, and while I'm here, give me a kiss.

DAVID

Darling, let me explain the mystery to you.

The SERGEANT and the BURGLAR walk up and down.

DAVID

The reason why these handcuffs fall off is because
I am extremely thin due to malnutrition brought on
by VAT.

SPIKE

This man needs a VAT-free diet. We must hurry.
That joke didn't get a laugh. We must get this
man to a criminal wrist-fattening restaurant as
soon as possible, or else he may die, and then the
charge would be … MURDER.

Camera ZOOMS IN on SPIKE and crashes into him. JOHN comes
to the front of scene, singing 'Rose Marie' in the style of
Nelson Eddy. Behind him a table is being set with a checked
tablecloth.

SPIKE

Heel, Fang.

JOHN
[Running back to the table]

Heel, Fang, he says.

SPIKE

I say, I say, waiter. Do you serve wrist-fattening foods here?

PETER

Yes sir, sit down, we serve anybody.

CHRIS

I say, I say, what's this fly doing in my soup?

PETER

That was no lady, that was my wife.

JOHN

Waiter, waiter, why did the chicken cross the road?

PETER

Because no power on earth can bring it down.

DAVID

Waiter, waiter, why has my dog got no nose?

PETER

To get to the other side. Now, any particular wine?

SPIKE

Yes, any particular wine?

[Shouts vague tuneless fanfare]

Now listen, it's time for the cabaret.

CUT TO STUDIO. MAGICIAN'S TRICK

LOTUS BLOSSOM (Julia Breck), a magician's assistant, stands beside a magician's sword-trick cabinet made from tea chests. A public address system comes to life.

PA

And now testing, testing, testing, 'ello, 'ello, and now the Riviera, Catford, is proud to present from merry Hong Kong, the cabaret sensation of 1929, Miss World. And here he is, China's very own Grot-Tee Thing.

                            SPIKE
                         [Inside box]

        OK, Lotus Blossom, take it away.

LOTUS BLOSSOM removes swords and finally SPIKE emerges, in
Chinese costume and Charlie Chan moustache.

                            SPIKE
            Herro folks, it are great to be back. Funny thing
            happen to me on way to studio. I go in fish and
            chip shop. I say, 'Have you any chip left?' He
            say, 'Yes.' I say, 'Serve you bloody right for
            making so many.' Ah well, can't win 'em all.
            For my first trick, is there a thin criminal in
            audience?

                            DAVID
                [Jumping into the sword-trick box]

        This could be my lucky night.

                            SPIKE
        Lucky night! A big hand for lucky night.

            [Drops Chinese accent and removes moustache]

        I am not really Grotty Thing. I am really a police
        officer and I have trapped this English criminal
        in his lair. Don't come out, because I'm coming
        in.

LOTUS BLOSSOM inserts the sword, an 'Ow!' is heard.

CUT TO EXT.

An Eskimo is fishing. SPIKE, in blood-spattered Chinese
costume, walks into shot. The Eskimo is laughing.

                            SPIKE
            Ladies and gentlemen, I have been in many police
            sketches in my time, and this has been one of
            them. Evening all.

# George and Mildred (1976)

## 'Moving On'

### Johnnie Mortimer and Brian Cooke

Between 1973 and 1976, *Man About the House* was one of the top sitcoms on the ITV network. Ostensibly the show was about three young flatmates Chrissy, Jo and Robin. However, their landlord and landlady, George and Mildred Roper, were soon elevated from supporting to equal top billing. It was natural, then, that they should be given their own series when *Man About the House* came to an end. The premise was that their house in Earl's Court had been compulsorily purchased, so they had to move, with Mildred favouring a move to an upmarket location in the suburban oasis of Peacock Crescent, Hampton Wick. George, an impotent layabout with an advanced case of inverted snobbery, was not in favour.

In this excerpt from the first episode of the spin-off series, Mildred's pretensions are on display, as is George's intent to sabotage the whole process so they can move somewhere he'll feel more at home. Showing them around is an estate agent who turns out to be their new next-door neighbour. He never quite comes to grips with George, but his wife and Mildred become the best of friends.

**Series:** *George and Mildred* (Thames Television, thirty-eight shows over five series, 1976–9), series 1, show 1.

**Original transmission:** ITV, Monday 6 September 1976, 8 p.m.

**Cast in excerpt:** Yootha Joyce (Mildred Roper), Brian Murphy (George Roper), Norman Eshley (Jeffrey Fourmile), Sheila Fearn (Ann Fourmile), Nicholas Bond Owen (Tristram Fourmile), Roy Kinnear (Jerry).

**Producer/director:** Peter Frazer-Jones.

INT. CHINTZY SUBURBAN LIVING ROOM - DAY

ANN is sitting on the sofa, reading a magazine. Her husband
JEFFREY walks in.

                    ANN
        Jeffrey?

                    JEFFREY
        Hello darling.

                    ANN
        Was I expecting you home?

                    JEFFREY
        I doubt it, otherwise you'd have been vacuum-
        cleaning and looking harassed.

                    ANN
        I've just this minute …

                    BOTH
        … sat down.

They embrace.

                    JEFFREY
        Yes.

                    ANN
        Lunch, or a five-minute frolic?

                    JEFFREY
        Careful, not at half-term. No, I'm just showing
        some people round next door.

                    ANN
        Ah, it'll have to be the window cleaner again.

                    JEFFREY
        You couldn't, not with the window cleaner. He
        drops his aitches.

                    ANN
        He drops everything when I whistle.

                    JEFFREY
        I'd rather not know, it's difficult to get window
        cleaners.

A vehicle is drawing up outside. ANN and JEFFREY walk to the window.

> JEFFREY
> Oh dear. That can't be them, can it?

EXT. STREET - DAY

A knackered flatbed truck is pulling up outside the row of smart new houses. As it stops suddenly, a pram falls off the back. Tn the cab are GEORGE and MILDRED, driven by GEORGE's friend JERRY.

> MILDRED
> Oh, this is going to make a lovely impression on the new neighbours.

> GEORGE
> [Looking at the house]

> Is that it?

> MILDRED
> Yes.

> GEORGE
> I don't like it.

> MILDRED
> Get out.

They get out of the truck.

> JERRY
> Oh dear. Look at them net curtains. Waving about like they're cemetery flags.

> GEORGE
> Yeah, I know their sort. They think they're God because they've got two bogs.

> MILDRED
> George, I have been sitting on sausage sandwiches.

> JERRY
> [Taking package from MILDRED]

> That's my lunch. Still warm.

JERRY begins eating the sandwiches with an utter lack of
decorum. JEFFREY approaches.

                    JEFFREY
    Mrs Roper?

                    MILDRED
    Yes.

                    JEFFREY
    We spoke on the telephone. Jeffrey Fourmile from
    the estate agents.

                    MILDRED
    Yes, absolutely.

                    JEFFREY
                 [To JERRY]

    Would you be Mr Roper?

                    JERRY
    Not for a big clock.

                   GEORGE
           [Very pleased with himself]

    Is that Fourmile as in the length of the Boat
    Race?

                    MILDRED
    Shall we go inside?

                    JEFFREY
    Of course.

                    JERRY
    I'll hang back for you, George. Might go on the
    knocker, see if I can get a few pickings.

Yootha Joyce and Brian Murphy knew each other well even before *Man
About the House*, having worked together extensively as members of Joan
Littlewood's Theatre Workshop at the Theatre Royal in Stratford, east London.

>               MILDRED
>     George. Don't chat to the driver.

GEORGE, MILDRED and JEFFREY enter the house, leaving JERRY outside. A small boy is examining the detritus that has fallen from JERRY's truck.

>               JERRY
>     Come on, son. Now, listen. Any daft old ladies
>     around here?

INT. HALLWAY - DAY

>               JEFFREY
>     This is the last remaining unit in this small,
>     rather exclusive development, and I may say they
>     are much sought after.

>               GEORGE
>     Yeah, we had trouble finding the place.

>               JEFFREY
>     This is the entrance hall, leading through to the
>     cloakroom, through lounge and affording access to
>     the first floor by means of a staircase.

>               GEORGE
>     Oh, that's a novelty.

>               JEFFREY
>             [Disdainfully]

>     Lounge.

JEFFREY goes through the door into the lounge. MILDRED glares at GEORGE.

>               GEORGE
>         [Still pleased with himself]

>     Fourmile, as in Boat Race.

>               MILDRED
>     Watch it.

GEORGE and MILDRED follow JEFFREY into the lounge.

INT. LOUNGE - DAY

                    MILDRED
                   [Delighted]

Oh! I mean it's so light and spacious. Such big
windows.

                    JEFFREY
Yes, but the local window cleaner's very willing.
Or so I'm told.

                    GEORGE
           [Looking at spec sheet]

What's this? The pay-tee-oh. Ideal for late night
barber's queues.

                    MILDRED
Barbecues, George.

                    GEORGE
What?

                    MILDRED
You shove sticks into things and roast them over
red-hot charcoal. As I will shortly prove to you
if you don't stop showing me up.

JEFFREY beckons GEORGE to the window.

                    JEFFREY
The garden is very manageable. Are you keen on
gardening?

                    GEORGE
Nah, I let 'em run to weed. I grew a nettle once.
Oh, it was about …

[Gestures to roughly own height; then notices something out
                of the window]

… ooh, I say, she's a bit of alright, isn't she?
Next door, too, eh?

                    JEFFREY
Yes, yes, she is.

GEORGE
Yeah, a bit on the skinny side, but there you go.
I like a bit of meat on them meself.

JEFFREY
That's my wife.

GEORGE
Well, there's a lot to be said for skinny women.

MILDRED
Oh, so do you live next door?

JEFFREY
Yes.

MILDRED
Oh, I'm so pleased. I think it's so important to
have nice neighbours.

JEFFREY
Yes. Yes, it is indeed.

GEORGE
[Still looking at spec sheet]

A damn fireplace?

JEFFREY
Eh? Adam.

They move through to the kitchen, but JEFFREY manages to shut
GEORGE out.

JEFFREY
Kitchen, fully fitted, plenty of cupboard space.

GEORGE
Eh!

JEFFREY
Bottle rack, for your wine.

[Looks at GEORGE]

Or your brown ale. A large space for all your
equipment. How big is your freezer?

MILDRED
Oh, it varies. Depending on how optimistic I feel.

GEORGE
Here, what's this big hole in the sink?

JEFFREY
Waste disposal. You put your waste down there,
potato peelings and so forth.

GEORGE
But they'd fall in the cupboard. Nah, I don't
know, Mildred. It's a bit posh for us, innit?

MILDRED
Oh, don't worry about it, George. When you sit
there in your vest, scratching yourself, it'll be
instant *Coronation Street*.

MILDRED walks away.

GEORGE
[To JEFFREY]

I mean, it don't feel like home.

JEFFREY
Well, it's not home.

GEORGE
Yeah, well, I like the place we live in, see.

JEFFREY
And why are you moving?

GEORGE
Oh, that's the council, you see, they want to
knock me down.

> JEFFREY
> Yes.

> GEORGE
> Yeah, well, it's compulsory purchase order, you see, they want to build flyunders or something.

MILDRED returns.

> MILDRED
> Yes, well, you see, the area has gone down dreadfully since we moved there. It hasn't felt the same since the young ones left.

> JEFFREY
> It is a sad time for a mother, when they leave.

> GEORGE
> You what?

> JEFFREY
> Well, and the father too, of course.

> GEORGE
> I wasn't their father.

> JEFFREY
> No?

> GEORGE
> No. They had three or four different fathers as far as I know. They were our lodgers.

> JEFFREY
> Er, shall we move upstairs?

They leave the kitchen. Once again, JEFFREY shuts the door behind him, leaving GEORGE.

# *Rising Damp* (1977)

## 'Clunk Click'

Eric Chappell

**Series:** *Rising Damp* (Yorkshire, twenty-eight shows over one pilot and four series, 1974–8), series 3, show 3.

**Original transmission:** ITV, Tuesday 26 April 1977, 8.30 p.m.

**Cast in excerpt:** Leonard Rossiter (Rigsby), Frances de la Tour (Miss Jones), Don Warrington (Philip), Richard Beckinsale (Alan).

**Producer/director:** Ronnie Baxter.

When Yorkshire Television's head of light entertainment, John Duncan, returned to the BBC in 1974, he left his successor Duncan Wood a present, in the form of a situation comedy set in a university-town boarding house run by a lecherous, racist misanthrope. This would turn out to be one of the ITV network's finest comedy series. In Eric Chappell's original play, *The Banana Box*, the landlord had been called Rooksby, but in the TV version, he became Rupert Rigsby, a miserly coward in a threadbare cardigan. His closest friend was a wayward fleabag of a cat called Vienna, so named because when he saw another pair of eyes in the dark it was 'goodnight Vienna'. Occupying his rooms were a black student called Philip (who claimed to be the son of a tribal chief), a sexually frustrated Brummie called Alan, and the spinster Ruth Jones, on whom Rigsby had designs.

Occasionally, the scripts relied a little too much on Rigsby's racist jibes at Philip, but the performances of the principals made up for any shortcomings. In particular, Leonard Rossiter as Rigsby captured an exasperated seediness perfectly and made a loathsome character almost sympathetic.

INT. CORRIDOR BY RIGSBY'S ROOM - NIGHT

RIGSBY is dressed in dinner jacket, ready to take Miss Jones to The Country Club. He is singing 'Moonlight and Roses'.

> PHILIP
> Rigsby, you could have killed me!

> RIGSBY
> What?!

> PHILIP
> You nearly ran me down out there. You missed me by inches.

> RIGSBY
> Ooh, as close as that, was it? It's alright, it was nothing personal. I was trying to avoid the cat.

> PHILIP
> The cat?! What about me? That's typical of you, Rigsby. You'd swerve to avoid the cat, and run down a dozen pedestrians!

> RIGSBY
> No, no, it's not like that. It's just that I can see him better. His eyes light up in the dark, yours don't - which in your case is a definite drawback.

> PHILIP
> What do you need a car for anyway? They cause pollution, use up the world's resources and in the wrong hands can be as lethal as a loaded revolver!

The final episode of the first series, 'Stand Up and Be Counted', was the subject of legal action from Labour MP Tom Pendry. The plot concerns an election campaign in which the Labour candidate is called Pendry. The staunchly Tory Rigsby suggests that the man is homosexual. The real Pendry's suit was successful, and Yorkshire Television destroyed the master tape. A copy was recovered from Canada, and is now available on DVD with references to Pendry's name edited or pixellated out.

RIGSBY

You don't understand, do you? A car is essential in this country. You can't travel by jungle creeper round here, you know.

PHILIP

You could use a bicycle.

RIGSBY

A bicycle?! I'm taking Miss Jones to the Country Club. What do you suggest we do, go by tandem? I can just see me handing in my clips to the commissionaire. No, I know what's up with you, mate. You are jealous because I'm taking Miss Jones out for the evening, and as soon as I've finished filling my cigarette case I'll be away, and I won't be back until dawn.

He slams the cigarette case shut in PHILIP's face. RUTH enters.

RUTH

Do I look alright, Mr Rigsby?

She is wearing a posh dress, black straw hat and a fox-fur stole, complete with head and legs, draped around her shoulders.

RIGSBY

Alright, Miss Jones? You look ravishing!

RUTH

Well I was wondering about this.

[She indicates the stole]

Don't you think it looks a bit odd?

RIGSBY

Why should it look odd, Miss Jones?

RUTH

Well, it's Aunt Ada's. It's a bit old-fashioned now. I think it's the head. I keep thinking something's leapt on me from behind.

RIGSBY

I shouldn't give it a moment's thought, Miss Jones. It suits you.

RUTH

What do you think, Philip?

PHILIP

What do I think of it? I think it's just another example of the way so-called civilized countries are decimating the animal kingdom, just to satisfy the whims of fashion, to grace the idle, pampered shoulders of Western women.

RUTH

You don't like it?

PHILIP

I think it's disgusting!

RUTH

Well I didn't kill it, and I'm sure Aunt Ada didn't!

PHILIP

You can't transfer your guilt as easily as that, Ruth. You're wearing it!

RIGSBY

Ah, just a minute. How do you know he didn't die of old age? He looks contented enough to me.

[He lifts the fox's head]

Are you feeling alright? 'Course I am!' There you are!

PHILIP
It's obscene, Rigsby. At least we only kill for food and warmth. Not for the Country Club.

RUTH
Oh God, now I've upset him. Perhaps I ought not to wear it.

RIGSBY
Nonsense, it is perfectly acceptable, Miss Jones. As long as Peter Scott doesn't turn up.

RUTH
Do you really think it suits me?

RIGSBY
Miss Jones, I promise you that when we walk through that door, every head will turn. And do you know what they will be thinking? 'Beauty and The Beast'!

RUTH
Oh I don't know, Mr Rigsby, you look very nice too!

RIGSBY
I was referring to the fox actually. Well, shall we go, Miss Jones? Those seatbelts are a bit tricky, and I want to get you strapped down … er, strapped in as safely as possible.

The pilot was produced and directed by *Monty Python* producer Ian Macnaughton. When the series got underway, Macnaughton was back at the BBC, busy with Spike Milligan's *Q6*, so the production duties passed to Yorkshire Television staffer Ronnie Baxter.

# The Good Life (1977)

## 'The Anniversary'

## John Esmonde and Bob Larbey

Having made their names as front-rank comedy writers
with the LWT school sitcom *Please Sir!* and its spin-off
*The Fenn Street Gang*, John Esmonde and Bob Larbey
moved to the BBC for their next major series. Larbey
turned forty in 1974, and began to think about how
different people react to the milestone. Eventually, he
and Esmonde had the idea of a draughtsman hitting
forty and deciding to jack in his job and live off the
land – 'land', in this case, meaning the front and rear
gardens of the Surbiton semi he shared with his wife.
Meanwhile, next door to the suburban farmers were
a quintessential sitcom couple: a rising executive and
his snobby wife. It would have been easy to make the
two couples enemies, but the joy of the series was the
sometimes uneasy but undoubtedly deep and warm
friendship between the Goods and the Leadbetters.
Margo and Jerry thought Tom and Barbara's agrarian
dream was the height of folly, but woe betide anyone
else who dared to criticize them.

Tom and Jerry – now where have we heard those names
before? – had been colleagues and contemporaries at the
same firm, and the ambitious Jerry tried repeatedly to get
Tom to come back into the fold. In this final episode of the
fourth series, Jerry suspected he was about to be passed over
for the managing director's job, and was himself considering
resigning.

**Series:** *The Good Life*
(BBC1, thirty shows
over four series and two
specials, 1975–8), series 4,
show 7.

**Original transmission:**
BBC1, Sunday 22 May
1977, 8.05 p.m.

**Cast in excerpt:** Richard
Briers (Tom Good), Felicity
Kendal (Barbara Good),
Paul Eddington (Jerry
Leadbetter), Penelope
Keith (Margo Leadbetter),
Reginald Marsh (Andrew/
Sir).

**Producer/director:**
John Howard Davies.

INT. LEADBETTER LIVING ROOM - DAY

MARGO is writing a letter.

> MARGO
>
> Jerry, what do you prefer? Wanton or
> irresponsible?

> JERRY
>
> Wanton, I think.

> MARGO
>
> Yes.

> [She writes it down]
>
> Wanton behaviour. Yes.

> JERRY
>
> Who are you writing to? Miss Mountshaft?

> MARGO
>
> No, it's to *The Times*, actually.

> JERRY
>
> What are you writing to *The Times* about?

> MARGO
>
> You.

JERRY stands up, open-mouthed.

> MARGO
>
> Listen.

> [Reads]
>
> 'Sir, is it any wonder that British industry is
> the lame dog of Europe when so-called managing
> directors are incapable of making rational
> decisions? How can Great Britain become great
> again when such wanton behaviour and crass
> stupidity as ...' and then I'm going on to say how
> Andrew didn't give you his job.

> JERRY
>
> That's libel.

MARGO

The truth is never libellous. You are worth ten of
Snetterton.

JERRY

I'll say, darling. I do appreciate the way you're
backing me up in all of this.

MARGO

I'm your wife, Jerry. Is hobble-de-hoy hyphenated?

JERRY

Twice, probably. Margo, what would you say if I
were to resign?

MARGO
[Concerned]

Are you thinking of resigning?

JERRY

It has crossed my mind. I don't really like
Snetterton. In fact, I loathe him. It would stick
in my craw to have to call him 'Sir'. I could call
him 'cur'.

MARGO snorts with laughter.

MARGO

I don't usually like puns, Jerry, but that is
brilliant.

JERRY

It's a very big step of course. Might have to
lower our sights a bit.

The Good and Leadbetter residences were not really in Surbiton. The location
filming for the series took place in Northwood, Middlesex, with the houses in
Kewferry Road.

                    MARGO

Jerry, if it meant retaining our self-respect, I
would be willing to start all over again. Even if
it meant moving to Epsom.

                    JERRY

Thank you, darling.

Doorbell rings.

                    JERRY

I'll go.

               [Exits to hallway]

                    MARGO
                   [To self]

Now. Riff-raff, yes, that's good.

                    JERRY
             [Out of shot in hallway]

Oh it's you, sir. Come on in.

JERRY enters with his boss.

                    JERRY

It's Andrew, darling.

                    ANDREW

Evening, Margo.

                    MARGO

Evening.

                    ANDREW

Well, I suppose I'm a bit of a surprise package,
aren't I?

                    MARGO

That's one way of putting it.

                    JERRY

You'd better sit down, I'll get you a drink.

                    ANDREW

That's very civil of you, Jerry.

MARGO

Yes, civility is a quality that Jerry has never lacked.

ANDREW

Well, I had a very pleasant dinner with Snetterton last night.

MARGO

Did you really?

ANDREW

Yes. Very pleasant. Mostly business, of course. We talked quite a lot about you, Jerry.

JERRY
[Handing him his drink]

Yes, I imagine you would have done.

ANDREW

Thank you. Do you want to know what I said?

JERRY

Well, you're obviously going to tell me, but if you think I'm going to jump through hoops to hurry you up, you're very much mistaken.

MARGO

Bravo, Jerry.

TOM and BARBARA knock at the French windows. JERRY lets them in.

TOM

Hello, Margo. Sorry to barge in, but we thought we'd— [notices Andrew] Oh. Nnnnn. Sorry, you're busy, we'll come back later.

MARGO

No, no, no. Dear Tom and Barbara, come in. We're never too busy to entertain real friends.

JERRY

Sit down, I'll get you some good brandy.

ANDREW looks into his glass.

TOM

Come round to have a bit of a gloat, have you?

ANDREW

Oh, never mince words, eh?

TOM

I don't have to, mate.

BARBARA

Neither do I, you're crackers.

ANDREW

Oh, and the little woman too.

BARBARA

Don't you patronize me.

ANDREW

Well, old Andy doesn't seem to be the flavour of
the month, does he?

TOM

Not unless this month's flavour is yuk.

JERRY

It's all over now, Tom.

MARGO

No, you carry on, Tom.

TOM

I was going to. I'll tell you one thing. Choosing
Snetterton was the biggest clanger you've ever
dropped, and you've dropped some.

ANDREW

I didn't.

TOM

You did. What about serving roast suckling pig to
that trade delegation from Israel?

ANDREW laughs.

ANDREW

No, I mean I didn't choose Snetterton.

JERRY

Then why did you take him to dinner, sir?

ANDREW

Well, old softy, I suppose. If you're going to
tell a fellow he's lost, you might as well soften
the blow with a decent meal.

JERRY

Then …?

ANDREW

Yes, Jerry, you are JJM's new managing director.

MARGO

Oh, Jerry.

[Rushes over to embrace him]

                    JERRY
Thank you very much indeed, Andrew.

                    ANDREW
You assume the crown as to the manner born, Jerry.

                    BARBARA
Next stop, the Palace.

TOM sinks to his knees.

                    TOM
My noble liege.

                    JERRY
Quiet please. Would it be indiscreet, Andrew,
to ask you what it was that finally swayed your
decision?

                    ANDREW
Not at all. No, it was that format that you gave
me a couple of weeks ago. A fine piece of work,
that. I liked the fact that you did it in your own
time as well. And you didn't use company paper.

                    TOM
Sorry I was a bit snappy, Andy.

                    MARGO
Yes, Tom, you really must think before you speak.

                    TOM
No, call it a fault if you like, but I actually
find acrimony quite entertaining.

                    BARBARA
Well, what are you going to do now you've retired?
Take up all-in wrestling?

                    ANDREW
No, I will tell you what I'm going to do, and this
is going to come as a shock to all of you. I'm
going to follow the example of two young people
that I hold in the very highest esteem.

                        BARBARA
    Who?

                        ANDREW
    You two.

                         TOM
    Us?

MARGO laughs uproariously.

                        MARGO
    I've always said you were one of the wittiest men
    in London. That is priceless.

                        ANDREW
    I'm quite serious. No, I'm casting the mask aside
    now. This is the real me talking now. I'm going to
    try the old hand at self-sufficiency.

                        BARBARA
    I was right. You are crackers.

                        ANDREW
    Are you two crackers?

                         TOM
    Yes, but we admit it.

                        JERRY
    This appointment of mine. It is official, isn't
    it? It has been confirmed?

                        ANDREW
    Yes, of course. Oh I know what you're thinking,
    that the old warhorse has pulled a hamstring in
    his last charge. Oh no. I'm in deadly earnest.

                        MARGO
    But, Andrew, it will have the effect of burning
    your social credentials.

                        ANDREW
    Did Tim and Fatima worry about that?

                         TOM
    No, but we didn't have very many to start with.


                                    *The Good Life* (1977)   **145**

ANDREW

Ohhhhh, no. No, I've come to realize there's a
lot of you two in me. After all these years in
commerce, it's oh so …

JERRY

Grubby?

ANDREW

Basic. The soil. The air. Reproduction. I'm not
going to insulate myself from reality any more.
I'm going to touch it every day. That's where I'm
going. Out there. A free spirit at last.

ANDREW goes to leave by the French windows and sets off the
burglar alarm.

JERRY

The burglar alarm.

ANDREW

Oh, any chance of the good brandy now? Where was I?

TOM

You were ringing the bells of freedom, Andy.

ANDREW

Oh yes. Very aptly put, Tim.

MARGO
[On the phone]

Excuse me just a moment. Oh hello, police? This
is Mrs Leadbetter speaking. One assumes that you
haven't got around to sending out a … oh, you
have. Oh well in that case it was a false alarm.
Yes, again. My ideas are bucked up, thank you very
much. It could happen fifty times, the burden of
responsibility is still yours. Goodbye.

[Puts phone down]

I'm so sorry.

TOM

So, Andy, you're not really serious about all this?

The show returned after the 1977 Christmas special for a one-off performance in front of Her Majesty Queen Elizabeth II and the Duke of Edinburgh. After the recording, the royal party were introduced to the cast and crew. The show was transmitted in an extended 45-minute slot, with the episode 'When I'm 65' bookended by the royal arrival and the presentation, complete with commentary by Brian Johnston.

> ANDREW
> Totally, Tim.

> TOM
> There's a lot of trouble with the neighbours.

> ANDREW
> Won't bother me. I'm cutting myself off. I've
> bought a little place in Devon. I've got a
> photograph of it somewhere.

> TOM
> Good grief.

> ANDREW
> Viscount Plymouth's old place. Just a manor house
> and a couple of hundred acres. Pedigree dairy
> herd.

> BARBARA
> You're really going to rough it, aren't you?

> ANDREW
> Only twelve staff, you know.

> TOM
> It's all that overseeing.

> ANDREW
> Won't bother me. Buy myself a hat.

> TOM
> Are you sure you got the idea from us?

ANDREW

Yes. See one, play one. From now on, we are birds
of a feather, we three. Sons of the sod.

TOM

If you want to come round and borrow a fork …

ANDREW embraces TOM and BARBARA.

ANDREW

Thanks, Tim. Well, I must push now. Ordered myself
a new tractor. Want to see what the chap's given
me. Congratulations, Jerry.

[Shakes JERRY's hand]

JERRY

Thank you, Andrew. Same to you.

ANDREW
[To MARGO]

You know, Napoleon once said that every soldier
carries a marshal's baton in his knapsack. I want
you to know, Margo, that I've always thought of
you as Jerry's baton.

MARGO
[Strained]

Thank you very much.

ANDREW

Barbara.

[Embraces Barbara]

BARBARA

You called me Barbara. You've always known my real
name, haven't you?

ANDREW

Yes, sorry about that. Bit of a habit. Call people
by the wrong name, puts them at a disadvantage,
old executive ploy.

[To TOM]

Cheerio, Tim.

                    TOM
Cheerio, Fred.

ANDREW exits.

                    JERRY
Will you excuse me for a moment?

            [Jumps in the air]

Wahey!

                  BARBARA
Oh Jerry, that's no way for a managing director to
behave, but we're so pleased.

                   MARGO
I'm so excited. I want to do something.

                    TOM
Alright, tell you what, let's go next door and
have a double celebration.

                   JERRY
Oh, yes, it's your seventy-eighth birthday or
something.

MARGO and BARBARA exit, except for TOM who goes over to the
drinks cabinet and produces two bottles of champagne.

                    TOM
Sir, haven't you forgotten something?

                   JERRY
Oh yes, of course.

Hands them to JERRY who hands them back.

                   JERRY
Happy birthday.

                    TOM
Oh Jerry, you shouldn't have.

# The Fall and Rise of Reginald Perrin (1977)

## 'Jimmy's Offer'

### David Nobbs

**Series:** *The Fall and Rise of Reginald Perrin* (twenty-one shows over three series, 1976–9), series 2, show 3.

**Original transmission:** BBC1, Wednesday 5 October 1977, 9.25 p.m.

**Cast in excerpt:** Leonard Rossiter (Reginald Perrin), Geoffrey Palmer (Jimmy Anderson).

**Producer/director:** Gareth Gwenlan.

The futility of existence, and executives on the verge of nervous breakdowns are not natural material for situation comedies, but David Nobbs – by turns a serious novelist, a playwright and a supplier of sketches to the *Two Ronnies* and *Les Dawson* – made them the subject of one of the great hits of 1970s television. Reginald Iolanthe Perrin, who is in middle-management with Sunshine Desserts, wonders where his life is leading. His boss is an appalling autocrat called CJ who enjoys playing mind games with his staff and responding to every assertion or claim by saying 'I didn't get where I am today without …', his juniors are crawlers, he fancies his secretary, and he thinks his mother-in-law resembles a hippopotamus. Over the course of the first series, Perrin gets madder and madder, before leaving his clothes on a Dorset beach and faking his own death. In subsequent series, Perrin returns to civilization, first opening a chain of shops selling useless items, then starting a suburban retreat for people in need of relief from the rat race.

Although despair underpinned much of *The Fall and Rise of Reginald Perrin*, the scripts were also full of superb laughs. In this excerpt from the second series, the comic value of a good list becomes obvious. Well, two good lists, as it happens. It concludes with the moment when Reggie has the inspiration to found his chain of Grot shops.

INT. JIMMY'S BEDSIT - DAY

The door opens. REGGIE and JIMMY enter.

                    JIMMY
     Not much of a place. A lifetime in the army. Bit
     of a greenhorn in civvy street. Stay for lunch?

                    REGGIE
     Yes.

                    JIMMY
     Scrag end of lamb, sprouts, cheese.

                    REGGIE
                    [Aside]

     God, it'll all be off by now.

                    [Aloud to JIMMY]

     Yes, sounds lovely.

                    JIMMY
     Fancy a whisky?

                    REGGIE
     Yes, yes, please, I do.

                    JIMMY
     So do I. Wish I had some. Cock-up on the liquid
     refreshment front.

                    REGGIE
     Well, who's this mysterious colleague of yours you
     wanted me to meet?

                    JIMMY
     Better you don't know.

                    REGGIE
     Ah. It's going to be a little difficult not to
     guess who he is when I meet him, isn't it?

                    JIMMY
     Aren't going to. Wants to remain in background
     until we're sure of you.

The first series was adapted from David Nobbs' novel *The Death of Reginald Perrin* and could have been very different if Nobbs' agent hadn't refused the first TV offer. Granada wanted to make it into a two-part drama, starring Ronnie Barker. Instead, it went to James Gilbert at the BBC as a situation comedy.

                    REGGIE
What are we planning to do? Rob a train? Invade
Poland?

                    JIMMY
Something I want to show you.

                    REGGIE
I see you still keep a bedpack army-style, Jimmy.

                    JIMMY
Habit of a lifetime. Old soldiers die hard.

                    REGGIE
Yes, old habits never die, they only fade away.

JIMMY reaches under the bed. Produces a dead mouse.

                    REGGIE
Ah, a dead mouse, fascinating. I am glad you asked
me over, Jimmy. The tension rises. Ah, a khaki
chamber pot. We are going to invade Poland.

                    JIMMY
Here we are, give me a hand, Reggie.

REGGIE crouches down to help JIMMY with a heavy item.

                    JIMMY
You've got it?

They lift a crate onto the bed. JIMMY opens it.

                    REGGIE
Good God.

                    JIMMY
Know what those are?

REGGIE
[Holding up a gun]

Rifles? Who on earth are these for, Jimmy?

JIMMY
Army. Equipped to fight for Britain when the balloon
goes up.

REGGIE
What army? What balloon? Up what? Fight against whom?

JIMMY puts a finger to his lips, takes the rifle from REGGIE
and replaces it in the crate.

REGGIE
Come on, Jimmy. Who are you going to fight against
when this balloon of yours goes up?

JIMMY
Forces of anarchy. Wreckers of law and order.

REGGIE
Ah, I see.

JIMMY
Communists, Maoists, Trotskyists, neo-Trotskyists,
crypto-Trotskyists, union leaders, communist union
leaders.

REGGIE
I see.

JIMMY
Atheists, agnostics, long-haired weirdos, short-
haired weirdos, vandals, hooligans, football
supporters, namby-pamby probation officers, rapists,
papists, papist rapists, foreign surgeons, head-
shrinkers, who ought to be locked up, Wedgwood Benn,
keg bitter, punk rock, glue-sniffers, Play for Today,
squatters, Clive Jenkins, Roy Jenkins, Up Jenkins, up
everybody's, Chinese restaurants. Why do you think
Windsor Castle is ringed with Chinese restaurants?

REGGIE
Is that all?

When a second series was commissioned, Nobbs planned to write it purely for television, but was persuaded by Leonard Rossiter to write a novel first, then adapt the series from that. Rossiter felt it added depth to the characters, and enabled him to understand better the man he was playing and the world around him.

                          JIMMY
    Yes.

                          REGGIE
    I see. You realize the sort of people you're
    going to attract, don't you, Jimmy? Thugs, bully-
    boys, psychopaths, sacked policemen, security
    guards, sacked security guards, racialists, Paki-
    bashers, queer-bashers, chink-bashers, basher-
    bashers, anybody-bashers, rear Admirals, queer
    Admirals, vice-Admirals, fascists, neo-fascists,
    crypto-fascists, loyalists, neo-loyalists, crypto-
    loyalists.

                          JIMMY
    You really think so? I thought support might be
    difficult. Well, Reggie, are you with us?

                          REGGIE
    I certainly am not. I've never heard such absolute
    rubbish. It is all rubbish. Absolute and utter
    rubbish. Not only that, Jimmy, it is neo-rubbish
    and crypto-rubbish.

            [Gets to door, then turns back]

    Rubbish. Rubbish. RUBBISH. Jimmy, thank you very
    much indeed.

REGGIE shakes JIMMY's hand.

                          JIMMY
    What for?

                          REGGIE
    Can't tell you. Hush hush. Not time or place.

REGGIE leaves.

# *Fawlty Towers* (1979)

## 'Communication Problems'

### John Cleese and Connie Booth

A location filming trip for *Monty Python's Flying Circus* provided the inspiration for one of the most enduring British situation comedies. The cast and crew had been booked into the Gleneagles Hotel in Torquay, run by a former naval officer called Donald Sinclair, but after experiencing his rudeness, the whole party moved to a different hotel. Apart from, that is, John Cleese, who found Sinclair fascinating and stayed on to observe him. With his then-wife Connie Booth, Cleese turned Sinclair into Basil Fawlty, Korean war veteran, snob, bully and coward, for six episodes on BBC2 in 1975. Four years and a divorce intervened before Booth and Cleese returned to Torquay for six more episodes, all maintaining the high standard of the first run.

Fawlty was married to Sybil, as appalling in her own way as he was in his, with her hyena-like laugh. The contempt in which the Fawltys held each other led viewers to wonder not just why they stayed together, but how they had come to be married in the first place. The staff was completed by Spanish waiter Manuel – a gift to impressionists then and now – struggling artist-cum-waitress Polly and Terry the chef. In this excerpt, an elderly, imperious, deaf female guest arrives to test Basil's already short patience.

**Series::** *Fawlty Towers* (BBC2, twelve shows over two series, 1975–9), series 2, show 1.

**Original transmission:** BBC2, Monday 19 February 1979, 9 p.m.

**Cast in excerpt:** John Cleese (Basil Fawlty), Prunella Scales (Sybil Fawlty), Connie Booth (Polly), Andrew Sachs (Manuel), Joan Sanderson (Mrs Richards), Johnny Shannon (Mr Firkins), Robert Lankesheer (Mr Thurston).

**Producer:** Douglas Argent.

**Director:** Bob Spiers.

INT. FAWLTY TOWERS RECEPTION - DAY

A guest, Mr THURSTON, approaches POLLY at the reception desk.
MRS RICHARDS comes in through the main door, followed by a
taxi driver carrying her case.

> POLLY
> [To THURSTON]

Oh, hello … can I help you?

> MRS RICHARDS

Girl! Would you give me change for this, please.

> POLLY

In one moment – I'm just dealing with this
gentleman. Yes, Mr Thurston?

> MRS RICHARDS

What?

> THURSTON

Thank you. I was wondering if you could …

> MRS RICHARDS

I need change for this.

> POLLY

In a moment – I'm dealing with this gentleman.

> MRS RICHARDS

But I have a taxi driver waiting. Surely this
gentleman wouldn't mind if you just gave me
change.

> POLLY
> [To THURSTON]

Do you?

> THURSTON

No, no, go ahead.

> POLLY
> [Giving MRS RICHARDS her change]

There you are.

THURSTON

Can you tell me how to get to Glendower Street …

MRS RICHARDS pays the driver, who exits. She turns back to POLLY.

MRS RICHARDS

Now, I've booked a room and bath with a sea view for three nights …

POLLY
[To THURSTON]

Glendower Street?

[Gets a map]

THURSTON

Yes.

MRS RICHARDS

You haven't finished with me.

POLLY

Mrs … ?

MRS RICHARDS

Mrs Richards. Mrs Alice Richards.

POLLY

Mrs Richards, Mr Thurston. Mr Thurston, Mrs Richards.

[MRS RICHARDS, slightly thrown, looks at MR THURSTON]

Mr Thurston is the gentleman I'm attending to at the moment.

In the opening titles of each episode after the first, in which they appeared unmolested, the letters on the sign saying 'Fawlty Towers' had been rearranged by a creative vandal. The hotel was known variously as 'Farty Towels', 'Fatty Owls', 'Flowery Twats' and 'Flay Otters'.

                    MRS RICHARDS
What?

                    POLLY
                    [Loudly]

Mr Thurston is the gentleman I'm attending to—

                    MRS RICHARDS
Don't shout, I'm not deaf.

                    POLLY
Mr Thurston was here before you, Mrs Richards.

                    MRS RICHARDS
But you were serving me.

                    POLLY
I gave you change, but I hadn't finished dealing
with him.

                    [To THURSTON]

Glendower Street is this one here, just off
Chester Street.

                    MRS RICHARDS
Isn't there anyone else in attendance here?
Really, this is the most appalling service I've
ever—

                    POLLY
                    [Spotting MANUEL]

Good idea! Manuel! Could you lend Mrs Richards
your assistance in connection with her
reservation.

                    [To THURSTON]

Now …

    [She continues to give THURSTON directions]

MRS RICHARDS
[To MANUEL]

Now, I've reserved a very quiet room, with a bath
and a sea view. I specifically asked for a sea
view in my written confirmation, so please be sure
I have it.

MANUEL

*Qué?*

MRS RICHARDS

What?

MANUEL

*Qué?*

MRS RICHARDS

K?

MANUEL

*Si.*

MRS RICHARDS

C?

[MANUEL nods]

KC?

[MANUEL looks puzzled]

KC? What are you trying to say?

MANUEL

No, no - *Qué* - what?

MRS RICHARDS

K - what?

MANUEL

*Si! Qué* - what?

MRS RICHARDS

C.K. Watt?

MANUEL

Yes.

MRS RICHARDS  
Who is C.K. Watt?

MANUEL  
*Qué?*

MRS RICHARDS  
Is it the manager, Mr Watt?

MANUEL  
Oh, manager!

MRS RICHARDS  
He is.

MANUEL  
Ah … Mr Fawlty.

MRS RICHARDS  
What?

MANUEL  
Fawlty.

MRS RICHARDS  
What are you talking about, you silly little man.

[Turns to POLLY, THURSTON having gone]

What is going on here? I ask him for my room, and he tells me the manager's a Mr Watt and he's aged forty.

MANUEL  
No. No. Fawlty.

MRS RICHARDS  
Faulty? What's wrong with him?

POLLY  
It's all right, Mrs Richards. He's from Barcelona.

MRS RICHARDS  
The manager's from Barcelona?

MANUEL  
No, no. He's from Swanage.

POLLY

And you're in twenty-two.

MRS RICHARDS

What?

POLLY

[Leaning over the desk to get close]

You're in room twenty-two. Manuel, take these
cases up to twenty-two, will you?

MANUEL

*Si.*

He goes upstairs with the cases. MRS RICHARDS follows. Mr
FIRKINS arrives at the desk as BASIL emerges from the office.

FIRKINS

Very nice stay, Mr Fawlty.

BASIL

Ah, glad you enjoyed it. Polly, would you get
Mr Firkins' bill, please. Well, when will we be
seeing you again?

FIRKINS

Not for a few weeks.

BASIL

Oh.

FIRKINS

You … you're not by any chance a betting man, Mr
Fawlty?

BASIL

Er …

[Looks towards the office; then, more quietly]

Well, I used to be.

FIRKINS

Only there's a nice little filly running at Exeter
this afternoon.

                    BASIL
Really?

                    FIRKINS
Dragonfly.

          [POLLY gives him his bill]
Ah.

                    BASIL
Dragonfly?

                    FIRKINS
Yes, it's well worth a flutter … but pay the tax
on it before …

                    BASIL
          [Seeing SYBIL approaching]

Ssssshhhh … Well, I'm delighted you enjoyed your
stay.

                    FIRKINS
Very nice.

                    BASIL
Hope to see you again before long.

                    FIRKINS
          [Paying his bill]

There you are.

                    BASIL
Thank you.

                    FIRKINS
Bye, Mr Fawlty.

                    SYBIL
Goodbye, Mr Firkins.

                    BASIL
          [To SYBIL]

A satisfied customer. We should have him stuffed.

FIRKINS
[From the main door]

Oh, Mr Fawlty. Three o'clock Exeter. Dragonfly.
Right?

[He leaves]

BASIL
… Yes. Good luck. Jolly good luck with it.

He busies himself. SYBIL stares at him. THE MAJOR wanders up.

BASIL
Morning, Major.

THE MAJOR
Morning, Fawlty.

BASIL
[Catching SYBIL's eye]

Yes, dear?

SYBIL
What was that about the three o'clock at Exeter,
Basil?

BASIL
Oh, some horse he's going to bet on I expect,
dear.

[To THE MAJOR]

You're looking very spruce today, Major.

THE MAJOR
St George's Day, old boy.

BASIL
Really?

THE MAJOR
Got a horse, have you? What's its name?

BASIL
Um …

[To SYBIL]

Did you catch it, dear?

SYBIL

Dragonfly, Major.

THE MAJOR

Going to have a flutter, Fawlty?

BASIL

No-o, no, no …

SYBIL

No, Basil doesn't bet any more, Major. Do you, dear?

BASIL

No dear, I don't. No, that particular avenue of pleasure has been closed off.

SYBIL
[Quietish]

And we don't want it opened up again, do we, Basil?

[She goes into the office]

BASIL

No, you don't dear, no. The Great Warning-Off of May the 8th. Yes. Good old St George, eh, Major?

THE MAJOR

Hmmm.

BASIL

He killed a hideous fire-breathing old dragon, didn't he, Polly?

POLLY

Ran it through with a lance, I believe.

MANUEL
[Running in]

Mr Fawlty, Mr Fawlty. Is Mrs … er, room, no like … she want speak to you, is problem.

                              BASIL
                          [Moving off]

            Ever see my wife making toast, Polly?

      [He mimes breathing on both sides of a slice of bread]

                           THE MAJOR
            Why did he kill it, anyway, Fawlty?

                              BASIL
            I don't know, Major. Better than marrying it.

                  [He follows MANUEL upstairs]

                           THE MAJOR
            Marrying it? But he didn't have to kill it though,
            did he? I mean, he could have just not turned up
            at the church.

Upstairs, BASIL follows MANUEL at a good pace towards MRS
RICHARDS' room. They go in.

INT. MRS RICHARDS' GUEST ROOM - DAY

                              BASIL
            Good morning, madam - can I help you?

                         MRS RICHARDS
            Are you the manager?

                              BASIL
            I am the owner, madam.

                         MRS RICHARDS
            What?

                              BASIL
            I am the owner.

                         MRS RICHARDS
            I want to speak to the manager.

                              BASIL
            I am the manager too.

                         MRS RICHARDS
            What?

                    BASIL

I am the manager as well.

                    MANUEL

Manaher! Him manaher!

                    BASIL

Shut up!

                MRS RICHARDS

Oh … you're Watt.

                    BASIL

I'm the manager.

                MRS RICHARDS

Watt?

                    BASIL

I'm … the … manager.

                MRS RICHARDS

Yes, I know, you've just told me, what's the
matter with you? Now listen to me. I've booked a
room with a bath. When I book a room with a bath I
expect to get a bath.

                    BASIL

You've got a bath.

                MRS RICHARDS

I'm not paying seven pounds twenty pence per night
plus VAT for a room without a bath.

                    BASIL
            [Opening the bathroom door]

There is your bath.

                MRS RICHARDS

You call that a bath? It's not big enough to drown
a mouse. It's disgraceful.

            [She moves away to the window]

BASIL
[Muttering]

I wish you were a mouse, I'd show you.

MRS RICHARDS
[At the window, which has a nice view]

And another thing - I asked for a room with a
view.

BASIL
[To himself]

Deaf, mad and blind.

[He goes to window]

This is the view as far as I can remember, madam.
Yes, this is it.

MRS RICHARDS
When I pay for a view I expect something more
interesting than that.

BASIL
That is Torquay, madam.

MRS RICHARDS
Well, it's not good enough.

BASIL
Well … may I ask what you were hoping to see out
of a Torquay hotel bedroom window? Sydney Opera
House perhaps? The Hanging Gardens of Babylon?
Herds of wildebeest sweeping majestically—

The building used for the exterior of the hotel was nowhere near Devon.
It was the Wooburn Grange Country Club in Bourne End, Buckinghamshire.
Other exteriors were mostly shot in the area around Harrow.

MRS RICHARDS

Don't be silly. I expect to be able to see the
sea.

BASIL

You can see the sea. It's over there between the
land and the sky.

MRS RICHARDS

I'd need a telescope to see that.

BASIL

Well, may I suggest you consider moving to a hotel
closer to the sea. Or preferably in it.

MRS RICHARDS

Now listen to me; I'm not satisfied, but I have
decided to stay here. However, I shall expect a
reduction.

BASIL

Why, because Krakatoa's not erupting at the
moment?

MRS RICHARDS

Because the room is cold, the bath is too small,
the view is invisible and the radio doesn't work.

BASIL

No, the radio works. You don't.

MRS RICHARDS

What?

BASIL

I'll see if I can fix it, you scabby old bat.

BASIL turns the radio on loudly. MANUEL puts his fingers in
his ears. BASIL turns the radio off.

BASIL

I think we got something then.

MRS RICHARDS

What?

                         BASIL
I think we got something then.

                      MRS RICHARDS
[To MANUEL, who still has his fingers in his ears]

What are you doing?

                        MANUEL
                       [Loudly]

*Qué?*

                         BASIL
Madam … don't think me rude, but may I ask … do
you by any chance have a hearing aid?

                      MRS RICHARDS
A what?

                         BASIL
A hearing aid!!!

                      MRS RICHARDS
Yes, I do have a hearing aid.

                         BASIL
Would you like me to get it mended?

                      MRS RICHARDS
Mended? It's working perfectly alright.

                         BASIL
No, it isn't.

                      MRS RICHARDS
I haven't got it turned on at the moment.

                         BASIL
Why not?

                      MRS RICHARDS
The battery runs down. Now what sort of a
reduction are you going to give me on this room?

                    BASIL
                 [Whispering]

Sixty per cent if you turn that on.

                 MRS RICHARDS
What?

                    BASIL
                  [Loudly]

My wife handles all such matters, I'm sure she
will be delighted to discuss it with you.

                 MRS RICHARDS
I shall speak to her after lunch.

                    BASIL
You heard that alright, didn't you.

                 MRS RICHARDS
What?

                    BASIL
Thank you so much. Lunch will be served at half-
past twelve.

# *Butterflies* (1979)

## 'Leaving'

### Carla Lane

**Series:** *Butterflies* (twenty-eight shows over four series and one special, 1978–83), series 2, episode 1.

**Original transmission:** BBC2, Monday 29 October 1979, 9 p.m.

**Principal cast:** Wendy Craig (Ria Parkinson), Geoffrey Palmer (Ben Parkinson), Joyce Windsor (Ruby).

**Producer/director:** Gareth Gwenlan.

Carla Lane was a mother of two young sons when she joined the Liverpool Writers' Club in the 1960s. There she met Myra Taylor, with whom she struck up a friendship and a working partnership, submitting sitcom ideas to the BBC's then head of comedy, Michael Mills. They showed enough promise for Mills to call the pair in and ask them to write a script about two young female housemates. The result was *The Liver Birds*, which ran for nine series between 1969 and 1979, before returning for a final run in 1996, catching up with the characters in middle age.

The encroachment of middle age was at the centre of *Butterflies*, focusing on Ria and Ben Parkinson, a married couple with two sons on the cusp of adolescence and adulthood. Ben, a dentist with a penchant for collecting butterflies, is largely pleased with the state of his marriage, apart from Ria's appalling cooking, while Ria feels neglected by Ben, as a result of his work and his hobby. Seeking companionship and possibly something else, she strikes up an association with Leonard, a businessman she meets while taking a walk in the park. Leonard is keen to entice Ria into an affair. Ria, although tempted, resisted for four series, before realizing her heart remained with Ben.

INT. PARKINSON'S DINING ROOM - DAY

RIA walks in. BEN is at the dining table, dealing with some
false teeth.

                    RIA
     Ben, I must talk to you.

                    BEN
               [Showing her the teeth]

     Look at those. Aren't they perfect? This woman
     came to me, had a mouth like an old graveyard.

                    RIA
     Adam's making me anxious.

                    BEN
     Stop his pocket money immediately.

                    RIA
     Listen, if you don't listen to me, I'll go into
     that kitchen and I'll get that, some sort of
     pie, and I'll run amok with it in and around this
     house.

                    BEN
     I'm listening.

                    RIA
     You know Adam has been deeply involved with that
     girl Annie?

                    BEN
     I was aware that we were all being suffocated by
     my aftershave, yes.

                    RIA
     Well, she's left him.

                    BEN
     So?

                    RIA
     So now he's in bed, beneath the covers,
     motionless.

BEN

Well, it's a reasonable reaction for him. I mean
he never did move about with that sense of urgency
one associates with being awake.

RIA

He looks so thin, so vulnerable, lying there. And
I know what he's thinking. He's thinking he's
undesirable. Oh Ben. You must know what that's
like.

BEN looks round, affronted.

RIA

You've been a boy, you must know the awkwardness
of it.

BEN

When I was a boy, there was no time to wallow in
one's awkwardness. You had to assess yourself.
Find out what you were best at and thrust it at
the world. The young today haven't got that kind
of energy. He can't take the top off his boiled
egg without going back to bed to recuperate.

RIA

We're talking about love ending.

BEN

How can he possibly be in love? He's only known
her a week.

RIA

Well, I knew perfectly well how I felt about you
within the hour. You smiled and everything on your
face sort of moved over to make room for it. If
you'd have left me after that, I'd have felt just
the same as Adam.

BEN

Yeah. It's not like that today, is it? It's not
the smiles, the gestures, the little endearments.
It's a quick shake of the hand and straight into a
double nelson.

RIA

Is that all you're going to say? You're just going
to sit there worrying about other people's teeth,
while your own son fades away?

BEN

He won't fade away. In a few days time, another
voracious female will slither up those stairs and
that room of his will hold another dark and dreadful
secret.

In 2006, Lane – whose real name is Romana Barrack – claimed that she had not
been loyal to her husband like Ria in *Butterflies*, and had begun a long-running
affair with an un-named BBC comedy producer while still married. She and her
husband divorced, finally, in 1980.

                              RIA
Adam is going through a difficult stage in his life.

                              BEN
We're all going through a difficult stage in his
life.

                              RIA
His body is neither one thing nor another. His face
hasn't come to any definite decisions yet. His chest
has only managed to produce two hairs.

                              BEN
Two?

                              RIA
Two.

                              BEN
No, it's not a lot.

                              RIA
And now he's been told by Annie that he's boring.
Boring!

                              BEN
He's upstairs, you say?

                              RIA
Yes, there's a sort of mound under the bedclothes.

BEN gets up to go and give ADAM a fatherly chat. He leaves
through one door. As he does so, RUBY the cleaning lady enters
through the other.

                              RUBY
The cat's been on the landing.

For many years, Carla Lane ran an animal sanctuary from her West Sussex
home. In 2002, she returned her OBE to Prime Minister Tony Blair, in protest
at the awarding of a CBE to Brian Cass, the chief executive of Huntingdon Life
Sciences, a company involved in vivisection.

# End of Part One (1980)

## 'Nationtrite'

### Andrew Marshall and David Renwick

By 1980, Andrew Marshall and David Renwick already had a wealth of experience as comedy writers, having written, individually or in partnership, for Dave Allen, Les Dawson and the *Two Ronnies*, among many others. The work in which their distinctive surreal and satirical voice had been most clearly heard had been the Radio 4 comedy series *The Burkiss Way*, and when its original producer, Simon Brett, moved into television at LWT, he took Marshall and Renwick with him. They, in turn, took Burkiss principal Fred Harris to head the cast of their new show. While not actually a TV version of *The Burkiss Way*, *End of Part One* was clearly cut from the same cloth, with lacerating parodies of then current shows.

Bizarrely, *End of Part One*, which seemed a natural fit for a Sunday 10.30 p.m. slot, where ITV placed a lot of its edgier comedy, was transmitted on Sunday afternoons. Had someone mistaken it for a kids' show? Or had the decision been taken to just bung it out anywhere and get rid of it? Although not a hit at the time, the bizarre scheduling ensured it was watched by a lot of young comedy fans who still remember the series with great fondness thirty years on. One of the most readily spoofable programmes then on television was BBC1's early evening current affairs programme *Nationwide*. Perhaps unfairly, it had got a reputation for daft stories about unusual pets – skateboarding ducks and snails that drank beer – and for technical foul-ups when the many live contributions from the BBC regions came in. Marshall and Renwick did not

**Series:** *End of Part One* (LWT, fourteen shows over two series, 1979–80), series 2, show 4.

**Original transmission:** ITV, Sunday 2 November 1980, 4 p.m.

**Cast in excerpt:** Fred Harris (First male presenter), Sue Holderness (Sue Straightman), Denise Coffey (Mr Norman Woman), Tony Aitken (Second male presenter).

**Producer:** Humphrey Barclay.

**Director:** Geoffrey Sax.

flinch from their satirical duty in this 'Nationtrite' sketch. (Historical note: Horace Cutler was the Tory leader of the Greater London Council in those pre-Ken Livingstone days.)

```
                OVER OPENING CREDITS
                     ANNOUNCER
        And now on BBC2, Nationtrite.
```

Music: *Nationwide* theme ('The Good Word' by Johnny Scott) and spoof of the *Nationwide* opening titles. Regional opt-out programme names scroll past: 'It's the North', 'Scotland Now', 'South Today', 'Lake District in Focus', 'Up the West-East', 'East Anglia the Hard Way', 'Wales Kept Where It Belongs', 'No Sex Please, We're the Midlands', 'Duff Announcers in Exile'.

```
                END OPENING CREDITS
```

INT. STUDIO NEWSROOM

```
                      PRESENTER
        Hello. On Nationtrite tonight, we hear about
        GLC plans to stage the 1988 Olympics in Horace
        Cutler's mouth.
```

CUT to female presenter SUE STRAIGHTMAN, who is standing in front of a signwriter, wearing overalls marked 'BBC DUMMY CLOCK LTD', who is painting the time on the backdrop.

> SUE STRAIGHTMAN
> And at 6.25, I'll be cued in two seconds late, to tell you how the engineering union's elections were held up today, when one of the men counting the ballot papers lost his rubber. We'll also have an interview with the writer of the wacky new BBC comedy *Foot and Mouth*, starring Michael Foot and Michael Foot. And later on, the Nolan Sisters will all pick up their microphones and perform a viewer's request. All this after your own programmes cut me off sudden—

*Nationtrite* theme and titles cut in.

> PRESENTER
> Here on *Nationtrite* we've become conditioned over the past few years to the idea of unusual pets, but this week we heard about one so staggeringly unique, we just had to invite it along to the studio. And it's here now with its owner, Mr Norman Woman of Forsdick Spencer Street, Leicester. Good evening, Mr Woman.

MR WOMAN has a moustache drawn on her top lip and a dog on her lap.

> MR WOMAN
> Good evening.

The cast of *End of Part One* were actors, rather than comedians. Dudley Stevens had extensive experience as one of the music hall revivalists at the Players' Theatre in London. Denise Coffey had been one of the original cast members of *The Burkiss Way*, but had left after the first series. The cast was completed by David Simeon, Sue Holderness, Tony Aitken and the aforementioned Harris.

PRESENTER

Mr Woman, what's the name of your dog?

MR WOMAN

Eight hundred and fifty-seven pounds return.

PRESENTER

No, the name of your dog.

MR WOMAN

Oh, sorry. Eric.

PRESENTER

Now Eric really must be the most incredible animal we've ever had on *Nationtrite*. I understand he doesn't waterski, doesn't go hang-gliding, doesn't dance, doesn't talk, doesn't play the flute and doesn't go out canvassing for the Liberal Party?

MR WOMAN

Yes.

PRESENTER

Absolutely astonishing. He really just behaves like a dog all the time?

MR WOMAN

Yes.

PRESENTER

Well, perhaps Eric could give us a little demonstration?

MR WOMAN

Well yes, certainly. Come on then Eric, there's a good boy. Good boy. Be normal. Be normal. Be normal. Normal. Normal.

The dog is out of shot. MR WOMAN is getting increasingly agitated.

MR WOMAN

Oh, I'm ever so sorry.

PRESENTER looks at the floor, clearly disturbed.

                    PRESENTER
Oh, now look what he's gone and done, Mr Woman.

                    MR WOMAN
I'm sorry.

                    PRESENTER
He's written a thesis on quantum mechanics all
over the floor.

                    MR WOMAN
Leave it. Naughty Eric. You're a naughty boy.

                    PRESENTER
Well, back to you, Sue.

CUT to another male presenter with more than a hint of Frank
Bough about his manner and appearance. His flies are open.

                SECOND PRESENTER
Well, as you may have heard tonight on the news,
it is World War Three night.

Crew member in red t-shirt labelled 'FLIES GAFFER' skulks on,
and does up the presenter's trousers.

        Tonight's designated by the government for a
        nuclear onslaught on Russia and the Eastern Bloc
        countries. Now, it's important to remember on
        World War Three night with all the rockets going
        off, do please try and keep your pets indoors.
        Just follow the Ministry of Defence nuclear
        conflagration code. It's quite simple. Just use
        your common sense.

Fred Harris is the *Play School* presenter responsible for probably the most
famous out-take from the long-running series. Tasked with sitting all of the
show's toys upright on the floor, he has trouble with Big Ted and Little Ted,
who refuse to stay in position. After a couple of takes, he belabours both toys
around the head with his script and declares, in a mock-prima donna voice,
to the obvious delight of the crew, 'I'm an artist, how am I expected to work
with these amateurs, for God's sake?'

# *Not the Nine O'Clock News* (1980)

## 'Constable Savage'

### Paul W. Newstead

*Not the Nine O'Clock News* was, like *Monty Python's Flying Circus*, a product of the old culture of freedom and trust in BBC comedy commissioning. *Python* had been allocated a series of thirteen shows without a pilot, and *Not the Nine O'Clock News* was given a six-show try-out under similar conditions. Not that then head of comedy, John Howard Davies, and head of light entertainment James Gilbert were taking a risk on unknown quantities. The programme pitch came from John Lloyd, a vastly experienced producer of radio light entertainment. They teamed Lloyd with Sean Hardie, an irreverent, idiosyncratic, current affairs producer who had been working on the early evening magazine programme *Nationwide*.

**Series:** *Not the Nine O'Clock News* (twenty-seven shows over four series, 1979–82), series 3, show 2.

**Original transmission:** BBC2, 3 November 1980, 9 p.m.

**Cast in excerpt:** Rowan Atkinson (Inspector), Griff Rhys Jones (Constable).

**Producers:** John Lloyd and Sean Hardie.

**Director:** Bill Wilson.

The first series, originally scheduled for April and May 1979, was postponed due to the calling of a general election. The opening show – with Rowan Atkinson, Chris Emmett, Christopher Godwin, John Gorman, Jonathan Hyde and Chris Langham – had already been recorded, and Hardie and Lloyd took the opportunity to examine it and address any weaknesses. When it finally appeared in October 1979, it had been recast almost completely, with only Atkinson and Langham remaining; funnywoman Pamela Stephenson was the most notable addition to what had been a previously all-male show. It was an instant hit, and for three years it skewered home affairs, foreign affairs and the vernacular of current affairs with devastating accuracy. At the time, police brutality and racism was a hot topic with the 'Sus' law resulting in the arrest of many innocent black people. *Not the Nine O'Clock News* addressed the matter head-on.

★ ☆ ★

INT. POLICE STATION - DAY

A police INSPECTOR is at his desk in his office. There is a knock at the door.

> INSPECTOR
> Come.

A CONSTABLE opens the door and walks in.

> CONSTABLE
> You wanted to see me, sir?

> INSPECTOR
> Ah, Constable Savage. Come in, shut the door. Now then, Savage, I want to talk to you about some charges that you've been bringing lately. I think that perhaps you're being a little over-zealous.

> CONSTABLE
> Which charges do you mean, then, sir?

> INSPECTOR
> Well, for instance, this one. 'Loitering with intent to use a pedestrian crossing.' Savage, maybe you're not aware of this, but it is not illegal to use a pedestrian crossing. Neither is smelling of foreign food an offence.

> CONSTABLE
> You sure, sir?

> INSPECTOR
> Also, there is no law against urinating in a public convenience. Or coughing without due care and attention.

> CONSTABLE
> If you say so, sir.

The original scheduled dates for the first series of *Not the Nine O'Clock News* ran on from the second series of *Fawlty Towers*. The untransmitted first show opens with a cameo from John Cleese as Basil Fawlty dealing with someone on the telephone, who is wondering where Fawlty Towers has gone. Fawlty replies that the series has finished and has been replaced by a 'cheap, tatty revue'.

INSPECTOR
[Angrily]

Yes, I do say so, Savage. Didn't they teach you anything at training school?

CONSTABLE
Sorry, sir.

CONSTABLE SAVAGE gets out his notebook and starts to lick his pen.

INSPECTOR
[Shouting noises at CONSTABLE to make him stop]

Some of these cases are just plain stupid. 'Looking at me in a funny way.' Is this some kind of joke, Savage?

CONSTABLE
No, sir.

INSPECTOR
And we have some more here. 'Walking on the cracks in the pavement'. 'Walking in a loud shirt in a built-up area during the hours of darkness' and 'Walking around with an offensive wife'. In short, Savage, in the space of one month, you have brought 117 ridiculous, trumped-up and ludicrous charges …

CONSTABLE
Yes, sir.

INSPECTOR
… against the same man, Savage.

                    CONSTABLE
Yes, sir.

                    INSPECTOR
A Mr Winston Kodogo of 55 Mercer Road.

                    CONSTABLE
Yes, sir.

                    INSPECTOR
Sit down, Savage.

                    CONSTABLE
Yes, sir.

CONSTABLE SAVAGE sits down.

                    INSPECTOR
Savage, why do you keep arresting this man?

                    CONSTABLE
He's a villain, sir.

                    INSPECTOR
A villain.

                    CONSTABLE
And a jailbird, sir.

                    INSPECTOR
I know he's a jailbird, Savage. He's down in
the cells now. We're holding him on a charge of
possession of curly black hair and thick lips.

                    CONSTABLE
Well, well, there you are, sir.

                    INSPECTOR
You arrested him, Savage.

                    CONSTABLE
Thank you, sir.

                    INSPECTOR
Savage, would I be correct in assuming that Mr
Kodogo is a coloured gentleman?

CONSTABLE
Well, I can't say I've ever noticed, sir.

INSPECTOR
Stand up, Savage. Savage, you're a bigot. It's officers like you that give the police a bad name. The press love to jump on incidents like this and the reputation of the force can be permanently tarnished. Your time on duty is dominated by racial hatred and petty personal vendettas. Do you get some kind of perverted gratification from going around stirring up trouble?

CONSTABLE
Yes, sir.

INSPECTOR
There's no room for men like you in my force, Savage. I'm transferring you to the S.P.G.

CONSTABLE
Thank you, sir.

INSPECTOR
Now get out. And mind that—

As CONSTABLE SAVAGE leaves, there is a squelching noise underfoot.

CONSTABLE
Sorry, sir. Is this your hedgehog, sir?

The final show of the fourth and final series closes with a song suggesting that the American farewell 'so long' should be replaced with 'the memory kinda lingers', or just 'kinda lingers'. It soon becomes obvious that this is merely a pun on 'cunnilingus' and an attempt to sneak some surreptitious filth past the BBC decency police. Playgrounds the following day resounded to the phrase 'kinda lingers', with most of those using the expression having not the slightest clue what they were saying.

# *Yes Minister* (1981)

## 'The Compassionate Society'

### Antony Jay and Jonathan Lynn

The machinations of Whitehall might not seem like a natural subject for comedy, but ex-head writer on *The Frost Report*, Antony Jay, saw its potential in 1972 when he attended a lecture by former Labour minister Barbara Castle. Here, he noted the disparity between what government ministers – transient politicians – want to achieve, and what their ministries – the civil servants who remain no matter who's in power – allow them to do. John Cleese, Jay's partner in the Video Arts business training operation, introduced Jay to his old Cambridge Footlights friend Jonathan Lynn, by now an actor and writer of note. Jay, a Tory by inclination, brought his powers of analysis to the partnership, while the left-leaning Lynn brought his comic skills.

Jay and Lynn created the fictitious Department of Administrative Affairs, and gave it a Secretary of State, Jim Hacker. Hacker's political allegiance is never made clear, a deliberate policy by the writers to avoid accusations of bias. In most matters, Hacker seems to be a moderate who could sit quite happily with Tories or Labour members at the centre. Hacker is a triumph of character creation and portrayal: vain, sometimes pompous and out of his depth, but somehow immensely warm, sympathetic and likeable. Hacker's main dealings are with his Permanent Secretary, Humphrey Appleby, and his Principal Private Secretary, Bernard Woolley. Appleby represents the real power in the department, reshaping and amending Hacker's bright and sometimes not so bright ideas out of existence. Occasionally,

**Series:** *Yes Minister* (BBC2, twenty-two shows over three series, one special and one *Funny Side of Christmas* segment, 1980–84), series 2, show 1; followed by *Yes, Prime Minister* (sixteen shows over two series and one special, 1986–8).

**Original transmission:** BBC2, Monday 23 February 1981, 9 p.m.

**Cast in excerpt:** Paul Eddington (Jim Hacker), Nigel Hawthorne (Humphrey Appleby), Derek Fowlds (Bernard Woolley).

**Producer/director:** Peter Whitmore.

Hacker gets one over on Appleby, and sometimes, Woolley chooses to disobey Appleby, his boss, on a point of principle. Woolley is a key figure in many of the central scenes. While Hacker and Appleby dominate the conversation, it is often Woolley who comes in with the line that gets the biggest laugh.

Even if it hadn't been a ratings success, *Yes Minister*'s passage was guaranteed by its elevated fans. The then prime minister Margaret Thatcher was a devotee of the show, which came in handy at a time when the BBC was coming under considerable political pressure from her administration. 'The credit that programme brought to the BBC was extraordinary, from very influential people,' said Sir Bill Cotton, BBC1 controller at the time of the first series. Fortunately, however, the show was a hit from the start, and it ran for three series before Hacker was promoted to the top job for a further two series.

In this scene, Hacker has just been mauled in the Commons by a backbencher about some figures concerning the reduction of ministerial administrators, and railroaded into offering a full independent inquiry. On his way back to the Ministry, he hears from his chauffeur of a newly built hospital with 500 administrative staff but no patients.

INT. MINISTER'S OFFICE - DAY

                         JIM
        Humphrey, I'm appalled.

                    SIR HUMPHREY
        So am I, Minister.

                         JIM
        The incompetence of it, the stupidity.

                    SIR HUMPHREY
        I agree. I can't think what came over you.

JIM is startled.

                         JIM
        I beg your pardon?

                    SIR HUMPHREY
        Well, to concede a full independent inquiry.

                         JIM
        Humphrey.

                    SIR HUMPHREY
        Yes, Minister?

                         JIM
        That's not what I meant.

                    SIR HUMPHREY
        But you mentioned stupidity and incompetence?

                         JIM
        Yours, Humphrey, yours.

                    SIR HUMPHREY
        Mine, Minister?

                         JIM
        How could you drop me into it like that?

                    SIR HUMPHREY
        Well, a small omission from the brief. We can't
        foresee everything, but a full independent
        inquiry.

JIM

I don't want an inquiry any more than you do, but
if you're drowning and somebody throws you a rope,
you grab it.

SIR HUMPHREY

That wasn't a rope, that was a noose. You should
have stood up for the department. That's what
you're there for.

JIM

No, Humphrey it won't do. I prepared myself
thoroughly for yesterday's question time, but
nowhere in my brief was there any suggestion that
you've been juggling with the figures so that I'd
give misleading replies to the House.

SIR HUMPHREY

Minister, you said that you wanted the
administration figures reduced, didn't you?

JIM

Yes.

SIR HUMPHREY

So we reduced the figures.

JIM

But only the figures. Not the number of
administrators.

SIR HUMPHREY

Well of course not.

JIM

That's not what I meant.

From the second show onwards, the opening titles were hand-drawn
and painstakingly animated by the cartoonist Gerald Scarfe, with a
distinctive theme tune by Ronnie Hazlehurst. The first show, recorded as
the pilot, has cruder cartoon titles and a more obviously comic theme tune.

SIR HUMPHREY

Well, really Minister, one is not a mindreader, is
one? You said reduce the figures, so we reduced the
figures.

JIM

And another thing, how did this get out? Another
leak. This isn't a department. It's a colander.
How are we supposed to govern responsibly if
backbenchers get all the facts? Well, at least the
inquiry gives us a little time.

SIR HUMPHREY

So does a time bomb.

JIM

Well yes. Haven't you got a disposal squad?

SIR HUMPHREY

Disposal squad?

JIM

Couldn't we get the independent inquiry to exonerate
the department?

SIR HUMPHREY

Do you mean rig it?

JIM

No, no, no, no, no. Well, yes.

SIR HUMPHREY
[Mock-disapprovingly]

Minister. No, it all depends on who the chairman is.
He absolutely has to be sound.

JIM

How do you mean sound?

SIR HUMPHREY

Well, a sound man will know what is required. He
will perceive the implications. He will have a
sympathetic and sympathetic insight into the overall
problems. In short, he will be sound.

JIM

You mean bent.

SIR HUMPHREY

No, he will be a man of broad understanding.

JIM

How about a retired politician?

SIR HUMPHREY

And unimpeachable integrity.

JIM

Yes, I see what you mean. A businessman?

SIR HUMPHREY

Not really.

JIM

An academic?

SIR HUMPHREY

No, no, no, no, no, no, no.

JIM

Alright, who have you got in mind?

SIR HUMPHREY

Well, I thought perhaps a retired civil servant.

JIM

Good thinking, Humphrey.

SIR HUMPHREY

Sir Maurice Williams could be the man.

JIM

Might not he be too independent?

SIR HUMPHREY

Well, he's hoping for a peerage.

JIM

Well, he won't get one through this, will he?

SIR HUMPHREY

No, but the right finding will earn him a few more brownie points.

JIM

Brownie points?

SIR HUMPHREY
Yes, they all add up, until finally you get the
badge.

JIM
Very well, Sir Maurice Williams it is.

SIR HUMPHREY
Thank you, Minister.

JIM
Thank you, Brown Owl.

SIR HUMPHREY stands, and gives JIM HACKER a very pleased-
with-himself Brownie salute, but is stopped in his tracks by
the arrival of BERNARD WOOLLEY.

SIR HUMPHREY
Good morning, Bernard.

BERNARD
Just two points, Minister. The Cuban political
refugees.

JIM
Oh, not that again.

BERNARD
It looks as though there's a row blowing up over
our refusal to do any more for them.

JIM
Well, it's not my fault, it's the Treasury.

BERNARD
Yes, quite, Minister.

JIM
You can't beat the Treasury, Bernard. I shall just
say nothing. Oh dear. One more public humiliation
and I shall become a political refugee myself.
What was the other point?

BERNARD
Well, you asked me to find out about that alleged
empty hospital in north London.

The series was commissioned in 1977, but not put into production by the BBC until after the 1979 General Election, for reasons of political caution.

JIM

Oh yes.

BERNARD

Well, as I reminded you, Minister, the drivers'
network is not wholly reliable. Roy has got it wrong.

JIM

Thank heavens for that. How did you find out?

BERNARD

Through the private secretaries' network.

JIM

And?

BERNARD

Well, in fact, there are only 342 administrative
staff at the new St Edward's Hospital. The other 170
are porters, cleaners, laundry workers, gardeners,
cooks and so forth.

JIM

And how many medical staff?

BERNARD

Oh, none of them.

JIM

None?

BERNARD

No.

JIM

Bernard, we are talking about St Edward's Hospital,
aren't we?

BERNARD

Yes. It's brand new. It was completed fifteen
months ago and fully staffed, but unfortunately,

at that time, there were government cutbacks, so consequently there was no money left for medical services.

> JIM
> [Aghast]

A brand-new hospital with over 500 non-medical staff and no patients?

> BERNARD
There is one patient, sir.

> JIM

One?

> BERNARD
Yes, the deputy chief administrator fell over a piece of scaffolding and broke his leg.

> JIM
Good God, thank heavens I wasn't asked about this in the House. Why hasn't it got out?

> BERNARD
Well, actually, I think it's been contrived to keep looking like a building site, and so far, no one's realized it's operational. You know, scaffolding, skips still there. The normal thing.

> JIM
The normal thing? I think I'd better go and have a look at this before the Opposition does.

> BERNARD
Yes, it's surprising the press haven't found out by now, isn't it?

> JIM
Fortunately, Bernard, most of our journalists are so incompetent, they'd have the gravest difficulty in finding out that today is Wednesday.

> BERNARD
It's actually Thursday.

JIM points to the door.

# *Only Fools and Horses* (1982)

## 'A Touch of Glass'

## John Sullivan

In the early years of the first Thatcher government, television began to do a nice line in roguish, likeable petty criminals. Nothing too reprehensible, just knocking out hooky merchandise and satisfying the national need for a bargain. Over on ITV, Thames Television's subsidiary Euston Films had brought *Minder* to the small screen to great acclaim, while the BBC countered with a sitcom about two brothers and an elderly relative in a Peckham high-rise, trying to make a fortune from flogging legally dubious tat.

The series was written by John Sullivan, who had come to prominence as a comedy writer with his tales of a Tooting revolutionary in *Citizen Smith*. David Jason, previously better known for his work in ITV sitcoms like *Lucky Feller*, *A Sharp Intake of Breath* and *The Top Secret Life of Edgar Briggs*, starred as Del Trotter, using French phrases which he didn't know the meaning of. With their yellow Reliant Regal van, the Trotters slowly became firm favourites with the viewing public. The first series was not the hoped-for hit, but the show was given a second series to prove itself – an unthinkable luxury to most TV writers now.

**Series:** *Only Fools and Horses* (BBC1, sixty-five shows over seven series, nineteen specials a *Funny Side of Christmas* segment and a *Comic Relief* segment, 1981–2003), series 2, show 7.

**Original transmission:** BBC1, Thursday 2 December 1982, 8.30 p.m.

**Cast in excerpt:** David Jason (Del Trotter), Nicholas Lyndhurst (Rodney Trotter), Lennard Pearce (Grandad), Donald Bisset (Wallace).

**Producer/director:** Ray Butt.

INT. TROTTERS' LOUNGE - NIGHT

The atmosphere is tense. DEL is pacing the room. GRANDAD is in his chair. RODNEY is at the dining table.

> DEL
> Don't be a plonker all your life, Rodney! I've done the deal now. It's 350 quid just to take down and clean a couple of chandeliers.

> RODNEY
> And do you honestly think he's gonna pay us?

> GRANDAD
> Of course he's gonna pay us! He ain't one of your fly-by-night merchants. I mean he's a lord of the realm, he's got blue blood and – and mottos!

> RODNEY
> He didn't even pay us for that cat!

> DEL
> Oh shut up about that rotten cat!

> RODNEY
> Del, you need specialized equipment for a job like this – refined glass brushes, advanced soldering gear. What we gonna use, eh? Superglue and a bottle of Windolene, knowing you!

> DEL
> Look, I'll get the right equipment, Rodney. I know this panel beater and he owes me a favour. Look,

The first series of *Only Fools and Horses* had a different theme tune – an instrumental by Ronnie Hazlehurst – instead of the opening and closing themes usually associated with the show. John Sullivan was hoodwinked into singing the better known themes by being told that the booked session singer couldn't make it, so he'd have to sing his own lyrics. This had always been the intention, but Sullivan had refused, citing nerves.

once we've done this job our name will spread.
All those dukes an' earls they'll be crying out
for us. Just imagine it, eh? We'll be the toast
of the county set, eh? Just think of it, all the
hounds, you know, baying with excitement, as our
steeds bite on the rein eager for the chase.
Hello, Tally ho Sir Herbert. Did you ken John
Peel? Come on boy …

RODNEY
Take a look at him will yer! He's spent three
hours in a stately home and he thinks he's the
Earl of Sandwich! He can't wait to get a shotgun
and a retriever and go marching across the grouse
moors all done up like a ploughman's lunch, can
he?

DEL
No, that's right, Rodney. I deserve a bit of the
good life, worked hard enough for it, I mean I've
always been a trier. Where's it got me? Nowhere,
that's where it's got me! We live 'alf a mile up
in the sky in this Lego set built by the council.
Run a three-wheel van with a bald tyre. We drink
in wine bars where the only thing's got a vintage
is the guvnor's wife! That's why I want to grab
this opportunity with both hands, Rodney. You
know, he who dares wins. This time next year we'll
be millionaires.

RODNEY
Do you honestly believe that, Del? I mean, do you
really think we can make a success of this?

DEL
Of course we can, Rodney. The door will be
opened to a new world. It'll be like … like *Alex
Through the Looking Glass*. You will dine at the
finest  restaurants on … on steak chasseur and
sautée potatoes. Your shoes will be by Gucci, your
jewellery will come from Asprey's, your clothes
will be made by Man at C&A! What d'you reckon
Rodders, eh? What d'you reckon?

                         RODNEY
Man at C&A. Yeah, alright. I'll give it a whirl.

                          DEL
Good boy. You know it makes sense, don't you?

                         RODNEY
Oi, but we do a proper job, right. No bodging!

                          DEL
Of course not, what do you take me for, eh?

                               RODNEY
Oi!

                          DEL
I'll save the best bit for you.

                         RODNEY
I'll see you in the morning then.

                          DEL
Yeah, see you in the morning. Night.

                        GRANDAD
'No bodging.' I think he lacks faith in you, Del
Boy!

                          DEL
Always been his trouble, innit, eh? Oi, 'ere,
do me a favour, will you, Grandad? Pop out in
the kitchen, see if we've got any Windolene and
superglue left, will you?

INT. RIDGEMERE HALL, MAIN HALLWAY – DAY

RODNEY is carrying a pair of aluminium ladders. He puts them
down, then goes out to get another set. GRANDAD is carrying a
tool bag and a large canvas sheet. WALLACE the butler watches
disapprovingly.

                          DEL
    Righto, Grandad, you pop upstairs and get the
    floorboards up! Now, you know what you're doing
    don't you?

GRANDAD reaches into his tool bag and removes a hammer, a
large screwdriver and a spanner.

GRANDAD

Don't you worry, Del, leave it to me.

DEL
[To WALLACE]

Oh, he's a craftsman!

[Calls]

Oi, Grandad, d'you want a jemmy?

GRANDAD
No, I had one before we left.

WALLACE
Why does he have to remove the floorboards?

DEL
What is this, the International Year of the
Wally-Brain or something? Listen, my good man,
how do you think that great big heavy chandelier
stays up there on that ceiling, eh? It is not
by the power of prayer or double-sided sticky
tape! There is a long threaded bolt through that
chandelier, it goes through a wooden joist and is
held in position by a locking nut. Now in order
to undo the locking nut you must first lift up the
floorboards! Ordre du jour!

WALLACE
We learn something new everyday! If you need me I
shall be round at the garages.

DEL
Right. Here, while you're there give the van a
wash, will you?

WALLACE exits as RODNEY enters with the ladders.

DEL
Ah, talking of wally-brains. Come on. Here - watch
it!

RODNEY
I mean this is terrific, innit? His lordship's
nowhere to be seen and now even the butler's
having a moody! D'you reckon we're gonna get paid?

DEL and RODNEY move the ladders under one of the chandeliers.

>                    DEL
>      Look, his lordship is away on holiday, he'll pay us
>      when he gets back! Now come on, get these ladders
>      up. Yeah, you never know might be in for a bonus.

>                    RODNEY
>      Oh yeah, perhaps he might bring us back a nice
>      stick of rock each, eh?

>                    DEL
>      Well, just shut up moaning, will yer! Oi, Grandad,
>      how you doing?

INT. UPSTAIRS ROOM - DAY

GRANDAD has removed a floorboard and is levering off another.

>                    GRANDAD
>                    [Calls]

>      Alright, Del Boy. I've found it, Del!

MAIN HALLWAY

DEL and RODNEY are standing near the two ladders.

>                    DEL
>      Here you are. See, he's found the nut. I told you
>      we could trust him. Right, come on, get this out.

>                    GRANDAD
>              [Out of view upstairs]

>      I've started to undo it.

>                  DEL AND RODNEY
>      No!

>                    DEL
>                    [Calls]

>      Gordon Bennett, we ain't even up the ladders yet!

>                    RODNEY
>      Grandad - don't you touch nuffink till we tell you.

The story of how John Sullivan came to get his first break as a television writer is usually told as 'scene shifter writes script'. In fact, Sullivan took a job as a scene shifter purely so that he would have a legitimate reason to frequent the BBC Club at Television Centre and approach legendary producer and drinker Dennis Main Wilson with his script.

DEL

Come on, we'd better get up there.

Holding the canvas bag between them, DEL and RODNEY climb the ladders, carefully enveloping the first chandelier with the canvas bag.

DEL

Alright, Rodders? Is there anything you want?

RODNEY

Yeah, I wanna go home! This ladder's none too safe.

DEL

The ladder's alright. Look, this is the chance I've been waiting for. Now don't let me down Rodders - now don't let me down!

[Calls]

Alright, Grandad, we're ready! You can start undoing it now!

UPSTAIRS ROOM - INT.

GRANDAD places the spanner on the nut and begins easing it round.

GRANDAD

It's coming, Del Boy! One more turn, Del!

MAIN HALLWAY - INT.

DEL

Right. Now brace yourself, Rodney, brace yourself!

GRANDAD bangs the nut with the hammer. It comes free. The
other chandelier crashes to the floor. DEL and RODNEY stare
at each other in shock. Eventually, they turn to see what's
happened.

                        DEL
      Grandad was undoing the other chandelier!

                      RODNEY
      How can you tell?

They climb down the ladders, somewhat shocked, and walk
across fragments of shattered crystal to the broken
chandelier. GRANDAD is coming downstairs to join them,
unaware of what's happened.

                      GRANDAD
      Alright, Del Boy?

                        DEL
      Alright? What do you mean 'alright'? Look at it!

                      GRANDAD
      Did you drop it, Del?

                      RODNEY
      Drop it? How could we drop it? We wasn't even
      holding it! We were working on that one!

                      GRANDAD
      Well, I wish you'd said something. I was working
      on this one! Is it very valuable, Del?

                        DEL
      No, not really! It was bleedin' priceless when it
      was hanging up there though!

                      RODNEY
      What's his lordship gonna say when he finds out?

                        DEL
      Well, I think I can safely say that my invitation
      to the hunt ball has gone for a Burton!

                      WALLACE
      It's broken!

DEL

Look, what the hell do you know about chandeliers
anyway?

RODNEY

I think he's tumbled, Del!

WALLACE

I shall telephone his lordship at his cottage
immediately!

DEL

Yeah, well, tell him to phone us at home. Oh, by
the way, has his lordship got our home address and
telephone number?

WALLACE

No!

DEL

Good! Right, out of it. Go on.

# The Les Dawson Show (1983)

## 'Cissie and Ada'

### Terry Ravenscroft

**Series:** *The Les Dawson Show* (BBC1, thirty-three shows over five series, two specials and one *Funny Side of Christmas* segment, 1978–89), series 3, show 2.

**Original transmission:** BBC1, Saturday 22 January 1983, 8.20 p.m.

**Cast in excerpt:** Les Dawson (Ada Shufflebotham), Roy Barraclough (Cissie Braithwaite).

**Producer/director:** Ernest Maxin.

At one time, every street in the north of England had a Cissie Braithwaite and Ada Shufflebotham, swapping gossip over the backyard wall. Variety comedian Norman Evans had turned the type into rich comedy with his 'Over the Garden Wall' monologues, but it fell to Les Dawson to take them into the television age, with the pair making their debut in his *Sez Les* series in 1973. Dawson himself took the role of Ada, with her finely tuned ear for innuendo and tendency towards malapropisms; while playing Cissie, who liked to kid herself and Ada that she was somehow more refined, was Roy Barraclough.

The early Cissie and Ada sketches were written by a combination of Dawson, Barry Cryer and David Nobbs, but when Dawson moved to the BBC, he encountered Terry Ravenscroft. Ravenscroft had grown up with women like Cissie and Ada too, and moved seamlessly into providing the bulk of the material for the pair.

INT. DOCTOR'S WAITING ROOM - DAY

CISSIE is reading a leaflet. The surgery door opens, out comes ADA.

ADA
Thank you, doctor. Are the suppositories the same length?

[Spies Cissie]

Well, well, well, Cissie. Fancy seeing you at the doctor's. Is it the old trouble?

CISSIE
What trouble?

ADA
[Gurning, then pointing downwards]

Women's trouble. Last year, when you said you might have to have a hysterical rectomy?

CISSIE
No, no, it's not that. That cleared up after the manipulation. Mind you, I don't feel very well. In fact, if I put my mind to it, I could be very ill indeed. No, it's not me I've come about actually. I've come on behalf of Leonard.

ADA
So help me God, what's wrong with the lad?

CISSIE
Well, it's his verruca. You know he's got a very big one.

ADA
Fancy.

CISSIE
I mean he can hardly get his shoe on for it.

ADA
Has he tried tucking his trousers down his socks?

CISSIE
It's much too painful to do anything like that.

ADA

I bet he doesn't know what to do with it.

CISSIE

Well, he doesn't. He couldn't hop down here, you know. That's why I've come to see whether Dr Patel can give him anything for it.

ADA

I don't see why not. I've got a lot of faith in Dr Patel, even though he does come from Bombay. He's a chapati you know. But he did the same for me when I came about my Bert. I told him exactly what was wrong with my Bert.

CISSIE

And what did he give you?

ADA

His deepest sympathy.

CISSIE

Not surprised. Knowing your Bert, you deserve all the sympathy you get. I mean what's the matter with the scoundrel now?

ADA

It happened two days ago, well two nights ago actually, after he'd been to the pub.

CISSIE

I'm surprised he can afford to go to a pub, on the dole like he is.

Ada's tendency to mouth certain words, particularly those concerning illness or bodily functions, had been observed by Dawson in his youth, particularly among cotton mill workers, who became skilled lip readers to overcome the noise of the machines with which they worked. Dawson said it was impossible to keep a secret in front of these old dears, even if you whispered.

ADA

Anyway, he went down to the pub, and the landlord
likes my Bert you know, because he once cleared a
boil up on his whippet's neck. And between you and
I, he lets him suck the beermats.

CISSIE

So that's why he had all his teeth out.

ADA

He's got a very deep cavity at the back. He was
stood at the bar having a quiet suck when an old
friend of his from the army days came in. Well, you
know my Bert. I don't have to tell you, my Bert was
one of the unsung heroes of World War Two. His full
story may never be told. The Home Office slapped an
embargo on his memoirs. My Bert was very important.
Everywhere he went, he was chained to MPs, you know.
Well this army chum of his, and Bert of course, they
were together, they were trapped in a rainforest
near Rangoon, in the monsoon period, behind Japanese
lines, sheltering with remnants of the Fourteenth
Army.

CISSIE

Chindits?

ADA

Oh, they all had them. They had nothing to eat
but sedentary armadillos. Well, obviously, I could
understand it. They had a few drinks too many. Well,
my Bert came home about two o'clock in the morning,
and he just fell asleep sat on the lavatory. And he
was still there the following morning.

[Starting to cry]

Cissie, I didn't know what to do. He'd lost the use
of his legs.

CISSIE

I say, Ada.

ADA

Every time I picked him up, he fell back on the
[mouthing silently] lavatory.

CISSIE
Oh, I say, well perhaps it was psychosomatic?

ADA
No, it's the old fashioned sort with the chain
flush. Actually, we've got a crack in the
pedestal, have to have it grouted. But I sent for
Dr Patel and, do you know, he came straight away.

CISSIE
And what was the matter with him?

ADA
What?

CISSIE
With Bert, as he couldn't get off the l— er,
toilet? Was it some sort of muscular seizure?

Dawson's first television appearance was in June 1962 on a regional ITV show for the Midlands and North called *Saturday Bandbox*. The host of the programme was Norman Evans, Cissie and Ada's original inspiration.

ADA

Sort of. His braces were fastened round the cistern.

CISSIE

Typical. That's enough about your Bert. What about you, chuck?

ADA

Oh, I don't feel so bad in myself, you know. I've got this cluster of varicose veins at the back of my leg. I shall have to have them pulled through BUPA.

CISSIE

I was just thinking you look a trifle wan.

ADA

Well, let's face it, you know, I am at a funny age. I won't tell another living soul this, of course. I'm approaching the change.

CISSIE

Approaching the change? From which direction?

ADA

What do you mean?

CISSIE

Well, I would have thought your batteries had run out years ago, chuck.

ADA

I'll have you know that my family has a tradition of fertility. We're a very fertile family. Very fertile. My cousin Bertha got copped when she was fifty-nine and she swears she only walked past a sausage factory.

CISSIE

Well, any road, changing the subject, what are you
here at the doctor's for?

ADA

I've got a lot of confidence in Dr Patel, even
though he's a poppadommi. Our Miriam came here for
an X-ray, and to find where the blockage was, he
gave her a Bavarian meal.

CISSIE

You mean barium?

ADA

No, she kept her bra and knickers on. Well, I came
in because I've got the most … I can tell you,
can't I?

CISSIE

Oh, my lips are sealed.

ADA

I've got the most peculiar complaint. Every winter
I get very heavily chapped legs, especially on
the inner thigh, and it's very embarrassing when
I'm wearing a hoorah skirt, with a handkerchief
hem. Now, I've tried rubbing myself with Algy's
pan, and it doesn't seem to work, and this happens
every time the clocks go back. I've been in to see
him today, that Dr Patel, wonderful, and he cured
my chapped legs in five minutes.

CISSIE

Did he give you an injection?

ADA

No, he took two inches off my wellington boots.

# *Chance in a Million* (1984)

## 'Stuff of Dreams'

### Richard Fegen and Andrew Norriss

Coincidences and misunderstandings abound in the world of situation comedy. Almost any opportunity to embarrass a character and leave them with a heap of explaining to do is seized upon gleefully by writers. *Chance in a Million* took this tendency to its bizarre but (usually) logical conclusion, centring on Tom Chance, a man who was plagued by unfortunate coincidences at every turn. Starting on Channel 4, it gained a wider following when repeated on the main ITV network. Somehow, it managed to send up the whole genre of sitcom, perhaps for the benefit of the Channel 4 audience, while working as a broad farce, which appealed more to the ITV punters. Richard Fegen and Andrew Norriss' scripts were knowing, but never arch.

**Series:** *Chance in a Million* (Thames Television for Channel 4, eighteen shows over three series, 1984–6), series 1, show 6.

**Original transmission:** Channel 4, Monday 15 October 1984, 8.30 p.m.

**Cast in excerpt:** Simon Callow (Tom Chance), Brenda Blethyn (Alison Little), Marc Sinden (Paratrooper).

**Producer/director:** Michael Mills.

The series benefited hugely from having Simon Callow playing Tom, and Brenda Blethyn as his girlfriend Alison, an apparently demure librarian with (barely) concealed torrents of passion raging inside her. Tom, of course, was oblivious to, or baffled by, her overtures, remaining more interested in cricket (one of his prize possessions was a cricket bat signed by Alec Bedser – later just 'Alec Bed' after it was used by Alison's mother to see off a savage dog), playing the tuba badly and downing pints of lager in one.

INT. LIVING ROOM - DAY

TOM walks in clutching a pint of milk. ALISON is at the breakfast table.

> TOM
>
> Done it again.

> ALISON
>
> Done what, Tom?

> TOM
>
> Kids. Swapped street signs. Now says Clivewood Avenue.

> ALISON
>
> Oh, not again.

> TOM
>
> Yes, must phone someone. Report it.

> ALISON
>
> Yes, well, you finish your breakfast first, Tom.

> TOM
>
> Yes, Alison. Must say. Enjoyed having you here, past few weeks, really.

> ALISON
>
> It's been very nice for me too, Tom. It was very good of you to let me.

> TOM
>
> Any luck, your search for new flat?

> ALISON
>
> No. No. But there's no particular rush, is there?

> TOM
>
> No, no, no rush at all. Just thought you might be happier. New flat. You know what I mean? Might stop these nightmares.

> ALISON
>
> Well, they're not that bad, Tom.

                              TOM
          Well, bad enough, Alison. Four days in a row now,
          had to come to my bed to calm down. Thought you
          might just be more settled, flat of your own.

                            ALISON
          Ah well, I'll keep looking, Tom.

                              TOM
          Yes.

TOM walks away from the table and picks up a newspaper.

                            ALISON
          Tom, you haven't forgotten about lunchtime, have
          you?

                              TOM
          No. Your friend? Her husband? Looking forward to
          it.

                            ALISON
          No, Roger isn't her husband, Tom. They just live
          together.

                              TOM
          Ah, modern couple.

                            ALISON
          Well, Susan's always saying two can live cheaper
          than one, and I must say the arrangement seems to
          work out very well.

                              TOM
          Good, good, good, good. Ah, found it.

                            ALISON
          What's that?

Michael Mills had been the producer of the first television programme to be
described as a 'situation comedy', *Family Affairs*, which ran for one series on
BBC TV in late 1949 and early 1950.

                          TOM
        Flats vacant column.

                        ALISON
        Don't you think it's a tricky time of year at the
        moment to find flats?

                          TOM
        Mustn't lose hope, Alison. Persist. Something's
        bound to turn up.

Suddenly a pair of feet dangle outside the window.

                          TOM
        Need to go hunting for it. Can't expect anything
        to fall out of the sky. Can't expect things just
        to plop at your feet.

The feet have been joined by the face of their owner, hanging
from a harness. He knocks at the window. TOM and ALISON turn
to see what's going on.

                          TOM
        Ahhh, yes. Help you at all?

                      PARATROOPER
        I think this 'chute's got caught up in your
        chimney.

DISSOLVE to the PARATROOPER sitting at the breakfast table,
dipping a soldier in a boiled egg.

                      PARATROOPER
        Funny you should mention flats.

                          TOM
        Why?

                      PARATROOPER
        Wife's sister's got a cousin with a house full of
        flats. She says one of them's coming vacant this
        week.

                          TOM
        Sounds marvellous, Alison.

                    PARATROOPER
I'll jot the address down for you, if you like.

ALISON looks sad.

                     ALISON
                [Unenthusiastically]

Thanks very much.

                      TOM
Corporal, this parachuting. Army exercise, is it?

                    PARATROOPER
Not an exercise, as such. More an initiative test.
They give us a list of items, and we have to get
back to base before sunset with as many as we can
find.

                     ALISON
Like a treasure hunt?

                    PARATROOPER
That's right. The training instructors usually
win. Or the sergeants. We don't usually do very
well. We're the regimental band, you see?

                      TOM
                [Looking at his tuba]

Ah!

                     ALISON
What sort of things do you have to collect,
exactly?

                    PARATROOPER
I've got a list, actually, here. Nobody ever gets
them all, of course.

He produces a piece of paper from his pocket and passes it to
ALISON.

                     ALISON
                  [Incredulous]

A cricket bat signed by Alec Bedser?

                    PARATROOPER
Yeah, whoever he was.

                         TOM
Alec Bedser? Most famous cricketer who ever lived,
that's all.

                      ALISON
Tom's got a bat signed by him, haven't you, Tom?

                    PARATROOPER
You haven't?

                         TOM
Certainly have. Bits of it missing. Got chewed by
dog. Just says Alec Bed now.

                    PARATROOPER
That doesn't matter. I couldn't borrow it, could
I? I'll look after it for you.

                         TOM
Certainly. Fancy your knowing Alec Bedser.

                      ALISON
A Zulu war shield. Tom, didn't you say your great
aunt gave you one of those?

                         TOM
Great-grandmother, Alison, used to hang in hall.
No idea where it is now.

                    PARATROOPER
Two items? I don't believe it.

                         TOM
Probably in the attic somewhere. Back in a moment.

TOM leaves the room.

                      ALISON
Do you know, I think he's got a stuffed rhino's
head up there as well.

                 [Calls after him]

     TOM!

DISSOLVE to the living room, now full of curios and gewgaws.

                    ALISON
        Now, we've done the street map of Lima. Police
        handcuffs. Number 18 - a ship's bell.

                     TOM
        Yes. Got one of those. Boat, outside.

                    ALISON
        Oh no, Tom, it can't just be any old bell. It has
        to come from one of Her Majesty's warships.

                     TOM

        Frigate?

                 PARATROOPER
        Yes, it is a bit annoying, isn't it?

                     TOM
        No, no, no. Got another bell outside. Comes from
        frigate. HMS *Eagle*. 1707. Drowned off the Scilly
        Isles. Sir Cloudesley Shovell. Interesting story.
        Tell you one day.

TOM exits.

                 PARATROOPER
        This boat of his. Keen on that sort of thing, is
        he?

                    ALISON
        No, not really, he says he has enough trouble on
        dry land. He's trying to sell it actually.

                 PARATROOPER
        What did he buy it for, then?

Mills cast Callow on the basis of a single appearance in a 1975 episode of
*Get Some In!* that he had directed. In the intervening nine years, Callow
had become a celebrated stage actor and member of the Royal Shakespeare
Company, a pedigree of which Mills was largely unaware.

ALISON

Oh, he didn't buy it, he won it in a lager-
drinking competition in 1967.

PARATROOPER

He's still trying to sell it?

ALISON

Oh well, no, you see, it was stolen the day
after he got it. The police only brought it back
yesterday. Found it in Newport Pagnell. Some man
had been breeding pigeons in it.

PARATROOPER

Oh.

ALISON

I'd quite like him to keep it, actually. Do you
know, I've always had a thing about boats, ever
since I saw that film *High Society*.

PARATROOPER

Oh yeah?

ALISON

Mmmm. Bing and Grace are on their honeymoon on
their boat, the *True Love*, and they're just lying
there underneath the moon and the stars, and
water's lapping the side of the hull, and they're
all happy and contented, then suddenly, Bing
reaches down and he pulls out his accordion. And
they sing that song, 'True Love'. Oooh, it always
used to send shivers up and down inside my vest,
and I used to think maybe one day I'd be able to …
oh well, we all have our little dreams, I suppose.
Silly, isn't it? Could you pass the coffee,
Corporal?

TOM enters, ringing the bell.

TOM

Here we are. Yes, this is splendid. What's next? I
like this game.

PARATROOPER

I don't think even you could get the last two, Mr Chance. Number 19 is a pair of knickers with the words 'Hello big boy' written across the front.

TOM

[Embarrassed]

No, no. Not quite my line.

PARATROOPER

No, I didn't think it would be, you know. Number 20 is a picture of Shirley Williams in the nude.

TOM

Ah, difficult.

PARATROOPER

Yeah. I know one of the lads is prepared to give it a go with chloroform and a Polaroid, but …

ALISON

Vera Brittain!

PARATROOPER

Pardon?

ALISON

The photograph. It's in the new biography of Vera Brittain. She was Shirley Williams' mother, and there's a picture in it of Shirley at six months old, on a bearskin rug in the nude.

PARATROOPER

Good God.

TOM

Remarkable woman, Alison. Librarian, you know.

ALISON

I've got it upstairs. I'll run up and get it for you. I'm reading it at the moment. [Pause] I'll fetch the knickers down at the same time, if you like.

# Victoria Wood: As Seen on TV (1986)

## 'Acorn Antiques'

### Victoria Wood

By the time Lancastrian comedian Victoria Wood was given her own BBC2 show in the mid-1980s, she had a decade of television experience behind her, beginning with her appearance on the mainstream talent show *New Faces* while still a drama student at Birmingham University. She won but, perhaps thankfully in retrospect, was not propelled into the big time. Instead, she continued performing in cabaret and was taken under the wing of Peter Eckersley, a drama producer at Granada Television. Eckersley commissioned her first play, *Talent.* Among the actors cast was Julie Walters, whom Wood had first encountered professionally when they both worked on a revue at London's Bush Theatre. Wood and Walters hit it off both as friends and colleagues, and this led to their Granada comedy series *Wood and Walters.*

The association continued when Wood moved to the BBC, with Walters featuring in many sketches across *As Seen on TV*, but most notably as Mrs Overall in the soap opera spoof *Acorn Antiques.* Although various soap opera traits were explored, the sketches were primarily a backhanded homage to ITV's Midlands motel-based series *Crossroads*, with the wooden acting, wobbly sets, mis-cues and mis-readings of lines being only slightly exaggerated from the original inspiration. This selection sends up the inevitable media brouhaha surrounding the departure of an actor from a long-running series. Mrs

**Series:** *Victoria Wood: As Seen on TV* (BBC2, thirteen shows over two series and one special, 1985–7), series 2, show 6.

**Original transmission:** BBC2, Monday 15 December 1986, 9.35 p.m.

**Cast in excerpt:** Celia Imrie (Miss Babs), Julie Walters (Mrs Overall), Victoria Wood (Miss Berta), Duncan Preston (Clifford), Kenny Ireland (Derek), Rosie Collins (Trixie).

**Producer/director:** Geoff Posner.

Overall's exit from the studio, pursued by reporters, is equal
parts Gloria Swanson's final sweep down the staircase in
*Sunset Boulevard* and Noele Gordon leaving the motel.

★ ☆ ★

INT. CONTINUITY STUDIO - DAY

                    ANNOUNCER
          Local news. Brian Taylor, new go-ahead producer
          of the television soap opera, *Acorn Antiques*,
          today announced the sudden axing of two of the
          longest-running characters. The actors who play Mr
          Clifford and Mrs Overall are said to be hurt and
          dismayed. Winthrop Tuesday spoke to them earlier
          today.

CUT TO INT. BBC TV CENTRE, OUTSIDE STUDIO 1 - DAY

Press photographers are waiting as the actors emerge from the
studio.

                    REPORTER
          How do you feel?

                    PRESTON
          No comment, gentlemen.

                    REPORTER
          Were you expecting to be fired?

                    WALTERS
          Does a faithful dog expect to be kicked? That show
          was my life.

CUT BACK TO CONTINUITY STUDIO

                    ANNOUNCER
          And because *Acorn Antiques* is live, and our news
          is recorded three weeks in advance, settle back
          and watch the final performances of Mr Clifford
          and Mrs Overall as we go over to that little shop
          on the outskirts of Manchesterford.

CUT TO EXT. OUTSIDE ACORN ANTIQUES - DAY

MISS BABS gets out of a Citroen Dyane van marked 'Acorn Antiques', holding a vase. A small chip from it falls into the gutter. She picks it up resignedly and enters the shop. MRS OVERALL and BERTA are in the window.

INT. ACORN ANTIQUES - DAY

BERTA is ironing, while CLIFFORD, DEREK and TRIXIE sit on a sofa.

> BERTA
>
> So you and Derek weren't having an affair, after all?

> TRIXIE
>
> Oh, no. He was only lying on top of me to get the creases out of my negligée.

> BERTA
>
> I knew there must be a perfectly reasonable explanation.

> TRIXIE
>
> Anyway, I have to get back to the convent.

> BERTA
>
> Ooh! Convent, why?

> TRIXIE
>
> I forgot my teapot.

> DEREK
>
> I'll give you a lift.

> TRIXIE
>
> Well, alright. But don't crash through a grocer's window this time. Those tinned pears really hurt me.

> BERTA
>
> Bye.

> BIMBO
>
> Bye.

BERTA finishes ironing with a flourish.

BERTA

There. That looks a bit better.

MR CLIFFORD

Berta. I've been meaning to …

BERTA

Just unplug the iron for me, could you?

MR CLIFFORD

A pleasure.

BERTA

Only don't touch it with your bare hand because …

MR CLIFFORD touches the iron, and it starts buzzing.

MR CLIFFORD

Aaagh!

BERTA

Because it's faulty.

MRS OVERALL

Whatever was that heart-rending scream? It sounded
as if somebody was being electrocuted.

BERTA

Look.

MRS OVERALL

Oh, my good golliwog!

BERTA

Is he dead?

Wood reported later that it was difficult to persuade the highly professional
BBC crews to let their standards lapse for the duration of the sketches, their
natural inclination being to correct any mistakes instinctively and quickly as
they went.

MRS OVERALL

Well, put it this way, Miss Berta, I needn't have bothered rinsing out the extra mug.

BERTA

Clifford will never touch your macaroons again.

MISS BABS

What was that terrible noise? It sounded like a tray of coffee being dropped on someone who had just been electrocuted.

BERTA

Look.

MISS BABS

He's dead!

[Sobs]

MRS OVERALL

Crying won't bring him back, Miss Babs.

MISS BABS stops crying very suddenly.

MISS BABS

No, that's true.

MRS OVERALL

Why don't we all have a delicious mug of my home-made sherry, and a couple of sausage dumplings?

MISS BABS

Yes, Mrs O, why don't we?

They laugh, then hum the incidental music. MR CLIFFORD is on the floor, still very clearly breathing.

CUT TO EXT. OUTSIDE THE SHOP

A large box marked 'Fragile' and 'Venus de Milo' is being removed from the van.

INT. INSIDE THE SHOP

A pair of customers are leaving. MISS BABS waves goodbye to them in a stagey, regal manner. In her other hand, she is holding the telephone receiver.

MISS BABS

*Ah, oui, bien sûr. J'aime beaucoup. Le world cup aussi. Naturellement. Au revoir.*

DEREK

We've brought the Venus de Milo, Miss Babs.

TRIXIE

And we want to say goodbye.

MISS BABS

Goodbye? But why?

DEREK

We're going away.

MISS BABS

Away? Where?

TRIXIE

Together.

MISS BABS

Together? When?

DEREK

We're going overland to Morocco.

MISS BABS

You're going overland to Morocco? Why?

BERTA barges in, nudging TRIXIE.

TRIXIE

Ow!

BERTA

What's wrong, Babs?

MISS BABS

It's Derek and Trixie, they're going away, travelling overland to Morocco together.

BERTA

Derek and Trixie are overland travelling to Morocco. Why?

                    TRIXIE
Everyone says you can get really nice jumpsuits.
Bye.

DEREK and TRIXIE leave hurriedly.

                    MISS BABS
Right. Back to business. These antiques.

        [Quietly, and breaking character]

Here comes Fanny Overall. I'll just go, 'blah,
blah, blah'.

                    BERTA
Give the blithering old nuisance time to get to
the table.

                    MISS BABS
Oh, Mrs O, we didn't hear you. What happened to
the body?

                    MRS OVERALL
Mr Clifford? He's gone nice and stiff, so I've
propped him up by the ironing board.

                    MISS BABS
How lovely.

                    MRS OVERALL
Well, he's that tall, I hadn't room to hoover.

                    BERTA
What's that delicious smell?

                    MRS OVERALL
That will be my macaroons. I've had them on a
low light since Wednesday. Slice them finely or
somebody might choke to death. I don't think she
heard me.

                    MISS BABS
What's wrong, Mrs O?

                    MRS OVERALL
It was the tea leaves in my cup this morning.
Something's wrong somewhere.

MISS BABS

Why?

MRS OVERALL

It was a cup of Horlicks.

CLIFFORD appears in the background outside the shop window. he turns and waves to someone off-set and mimes that he is going for a drink.

MISS BABS

Strange to think of Clifford lying in the sitting room all alone.

MRS OVERALL

Oh, don't worry. When Mr Overall, no relation, was dying, he said, 'Well, Boadicea, I shall never have to play another game of Travel Scrabble.'

MISS BABS

Why did he call you Boadicea?

MRS OVERALL

He was barmy, Miss Babs.

BERTA

Mmm. Your macaroons smell delicious.

MISS BABS

Yes, Mrs O, you sample the first one.

MRS OVERALL

Well, yes, I will. But just in case something should happen when I bite into it, I'd just like to say what I feel for Acorn Antiques, and the folks what work here. I'm only a simple woman, got no O-levels, or life saving certificates. Never been abroad or fully participated in a summit conference, but I've got feelings. And what I feel for you, Miss Babs, and you, Miss Berta, is nothing more or less than plain and simple cove. Love.

MISS BERTA
She's choking on her own macaroon!

MRS OVERALL starts choking.

MISS BABS
Quick, get the family doctor!

MISS BERTA
I can't. He's being blackmailed in the Sudan.

MISS BABS
Oh, darn! What are we going to do, Berta?

MISS BABS
As far as Mrs O's concerned, it's far too late.

Credits begin: They slide up diagonally in a send-up of the *Crossroads* credits and bump into each other.

MISS BABS
Mrs Overall. That macaroon you just choked on. I'm going to send the recipe to the *Weekly News*.

MRS OVERALL
Oh, I am pleased.

Closing theme finishes.

MISS BERTA
Are we off?

MRS OVERALL
[Not in character, and starting to get up off the floor]

I thought that went quite well, didn't you?

FLOOR MANAGER
[Off-screen]

Still on air!

MRS OVERALL falls back down on the floor, and the others look concerned again.

# Blackadder the Third (1987)

## 'Dish and Dishonesty'

### Ben Elton and Richard Curtis

Following the success of *Not the Nine O'Clock News*, Rowan Atkinson was understandably in demand. His idea was for a situation comedy about an alternative history of the Middle Ages, in which Richard III was succeeded not by Henry VII but by Richard IV, whose idiot son Edmund, the Black Adder, had been responsible for Richard III's death at the Battle of Bosworth. The first series – written by Atkinson and Richard Curtis – received mixed reviews, and was an expensive production with a lot of location filming. A second series, set in the time of Queen Elizabeth I, with Atkinson as wily courtier Edmund Blackadder, was only greenlit with the proviso that it would be mostly studio based. Atkinson also took a back seat in the writing, handing over to Ben Elton. Subsequent series, continuing in the time of the Prince Regent and the First World War, proved to be massive hits.

Over the course of the four series, the various Blackadder characters became cleverer – the original having been a dunce. To make up for it, the servant Baldrick, who started out relatively intelligent and very sarcastic, became a simpleton, whose only interest lay in the acquisition of turnips. In this scene from the third series, Baldrick has been put up as a candidate in a rotten borough, charged with winning the election and ensuring that a deadlocked parliament is unable to remove the Prince Regent from the Civil List. It features a cameo from real-life BBC political reporter Vincent Hanna, and was, at one time, used

**Series:** *The Black Adder/ Blackadder II/Blackadder the Third/Blackadder Goes Forth* (twenty-five shows over four series and one special, 1983–9), series 3, show 1.

**Original transmission:** BBC1, Thursday 17 September 1987, 9.30 p.m.

**Cast in excerpt:** Rowan Atkinson (Edmund Blackadder), Tony Robinson (Baldrick), Hugh Laurie (Prince George), Vincent Hanna (Vincent Hanna, 'his own great-great-great grandfather'), Dominic Martelli (Pitt the Even Younger), Geoffrey McGivern (Ivor Biggun).

**Producer:** John Lloyd.

**Director:** Mandie Fletcher.

extensively by teachers with a love of comedy to explain the electoral system before the 1832 Great Reform Act.

★ ☆ ★

INT. ELECTION COUNT - NIGHT

                    HANNA
Good evening and welcome to the Dunny-on-the-Wold
by-election. The first thing I must tell you is
that the turnout has been very good. As a matter
of fact, the voter turned out before breakfast.
And I can bring you the result of our exclusive
exit poll, which produced a 100 per cent result
for 'Mind-Your-Own-Business-You-Nosy-Bastard'.

                VOICE (OUT OF VIEW)
Mr Hanna, are you going to talk to any of the
candidates?

                    HANNA
I certainly am, and I can see Prince George, who
is leader of what has become known as the 'Adder
Party'; Prince George, who is described in his
party news-sheet as a 'great moral and spiritual
leader of the nation', but is described by almost
everyone else as a 'fat, flatulent git'.

                  [To GEORGE]

Prince George, hello.

During the making of the first series, Brian Blessed, playing Richard IV, was required to knock down what appeared to be a solid oak door. A lightweight prop door was to be substituted, but before this could be done, Blessed mistakenly attempted a take with the real oak door. Blessed was injured slightly, but the door came off far worse.

GEORGE
[Holding a dachshund]

Good evening.

HANNA
[To the dog] And good evening, Colin.

Er, how do you see your prospects in this
campaign?

GEORGE
Well, er, first, I'd like a word about the
disgraceful circumstances in which this election
arose. We paid for this seat, and I think it's
a damn liberty that we should have to stand for
it as well. And another thing, why is it that
no matter how many pairs of socks a man buys, he
never seems to have enough?

[Leaves]

HANNA
Fitting words from the Prince Regent. And now
let's have a word from the Adder Party candidate,
Mr S. Baldrick, who so far has not …

[BALDRICK enters with a turnip in his mouth, the leaves
sticking out]

… commented on his policies in this campaign, but
with him is his election agent, Mr E. Blackadder.

BLACKADDER
Well, we in the Adder Party are going to fight
this campaign on issues, not personalities.

HANNA
Why is that?

BLACKADDER
Because our candidate doesn't have a personality.

HANNA
He doesn't say much about the issues, either.

BLACKADDER
No; he's got something wrong with his throat.

> HANNA
>
> Well, perhaps he could answer one question: What does the 'S' in his name stand for?

> BLACKADDER
>
> 'Sodoff'.

BLACKADDER leaves.

> HANNA
>
> Fair enough, er, none of my business, really. And now it's time, I think, for a result, and tension is running very high here. Mr Blackadder assures me that this will be the first honest vote ever in a rotten borough. And I think we all hope for a result which reflects the real needs of the constituency. And behind me … yes, I can just see the returning officer moving to the front of the platform.

> BLACKADDER
>
> As the acting returning officer of Dunny-on-the-Wold …

> HANNA
> [Cuts in]
>
> Er, the acting returning officer, Mr E. Blackadder, of course. And we're all very grateful, indeed, that he stepped in at the last minute, when the previous returning officer accidentally brutally stabbed himself in the stomach while shaving.

> BLACKADDER
>
> I now announce the number of votes cast as follows: Brigadier General Horace Bolsom—

> HANNA
> [Cuts in]
>
> Cheap-Royalty-White-Rat-Catching-And-Safe-Sewage Residents Party …

> BLACKADDER
>
> No votes.

BOLSOM pushes his way off the platform.

```
                    BLACKADDER
        Ivor 'Jest-ye-not-madam' Biggun—

                      HANNA
                    [Cuts in]

        Standing-At-The-Back-Dressed-Stupidly-And-Looking-
        Stupid Party …

                    BLACKADDER
        No votes.

IVOR laughs, plays a kazoo in BLACKADDER's ear and waves.

                    BLACKADDER
        Pitt, the Even Younger—

                      HANNA
                    [Cuts in]

        Whig …

                    BLACKADDER
        No votes.

                      HANNA
        Oh, there's a shock.

PITT the Even Younger turns to his mum and cries.

                    BLACKADDER
        Mr S. Baldrick—

                      HANNA
                    [Cuts in]

        Adder Party …
```

Although there is always talk of further Blackadder, the most recent occurrence was in *Blackadder: Back and Forth*, a special programme made for projection in the Millennium Dome, but also transmitted on Sky One on 31 December 1999.

                    BLACKADDER
Sixteen thousand, four hundred and seventy-two.

Cheers from the crowd.

                     HANNA
And there you have it: victory for the Adder
Party – a sensational swing against the Whigs.
I'll just try to get a final word from some of
the candidates as they come up from the stage.
Master William Pitt the Even Younger, are you
disappointed?

                     PITT
Yes! I'm horrified! I smeared my opponent, bribed
the press to be on my side, and threatened to
torture the electorate if we lost. I fail to see
what more a decent politician could have done.

PITT storms off.

                     HANNA
Quite. Now, Ivor Biggun, no votes at all for the
Standing-At-The-Back-Dressed-Stupidly-And-Looking-
Stupid Party. Are you disappointed?

                     BIGGUN
Ah, no, not really, no … I always say, 'If you
can't laugh, what can you do?' Ha-ha-ha-ha.

            [Squirts HANNA with flower]

                     HANNA
Take up politics, perhaps. Has your party got any
policies?

                     BIGGUN
Oh yes, certainly! We're for the compulsory
serving of asparagus at breakfast, free corsets
for the under-fives, and the abolition of slavery.

                     HANNA
Now, you see, many moderate people would respect
your stand on asparagus, but what about this
extremist nonsense about abolishing slavery?

**BIGGUN**

Oh, we just put that in for a joke! See you next year!

**HANNA**

And now, finally, a word with the man who is at the centre of this by-election mystery: the voter himself. And his name is Mr E. Bla— Mr Blackadder, you are the only voter in this rotten borough …?

**BLACKADDER**

Yes, that's right.

**HANNA**

How long have you lived in this constituency?

**BLACKADDER**

Since Wednesday morning. I took over the previous electorate when he, very sadly, accidentally brutally cut his head off while combing his hair.

**HANNA**

One voter, 16,472 votes – a slight anomaly?

**BLACKADDER**

Not really, Mr Hanna. You see, Baldrick may look like a monkey who's been put in a suit and then strategically shaved, but he is a brilliant politician. The number of votes I cast is simply a reflection of how firmly I believe in his policies.

**HANNA**

Well, that's excellent. Er, well, that's all for me – another great day for democracy in our country. Vincent Hanna, *Country Gentleman's Pig Fertilizer Gazette*, Dunny-on-the-Wold.

# *A Bit of Fry and Laurie* (1989)

## 'Cocoa'

## Stephen Fry and Hugh Laurie

Stephen Fry and Hugh Laurie are, like John Cleese, Graham Chapman, Eric Idle, Graeme Garden, Tim Brooke-Taylor and Jimmy Edwards, Cambridge Footlights alumni. The pair took part in the 1981 Footlights revue, *The Cellar Tapes*, which won the first Perrier award at the Edinburgh Fringe Festival, and also brought Emma Thompson and Tony Slattery to prominence. They served their television apprenticeship on shows like *Alfresco*, *The Young Ones*, *Happy Families* and *Saturday Live*. A 1983 BBC pilot, *The Crystal Cube*, did not progress to a series but, in 1987, they were offered another go on BBC2 with a pilot for a sketch show. The result was *A Bit of Fry and Laurie*.

Their allotted producer/director, Roger Ordish, seemed like a surprising choice, being better known for his work on *Jim'll Fix It*, but as a former university revue performer and director of surreal comedy shows like *World in Ferment*, he was actually ideal. Fry and Laurie later sent up the Jimmy Savile connection in the show by referring to Ordish as the producer of *Sir James Does His Level Best To Comply With Your Wishes*.

Fry and Laurie's comedy has always been notable for its gentle yet devastating mockery, particularly of pretentious academics ('"Hold the newsreader's nose squarely, waiter, or friendly milk will countermand my trousers." One sentence, common words, but never before placed in that order.') and incompetent businessmen ('Daaaaaaaaaaaaamn!'). However, the example chosen here owes more to the drama of Alan Bennett than anything else. The choice of the name for the

**Series:** *A Bit of Fry and Laurie* (BBC2, twenty-six shows over four series and one special, 1987–95), series 1, show 6.

**Original transmission:** BBC2, Friday 17 February 1989, 9 p.m.

**Cast in excerpt:** Stephen Fry (Attendant); Hugh Laurie (Very old northerner).

**Producer/director:** Roger Ordish.

cocoa manufacturer in this sketch may or may not be related
to that of Fry and Laurie's Footlights contemporary, Anthony
Berendt.

★ ☆ ★

INT. AN OLD PEOPLE'S HOME. MR SIMNOCK'S ROOM – DAY

          STEPHEN (ATTENDANT)
Alright, Mr Simnock?

       HUGH (VERY, VERY OLD NORTHERNER)
Eh?

           STEPHEN
I say, are you alright, Mr Simnock?

            HUGH
Smimble cocoa.

           STEPHEN
Yes, your cocoa's coming in a minute. I say
your cocoa is coming in a minute. I'll draw the
curtains, shall I? Be cosier then. You'll be more
cosy.

            HUGH
Aye. Draw the curtains, cosy that. Cocoa.

           STEPHEN
Yes, your cocoa's coming in a minute.

            HUGH
Curtains.

           STEPHEN
         [Drawing them]

Yes, I'll draw them for you. There you are.
That's a bit cosier, isn't it? Nights are getting
chillier all the time, aren't they? Only seems
like yesterday it was Christmas. I don't know, oh
look, you've dropped your magazines, look. I'll
pick them up for you.

HUGH

Didn't like them. Rubbish they were.

STEPHEN

See what they are. There we are, look.

As STEPHEN bends down to pick up the magazines, HUGH whacks
him with a newspaper.

STEPHEN

Ooh, now. There's no call to go doing that, was
there, Mr Simnock? That wasn't very nice was it?
Hitting me like that. What d'you want to go and do
that for?

HUGH

Where's me cocoa?

STEPHEN

Your cocoa's coming. I'm not so sure you deserve
it now, though. Acting up like I shouldn't wonder.
I'll tuck you in, look.

HUGH

Ninety-two years old.

STEPHEN

That's right, ninety-three come November.

HUGH

Ninety-two years old and I've never had oral sex.

STEPHEN

Well, I should think not indeed. Oral sex. The
idea.

HUGH

Never ridden a camel.

STEPHEN

You're just babbling now, Mr Simnock.

HUGH

I've never watched a woman urinate.

STEPHEN

I shall get very cross with you in a minute, I
shall really.

                         HUGH
Never killed a man.

                       STEPHEN
Well, there's a certain man that I shall be
killing if he's not very careful.

                         HUGH
Never been inside an opera house. Never eaten a
hamburger.

                       STEPHEN
You're a stupid silly old man and I won't have any
more nonsense.

                         HUGH
I'm fed up, me. Never done anything.

                       STEPHEN
Well, you're a bit chilly I shouldn't wonder. Your
cocoa'll be along in a minute.

                         HUGH
Don't want any stupid cocoa.

STEPHEN

Well, there's no call to be getting contrary, is
there? You love your cocoa, you know you do.

HUGH

I hate cocoa. Gets a skin on it.

STEPHEN

Not if you keep stirring it.

HUGH

Makes me kek that, makes we want to cat up. I
want to drink milk from the breasts of a Burmese
maiden.

STEPHEN

I don't know what's got into you today, Mr
Simnock? I don't really. I think we're going to
have to give you some extra Vitamin E. Burmese
maidens! In Todmorden.

HUGH

You've got bad breath you have.

STEPHEN

Well, there's no call to be personal, I hope.

HUGH

Like rotting cabbages.

STEPHEN

I'm very angry with you, Mr Simnock.

HUGH

You're a great nancy.

STEPHEN

I'm not a great nancy, Mr Simnock, and you're
wicked to say so.

HUGH

You're a great Mary-Ann, bum-boy nance. I bet
you've never even done it.

STEPHEN

I'm not going to take any more of this from you,
Mr Simnock, I'm not, really.

HUGH

You shouldn't be in a place like this, at your
time of life.

STEPHEN

Someone's got to do it, Mr Simnock. Dedication,
though why I bother I do not know.

HUGH

You should be out there having oral sex, killing
people, watching women urinate in opera houses and
eating hamburgers in opera houses. Drinking milk
from the breasts of Nepalese maidens.

STEPHEN

It was Burmese last time.

HUGH

Nepalese. I've changed my mind. Instead you're
stuck here taking rude talk from 'n old man. You're
a great bog-breath Nancy.

STEPHEN

You've really upset me today, Mr Simnock, you
have really. I'm going out to hurry along your
cocoa and when I get back I don't want any more
nonsense. Honestly!

Exit STEPHEN.

HUGH
[Calling after him]

You're a screaming great Bertie and you pong.

[To himself]

Ninety-two years old and I've never watched a
woman urinate. Tragic waste, that.

STEPHEN
[Re-entering]

Now, here you are, Mr Simnock, I managed to
intercept Mrs Gideon in the hall with the tray. So
don't say you aren't a lucky man to get it before
the others.

#### HUGH

Hooray!

#### STEPHEN

Yes, that's better, isn't it?

#### HUGH

Cocoa.

#### STEPHEN

That's right, but a certain naughty boy said some naughty things though, didn't he?

#### HUGH

I'm sorry, Brian. Right sorry.

#### STEPHEN

Well, I'm not sure you should have it now. As soon as you see your cocoa you mend your manners, don't you?

#### HUGH

Please, Brian.

#### STEPHEN

Alright. There you are. That's better, isn't it?

#### HUGH

Oh, it's a lovely drop of cocoa, that.

#### STEPHEN

It's Berent's: that's the best.

[Smiles at the camera; advert-style]

Good old Berent's cocoa. Always there. Original or New Berent's, specially prepared for the—

#### VOICE-OVER

—mature citizens in your life, with nature's added store of powerful barbiturates and heroin.

HUGH collapses with a grin on his face.

# *Alexei Sayle's Stuff* (1989)

## 'Democracy'

## Alexei Sayle, Andrew Marshall and David Renwick

**Series:** *Alexei Sayle's Stuff* (BBC2, eighteen shows over three series, 1988–91), series 2, show 3.

**Original transmission:** BBC2, Thursday 2 November 1989, 9 p.m.

**Cast in excerpt:** Alexei Sayle (Himself/man in cloth cap/second drinker), Tony Millan (First voter/first drinker), Jan Ravens (Poll clerk/exit pollster/barmaid), Angus Deayton (Second voter).

Alexei Sayle made his name and reputation as the MC at The Comedy Store when the London club opened in 1979, his aggressive manner keeping both the audience and his fellow comics firmly under control. Sayle was a Liverpool-born, art-school-trained son of a communist railway worker, and his unpredictable and sometimes menacing stand-up comedy combined his far-left politics with surrealism, all delivered from within a suit a couple of sizes too small for him, making him look far fatter than he really was. For television, he worked extensively on shows like *O.T.T.* and *The Young Ones* before being given his own BBC2 sketch show in 1988, helped by writers Andrew Marshall and David Renwick, and a cast including Angus Deayton.

In a similar move to Paul Jackson's a few years earlier, producer Marcus Mortimer had come to *Stuff* fresh from producing *The Two Ronnies*, bringing that show's high production values with him. Mortimer's background meant that when Sayle, Marshall and Renwick (along with musical director Simon Brint) wrote a lavish musical number, it looked and sounded superb. Watching the shows back, it can sometimes appear obvious where the dividing line is located between material by Sayle or Marshall and Renwick. A first-series item presenting Lowestoft as a hot holiday destination can only be Marshall and Renwick's work – Marshall hailing from the Suffolk town.

EXT. SUBURBAN LONDON STREET - DAY

ALEXEI is walking along street.

> ALEXEI
>
> The 70s. That's when it all started to happen for
> me, here in Stoke Newington. A very alternative
> part of the world, Stoke Newington. I actually
> worked here on an alternative listings magazine
> called *What's on in Stoke Newington*. It was a big
> piece of paper with 'bugger all' written on it.
>
> In the 70s, when the middle classes began to
> re-colonize these inner-city areas, like Stoke
> Newington, you could always spot the middle-class
> houses because they were the ones that had been
> painted blue and had those carriage lamps outside.
> It was like a big sign saying 'Please break in and
> steal my video recorder'. I could never understand
> those carriage lamps. I mean what's the idea of
> carriage lamps? Why put headlights on your house?
> It's not going anywhere, is it?
>
> In the 70s, you got all those grants. Government
> grants to make a mess of your house. And in one
> middle-class street in Stoke Newington, they all
> knocked their front and back rooms into one in the
> same week and the street fell down. Another way you
> could spot the middle-class houses was that they
> always had those Suzuki jeeps parked outside.
>
> [Poncy voice]
>
> 'Oh yes, I think it's so important to have four-
> wheel drive when you're going down to Sainsbury's.'

The first show of the series was described by a *Daily Express* reviewer as 'about as funny as an orphanage on fire'. By week five, the *Express* had upgraded its view to 'Hit and miss comedy'.

Have you noticed that with the top down those Suzuki jeeps all look like pedal cars? All pedalling away. You have to pedal them because they're all powered by Evian water.

A time of great political activity, the 70s, and I was in a political group called Cystitis Sufferers Against the Nazis. We'd march, well it was more of a mince, actually.

[Mimes discomfort]

'Oooh, ahhh, ow, ow, owwww, down with the Nazis.'

CUT to a patch of green in front of the previous houses.

ALEXEI
The left has an obsession with words, and changing words, like, where I live now has got one of those Labour left-wing councils, and they're always renaming things, usually after Nicaraguans and dead South Africans. That's going to worry the government in Pretoria, isn't it? 'Oh my God, they've named a taxi rank in Camden after Winnie Mandela. We'd better dismantle apartheid immediately, then.' They think that if you change the name of something, then it's going to make it somehow better. They think that if you took something like typhoid and you renamed it Fabulous Fun Happy-Time Jolly Feeling, then it'd be like loads of fun to have it.

CUT to ALEXEI standing in the middle of a street in front of a large gasometer.

ALEXEI
Of course, they say the only way to change society is democratically, through the ballot box. Crap. Can you think of anything more futile than going into a little booth once every five years to vote for some politician? Well, yeah.

CUT TO EXT. OUTSIDE POLLING STATION – DAY

A man is striding in purposefully.

INT. POLLING STATION - DAY

VOTER approaches the poll clerk's desk.

> VOTER
>
> Morning.

> POLL CLERK
>
> Good morning.

> VOTER
>
> I've come to stick my head in a bucket of
> something nasty, please.

> POLL CLERK
>
> Right, have you got your voter registration card
> with you?

VOTER produces card from pocket.

> POLL CLERK
>
> OK, there we are then. Now, there are four buckets
> in this constituency. Creosote, sump oil, liquid
> manure and cold rice pudding. If you'd just like
> to go into the booth and stick your head in the
> bucket of your choice. It's just over there.

> VOTER
>
> Thank you very much.

VOTER walks across to booth, disappears from view. There is a
squelching sound.

EXT. OUTSIDE POLLING STATION

An EXIT POLLSTER is waiting. The VOTER comes out, covered in
brown sticky liquid.

In the second show of the first series, Sayle's opening monologue was
delivered by Leslie Crowther (in a bald wig and an ill-fitting suit), with a
voice-over announcing that this was due to technical problems.

```
                    EXIT POLLSTER
     Excuse me, sir, may I ask which were you?

                       VOTER
       Yes, I went for creosote, and proud of it.

                    EXIT POLLSTER
     Have you always stuck your head in that?

                       VOTER
     I have. We've always been staunch creosote in our
     family. In fact, my grandfather served as a local
     alderman with his head in a bucket of coal tar for
     thirty-six years.

  CUT to black and white footage of a man standing on his head
  in a bucket, as another man in a cloth cap looks on.

                        MAN
        I think you politicians do a wonderful job.

  CUT BACK TO EXT. OUTSIDE POLLING STATION

  Another VOTER is leaving, with his head covered in creosote.

                    EXIT POLLSTER
     Excuse me, sir, may I ask which bucket you …

                    SECOND VOTER
     No, you may not.

                    EXIT POLLSTER
     We're just doing an exit poll.

                    SECOND VOTER
     Which disgusting substance I choose to stick
     my head in is between me and the bucket. Now
```

One show of the second series begins with an announcement that *Stuff* has been cancelled and replaced with an episode of the police drama *Juliet Bravo*. Only slowly does it become apparent that this is actually the opening sketch of *Stuff*, featuring a cameo from Anna Carteret, the real star of the cop show.

if you'll excuse me, I have to go and buy some
industrial solvents.

INT. PUB - NIGHT

The BARMAID is cleaning glasses, listening to TWO DRINKERS
talking about politics.

                    FIRST DRINKER
My son says he's not going to stick his head in a
bucket of anything this year. He's going to shove
it down the lavatory instead, as a protest.

                    BARMAID
Bloody hell. Anarchists.

                    SECOND DRINKER
He should be grateful that he don't live in
Russia, 'cause there they only have two buckets,
and they're both filled with hedgehog's urine.

                    BARMAID
I heard they were going to have a third bucket
this year, with some glasnost in it?

                    FIRST DRINKER
What's glasnost?

                    BARMAID
Well, it's a kind of very runny cheese. Smells
odd.

                    SECOND DRINKER
Thank God we live in a democracy.

# *Absolutely* (1990)

## 'Stoneybridge Olympic bid'

### Jack Docherty

*Absolutely* is probably the perfect example of a cult comedy show. Tucked away on late-night Channel 4, it reached a relatively small audience who took it to their hearts, thanks to characters like the Welsh DIY enthusiast, Denzil, his wife Gwynedd, the Nice family, a beige-clad Scots clan who prized being 'zenzible' above all else, and a vile saloon bar (well, pub lavatory) philosopher called Frank Hovis. The show's cult status was underlined fifteen years after it began when some of the original fans ran an ultimately successful Internet campaign to get the series released on DVD.

**Series:** *Absolutely* (Absolutely Productions for Channel 4, twenty-eight shows over four series, 1989–93), series 2, show 4.

**Original transmission:** Channel 4, Friday 12 September 1990, 10 p.m.

**Cast in excerpt:** Gordon Kennedy (Bruce), Moray Hunter (Wully), Morwenna Banks (Maigret), Jack Docherty (Erch), John Sparkes (Ek), Pete Baikie (Boaby).

**Producer:** Alan Nixon.

**Director:** Alistair Clark.

Jack Docherty, Moray Hunter, Pete Baikie and Gordon Kennedy had been friends since their schooldays at George Watson's College in Edinburgh, later forming a comedy sketch group called The Bodgers. BBC radio light-entertainment producer Alan Nixon had paired them with Welsh comedian John Sparkes – who had come to prominence as the bedsit poet Siadwell in BBC2's *Naked Video* – and Cornish-born Morwenna Banks for the 1986 Radio 4 series *Bodgers, Banks and Sparkes*. Sensing their TV potential, Nixon took the team to Channel 4, at the time doing very nicely from Radio 4 shows that the BBC opted not to develop for television, not least *Whose Line Is It Anyway?*

The councillors of the Scottish town of Stoneybridge were among the most popular of the recurring characters. Although usually absurd and surreal, their meetings, often held to discuss the attainment of an impossible goal, seemed to capture an essential truth about the pettiness, bickering,

horse-trading and power struggle present at any such gathering
of policy-makers.

★ ☆ ★

EXT. – DAY A NON-DESCRIPT STONE BRIDGE

> VOICE-OVER
> Stoneybridge. Described by Sir Walter Scott as …
> Stoneybridge.

CUT to still of same bridge from another unattractive angle.

> Stoneybridge, with its … stoney bridge. Stoneybridge.
> Prospective host for the 1996 Olympic Games. Just
> look at our facilities.

CUT back to first still of bridge.

> There's our stoney bridge.

CUT to still of grim-looking houses, seen across scrubland.

> There's our public park with plenty of scope for
> development of a track.

CUT to still of building site.

> Our swimming pool.

CUT back to still of grim-looking houses across scrubland.

> We don't have a velodrome yet but Maigret does have
> a bicycle, so you can't fault us for spirit in …
> Stoneybridge.

CUT to still of a tabby cat.

> Oh … I don't think you're entered in any
> competition, Tabby. You see, everyone wants to get
> in on the act in Stoneybridge.

CUT to still of an old man in flat cap, polishing a window
very self-consciously.

> If being old and quite interesting was an Olympic
> sport, then surely Wully MacPhee would be there or

thereabouts. If we could get him out of the pub.
Aha.

CUT to still of white building with 'HOTEL' on the side, with
the view obscured by a lamp-post.

> Oh … what's this? Of course, it's the Olympic
> Village. Or hotel as we call it … and outside, for
> the press …

CUT to still of telephone box, with a pile of black bin bags
next to it.

> … a first-class payphone with its own directory.
> Remember it's 0-4-1-2-2-6-5-0-6-1 for Stoneybridge.

CUT to still of the Leaning Tower of Pisa.

> All roads lead to Rome …

CUT to the grim houses we saw earlier from a different angle,
along a road.

> … apart from the B7193 which just skirts
> Stoneybridge.

CUT to new still of the road over the stoney bridge.

> Stoneybridge. Bang slap on the route of the No. 47
> bus.

CUT back to still of B7193.

> Except for Thursdays when you'd be advised
> to change at the Yetts of Muckart. Or walk.
> Stoneybridge.

CUT to still of Olympic flag.

> We're Games if you are.

The video ends. CUT to TV screen with the credits in wobbly
Letraset: 'STONEYBRIDGE OLYMPIC BID. © Scottyfilms (inc.
Haggisound), Music The MacMacs, narrated by Fraser Covey'.
There is much applause from the councillors.

                          ALL
> Marvellous, etc.

                    WULLY
Rubbish.

                    BRUCE
What's the matter, Wully?

                    WULLY
Too short. It was just getting going I thought.

                    BRUCE
Oh, Wully, we're on a tight budget, as you know.

                    MAIGRET
Eh, two points. Secondly, do I have to wear this
beard?

          [Indicates false pointy beard]

                    ERCH
Maigret, we've been through this before. It's
traditional. The secretary always has a beard.
Anyway, you look very handsome. Now, your point
please.

                    MAIGRET
Well, I don't want to be a wet blanket, but don't
you think we might be over-reaching ourselves a
wee bit with this Olympic bid?

                    ALL
Tut, tut, tut, Maigret.

                    BOABY
What would you have us bid for, Maigret?

                    MAIGRET
Well, what about the World Cup?

                    EK
What about the Commonwealth Games? They're crap.

                    ERCH
Oh no, I think there might be a danger there.
There'd be an influx of … er, you know … other
people, as they say?

                    BRUCE
I don't quite follow …

                                    WULLY
You know, the sort of people that your brother-in-law
doesn't care for.

                                    BRUCE
Oh, I see. Others.

                                    WULLY
Not that it bothers me.

                                    ALL
No, no, no.

                                    BOABY
Anyway, I don't think Big Jock allows them in the
hotel.

                                    BRUCE
Well look, we've shelled out the twenty quid for this
wee-dee-o. We've got to bid for something.

                                    EK
What about the Stoneybridge Highland Games?

                                    ERCH
I think it's jingle time!

                                    ALL
Oooooh …

Caption: 'SIX YEARS LATER'.

MAIGRET's beard is now extremely lengthy. WULLY's seat is empty.

                                    MAIGRET
It's just a wee bit impractical, that's all I'm
saying.

                                    BRUCE
Maigret, Maigret, shut up about the beard. Boaby
here's got the jingles. Well done, Boaby, by the way,
you've really rushed them through this time.

                                    BOABY
Thanks. OK, is everybody ready? Here we go.

JINGLE
It could be Timbuktu or Paris or even Thailand,

but there's only one place, and that's
Stoneybridge for the Highland … Games.

BOABY
Wait a minute! There's one more.

JINGLE
If you like tossing a caber

Or eating porridge

Have the Highland Games

At Stoneybridge

And not at Norwich.

ALL
Marvellous.

WULLY enters with a letter.

WULLY
[Excited]

Here we are! Here's our answer. 'Dear Stoneybridge
Town Council. After careful consideration we
are delighted to announce that this year's
Stoneybridge Highland Games will be held the week
commencing 19th July in the Yetts of Muckart'.

ERCH
Ah, no. What about Gilbert, our mascot?

[Holds up dead mouse by tail]

I killed him specially.

# *French and Saunders* (1990)

## 'Womanly World'

### Dawn French and Jennifer Saunders

Dawn French and Jennifer Saunders emerged in the early 1980s as part of The Comic Strip team, but, like Stephen Fry and Hugh Laurie, did not get their own series until the late 80s. Like Fry and Laurie, the duo had their own distinctive voice from the off, and when given their own showcase they made excellent use of the BBC's costume and make-up facilities in order to depict a plethora of characters. Perhaps the most extensive use of the BBC resources came when they began depicting a pair of fat sexist men.

Although the series came to be best known for the extended movie pastiches – Dawn and Jennifer's take on *Silence of the Lambs* being a particular highlight – the shows were rich in variety, and, for all their absurdity, many of the sketches had a kernel of acute observation. As with this extract. Anybody who has worked in magazine publishing will recognize elements of Fiona and Jilly's flustered discussion. The names of the celebrities and subjects may well be different, but this apparently daft skit nails some universal truths about working in the media and the casual desperation to fill space or air time it sometimes engenders.

**Series:** *French and Saunders* (BBC1/2, fifty shows over six series, nine specials and two *Comic Relief* segments, 1987–2005), series 3, show 2.

**Original transmission:** BBC2, Thursday 22 March 1990, 9 p.m.

**Cast in excerpt:** Dawn French (Fiona), Jennifer Saunders (Jilly).

**Producer:** Jon Plowman.

**Director:** Bob Spiers.

INT. MAGAZINE OFFICE - DAY

> JILLY
> [Bustling in with bags]

Morning.

> FIONA

Morning, Jilly.

> JILLY

Oh God, I've been thinking about it all night,
Fiona, and I think I might have got it. Since it's
our bumper Easter issue - bonnets.

> FIONA

Absolutely, of course.

> JILLY

Get lots of pictures of Princess Di in various
hats and stuff. It's absolutely perfect. Now,
straight down to business. What else have we got?
Any news on Tim Dalton?

> FIONA

Yes, his people have come back and said he'll do
it as long as he can talk about the new Bond.

> JILLY

So we'll put him in wellies and an Arran, and do a
sort of 'At home with Bond'.

> FIONA

Yes.

> JILLY

Good show.

> FIONA

Not at his home, I hope.

> JILLY

No, mine. I thought outside my French windows.
Rather like we did with Anthony Andrews.

> FIONA

And we'll call it?

JILLY
Bond, Bond, 'Tim talks'? 'Terrific Tim'?

FIONA
'Bond Voyage'? 'Premium Bond?'

JILLY
[Pointing at FIONA]

'Premium Bond'!

FIONA
I'll get back to Nigel Havers' people, shall I,
and say no?

JILLY
Say no, but say could he do a recipe this week?
And next week we'll do a sort of Nigel really is
terrific piece.

[Shouts out to outer office]

So Rumenda, Rumenda, that's no to Nigel Havers,
we're going with Timmy Dalton.

FIONA
Right, I'll write a few letters to Postbag saying
Timmy Dalton really is fab, when are we going to
have more of Nigel Havers? Something like that.

JILLY
Yes, perfect. Now, I wanted to talk to you about
the Problem Page. Not enough emotion.

FIONA
Oh, Jilly, there were three very emotional letters
this week.

JILLY
What?

FIONA
Oh yes. First letter: 'I fancy my best friend's
husband, what should I do?'

JILLY
Think he feels the same way?

**FIONA**

Yes, that sort of thing. Second one I've written: 'Think my best friend's husband has left her but I'm too embarrassed to ask.'

**JILLY**

She'll tell you in her own time.

**FIONA**

Yes, something like that. Third one: 'Not interested in sex anymore, am I abnormal?'

**JILLY**

No, perfectly normal, if you're worried, see doctor, he'll give you some pills. Oh, look, also, I'm wondering, should we do a sort of 'Think my daughter's on heavy drugs' thing? Sort of 'AIDS, is it all stuff and nonsense?' I don't know.

**FIONA**

That means we'd have to talk about sex.

**JILLY**

All right, then.

**FIONA**

No, dirty, dirty.

**JILLY**

Right, straight on now, moving on. Cover.

**FIONA**

Yes, we've got a choice this week, Jilly. We've got Princess Di or Jean Boht.

In a later show in the 1990 series from which this sketch was taken, a galaxy of music stars was assembled for a show trial dream sequence, after house band Raw Sex found a Ralph McTell songbook lacking in chord diagrams. David Gilmour from Pink Floyd, Lemmy from Motorhead, Mark King from Level 42, Mark Knopfler from Dire Straits and Gary Moore all testified against McTell, showing themselves to be unable to play properly without diagrams.

                         JILLY
No competition.

                         FIONA
Jean Boht?

                         JILLY
Absolutely.

                         FIONA
Now, another idea, Jilly. I thought we could get
the pottery chicken from *Bread*, take the top off
and fill it with lots of little Easter chicks.
What do you think?

                         JILLY
Oh, what, sort of 'Jean's Easter joy'?

                         FIONA
Yes.

                         JILLY
That's marvellous. Now love, I don't want to see
any primary colours on that cover. Only pastels
for the Easter.

             [Shouts to outer office]

Oh, and Gwen, Gwen! Something on conservatories.
Ask Susie Hampshire. No, Hannah Gordon.

                         FIONA
Jilly, had an idea. What about Shakira Caine on
multi-purpose sarongs?

                         JILLY
Good idea.

                         FIONA
And I thought that sarongs are a little bit like
saris, which gets us in nicely to Benazir Bhutto.

                         JILLY
That's our serious piece.

                         FIONA
And another idea, Jilly. I thought we'd get a
picture of Margaret Thatcher, picture of Benazir

Bhutto, swap the heads around, and that will show our readers exactly what two leading women look like in each other's clothes.

> JILLY

That's our politics.

> FIONA

Yes, absolutely wonderful, that's our politics covered.

> JILLY

Now, look, ads.

> FIONA

Yes.

> JILLY

Are we carrying tampons this week?

> FIONA

Very blatant, aren't they? What about panty pads?

> JILLY

Mmmm, yes, panty pads. After all there's only one place a tampon's going.

> FIONA

Yes. Oh, which reminds me. Sue Lawley on flans?

> JILLY

No, too spikey.

FIONA's phone rings.

> FIONA

Hello?

> [To JILLY]

It's Janie again.

> JILLY

Seymour or Asher?

> FIONA
> [Mouthing]

Asher.

[Into phone]

Yes, yes, mmmm hmmm.

                    JILLY
What does she want? What does she want?

                    FIONA
Hang on a minute.

          [To JILLY]

She wants us to cover her kitchen again.

                    JILLY
Oh no.

                    FIONA
          [Into phone]

Erm …

                    JILLY
Is there a new angle? Ask her. Is there a new
angle?

                    FIONA
Is there a new angle on your kitchen? We've done
it so many times, Jane. Yes, I see. Hand-painted
Mexican tiles.

                    JILLY
No, not Mexican. Oh, offer her the flan feature.

                    FIONA
Have to pass on the tiles, Janie. Bit too ethnic
for us. What about 'It's flantastic'? Yes, thank
you. Bye.

          [Puts phone down]

She's gone for it. Novelty flans, she says.

                    JILLY
I'm only worried, is that going to clash with
'Kids' Kitchen'?

FIONA
[Calls to outer office]

Suuuuuuuuuuuuuuuuuue, can we see the layout for
'Kids' Kitchen', please?

JILLY
Sue, if you're on your feet, you couldn't pop down
to Marks's for the lunch could you? Thank you.

FIONA
Now, what about Mandy Smith?

JILLY
[Very quickly]

No.

FIONA
Kate Adie?

JILLY
For a makeover?

FIONA
I know she needs one, poor darling, but I've
promised the makeover to Sarah's daughter this
week.

JILLY
Oh, well, maybe the travel feature. Romantic
hotspots I know.

FIONA
Beirut.

JILLY
I've also been thinking about Barbara Bush. I
think she'd be very good for something. A sort
of … 'Beautiful Bush', 'Big Bumptious Beautiful
Big Barbara Goes Grey Gracefully', or 'Gracious
Big Bumptious Beautiful Bosomy Barbara Goes
Grey Gracefully'. Something like a Big Beautiful
Bumptious …

FIONA gets up and starts walking around strangely. Looks out
of the window. Looks horrified.

> JILLY

What's the matter? Fiona? What's the matter?

> FIONA

It's happening again, Jilly.

> JILLY

What? Fiona?

> FIONA

It's just occurred to me it's all so trivial.

> JILLY

Come on, come on, pull through.

> FIONA

Why are we doing this? It doesn't mean anything. It's banal. It doesn't mean anything.

> JILLY

Come on, for heaven's sake, don't let this happen again. We're halfway through. We haven't even touched on horoscopes.

> FIONA

What?

> JILLY

We've got knits to do yet.

> FIONA

Yes, I don't like knits.

> JILLY

Come on. What about 'Bride of the Year', darling? 'Bride of the Year'?

> FIONA

That is someone's most important day. It is worth it. It is worth it.

> JILLY

Come on.

[Both sit down]

Story. What have we got?

FIONA

Fay Weldon. Thriller. 'He took me'. Seven hundred words.

JILLY

Oh, too racy. Cut it in half and call it 'Regrets'.

JILLY walks over to the sofa by the window.

JILLY

Right. On the sofa for a summary meeting.

FIONA

Right.

JILLY

And I think we might have got it. Right. We've got 'Jean's Joy' as cover, plus everything I've already mentioned, Easter bonnets, Tim Dalton at home. I know I say it every week, but can't we get Charles Dance to do something?

FIONA
[Calls to outer office]

Suuuuuuuuuuuuuuuue, get Charles Dance to do
anything.

JILLY
Now, 'Hodge Podge'. What's that?

FIONA
That's Patricia Hodge back in shape after baby.

JILLY
Lovely.

[Calls to outer office]

Knits are under control, aren't they, Miranda?

[To FIONA]

Politics?

FIONA
Yes, we've got Babs Bush, Bhutto and Lulu.

JILLY
Lovely. Now, science.

FIONA
Well we've got 'Flossing can be fun'. Flossing.
Fun. Something like that.

JILLY
OK, now, triumph over tragedy. I don't see anyone.

FIONA
Sarah Greene?

JILLY
Oh, yes, alright, that's lovely. And get her to
do a salad as well. That'll cover environmental
issues.

FIONA
Of course, because green's green's green.

JILLY
Absolutely. Now, coping with surgery?

FIONA

Well, Miriam's turned up trumps again.

JILLY

Yes?

FIONA

Stars and their secret scars?

JILLY

Marvellous.

FIONA

Yes.

JILLY

So, that, horoscopes, competition and the free
J-Cloth offer, that's the bulk of it.

FIONA

Yes, and we'll just pad with old items from back
issues as usual.

JILLY

As per normal. Well, I think that's lunch, Fiona,
and a quick afternoon's flick through Freemans.

[Calls to outer office]

Oh, chicken tikka sandwiches, Sue, if you're on
your way out.

FIONA

Yes and three bean salad. Oh, and go crazy, two
syrup sponges. Why not?

In 2006 French and Saunders announced that they had finished their TV
sketch shows, and in 2009 finished touring as a double act. They remain
close friends and turn up at Easter and Christmas on BBC Radio 2, hosting
shows together.

# *One Foot in the Grave* (1990)

## 'Timeless Time'

### David Renwick

For years, Richard Wilson had been a reliable supporting actor in various sitcoms, most notably as the consultant Dr Thorpe in *Only When I Laugh*. It took until 1990 before he was given his own starring role, as retired security guard Victor Meldrew in David Renwick's first solo creation. Meldrew is usually seen as grumpy, but it's fairer to say that he's a kind, helpful soul tested by circumstance and coincidence, which brings out his sometimes fearsome temper. His long-suffering wife, Margaret, played to perfection by Annette Crosbie, has to make excuses for him to the outside world, though rarely to his face, confronting his worst excesses.

**Series:** *One Foot in the Grave* (BBC1, forty-three shows over six series and six specials and two *Comic Relief* segments, 1990–2001), series 2, show 6.

**Original transmission:** BBC1, Thursday 15 November 1990, 9.30 p.m.

**Cast in excerpt:** Richard Wilson (Victor Meldrew), Annette Crosbie (Margaret Meldrew).

**Producer/director:** Susan Belbin.

In earlier series, Meldrew was inclined to greet each indignity with a shout of 'I don't believe it'. When this started to become a catchphrase, Renwick began rationing its use rigorously, using it as an occasional treat for viewers craving familiarity. Renwick was too interested in exploring other facets of the characters to rely on catchphrases. When Renwick felt the series had run its course, after ten years, he took the brave decision to kill Victor off, partially, he said, to remove any temptation he might feel to revisit the character with diminishing returns. The final episode, 'Things Aren't Simple Any More', was watched by 13 million viewers.

INT. MELDREWS' BEDROOM - NIGHT

                    VICTOR
    Are you asleep?

                [With a harsher tone]

    Margaret! I think I might buy one of those
    sweaters tomorrow that Noel Edmonds wears.

                    MARGARET
    You do, and I'll kill myself.

                    VICTOR
    What was that? Did you hear that?

                    MARGARET
                [Exasperated]

    What?

                    VICTOR
    That strange hooting sound.

                    MARGARET
    Probably Mrs Stebbings down the corner.

VICTOR gets up and goes to the bedroom window.

                    VICTOR
    No, it's that baby owl I told you about the other
    night. Sitting perched on the telephone wires.
    Look at him, perched right over my car roof. You
    just dare, matey boy. He's thinking about it, you
    can tell.

                    MARGARET
    Well, he will do if you keep staring at him.
    You'll make him nervous.

                    VICTOR
    Why don't they spatter someone else's car, why
    is it always mine? He is going to, too. Look at
    him, he's getting into position, shifting himself
    around. Any second now, he's definitely going to …
    there.

Car alarm goes off in the street outside.

                    VICTOR
Oh, I don't believe it. They told me they were
supposed to have fixed this thing. That's twice
I've had to take that back now because it was too
sensitive. You can't tell me there isn't something
wrong somewhere when your car alarm is set off by
a bird dropping.

         [VICTOR walks into the bathroom]

Well, that's their rations finished with. Any
stale pieces of toast now go into the dustbin.
What's this packet of Bisto doing in here?

                    MARGARET
What?

                    VICTOR
What's this packet of Bisto doing in the medicine
cabinet?

                    MARGARET
How do I know what it's doing? I can't even see
it.

                    VICTOR
I'll ring that garage in the morning, that'll be
the first job. Why is nothing in life ever simple?
What makes that last teaspoon cling for dear life
to the bottom of the washing-up bowl each night
when you pour the water away? Even if you haven't
used a bloody teaspoon. There's always one appears
from somewhere.

                    MARGARET
Will you just go to sleep?

                    VICTOR
Mysteries of the universe. Time and space. Life
and death. Mike Hope and Albie Keen. Never did
hear any more about them. Time. When you think
about it, nothing ever exists in fact. I was
working this out in the Post Office while I was
waiting for that woman to finish twanging her

elastic bands. The future doesn't exist because
it hasn't happened yet. The past doesn't exist
because it's already over. But the present doesn't
exist because as soon as you start to think about
it, it's already in the past, which doesn't exist
any more. Like that moment just then when I said
that. That's already in the past. Gone forever.
And so's that when I just said 'gone forever'. And
so's that when I said 'and so's that', that's gone
forever now. And so's that, when I said 'that's
gone forever now as well', that's gone forever now
as well.

                    MARGARET
Oh for God's sake, will you shut up, Victor?
Jabbering on all the while there like a rabid
parrot. Now I'm wide awake. Thank you very much.

                    VICTOR
What time is it? Are we in the single European
market yet?

MARGARET turns on bedside light.

                    MARGARET
Quarter past three. I'll finish this crossword.
That usually sends me off. Saw an old friend of
yours today. He came into the shop with a wilting
hibiscus. Charlie Masefield?

                    VICTOR
Oh yes. I haven't seen him in ages. I wonder how
he's getting on? Did he ask how I was?

                    MARGARET
No. Well not as such.

The series was remade for the American market under the title *Cosby*, starring
comedian Bill Cosby. The central character was considerably less grumpy and
irascible than in the British original, slightly missing the point of the series.

VICTOR
How do you mean 'not as such'?

MARGARET
Well, he seemed to be under the impression that
you were dead. In fact, we had quite an argument
about it. He was absolutely convinced that you
died last year, during Wimbledon fortnight. He
said he remembers it was the same day Jimmy
Connors got knocked out, so he was doubly shocked.
I said, 'No, no, I think you must be getting him
mixed up with someone else,' but he wouldn't
have it. You know, people that age, they get
something into their head, and it won't budge. He
said he distinctly remembered you'd asked to have
your ashes scattered across the floor in Allied
Carpets, to get your own back. To be honest, I
think he's going a bit [points to head], you know,
so in the end, to keep the peace, I agreed with
him. I said, 'Now you come to mention it, you're
right, he is dead.' He went off then, happy as a
sandboy. Oh, and then – talk about an afternoon
for characters – we had Broad Maude come in with
all her latest problems.

VICTOR
Broad Maude? Is she the one who always carries her
own toilet seat about with her?

MARGARET
In a Tesco's carrier bag. Frightened stiff of
public lavatories. Frightened stiff of everything.
Takes it all to heart. Everything she reads in the
papers, sees on the news. Salmonella, listeria,
poisonous algae, a man-eating fungus that comes up
through the drains.

VICTOR
Man-eating fungus?

MARGARET
She says she saw it on the news, but I reckon
it was *Doctor Who*. I think they all start to
blur in her mind a bit in the end. That was her
late husband, always had a morbid fear of giant

spiders. Every time he heard the cat flap go, he used to break out into a cold sweat.

> VICTOR
> [Yawning]

Can you imagine carrying your own toilet seat everywhere, though. It must be a bit of a handicap. What does she do if she's got two bags of shopping? Wear it round her neck?

> MARGARET
> [Folding up newspaper]

Well, that's that, and I'm still wide awake. Perhaps I'll go and make a milky drink. You want one?

> VICTOR

Yes, I suppose so, might as well. I'll try anything.

> [Shouting downstairs to MARGARET]

Put a drop of rum in it. Perhaps if I read something, that would help? What have we got? A *Brief History of Time* or the autobiography of Reg Varney. Bloody book clubs. I know what I could do. I could open last year's Christmas present from Ronnie and Mildred. [Reads label] 'To dearest Victor, just a little something to wish you a Merry Christmas and a prosperous 1990 from Ronnie and Mildred.' No, I'm not that bored yet.

Ohhhh.

Pulls fitted sheet back down so it covers mattress, then notices wonky picture over bed. Straightens it.

> No, still not straight. That's got it, that's straight.

Phone rings.

> VICTOR

4291? What? Yes it is straight. What do you mean not from where you're standing? You can't see from right across the road, I know. Anyway, what are you doing up at this time of— Oh, can't you? Yes, I'm sorry about that. They were supposed to have fixed it, but you know what it's like with garages. Yes. I hope you do too, goodnight.

[Waves out of window]

MARGARET

The rest of that milk was off, so I had to use powdered, and we're out of rum.

MARGARET and VICTOR return to bed.

VICTOR

God, this tastes revolting.

MARGARET

I know, it came through the front door. There are several Olympic pole-vaulters supposed to swear by it. That shampoo makes my hair all dry, I won't use that one again.

VICTOR

Which one was that?

MARGARET

Another new one on the market. That came through the front door as well.

VICTOR

Just as well they haven't got a sales push on for motorcycles or we'd have a Harley-Davidson coming through the front door, mowing us all to the ground when we came down for breakfast. The man from the local pet shop was coming round this morning delivering free trial offer chihuahuas, hammering them through people's letterboxes with a large mallet. I expect we'll get ours tomorrow.

MARGARET

More than likely. Is it alright if I put the light out now?

VICTOR

Yes.

Calm reigns briefly before VICTOR sits bolt upright in the dark.

In typical TV location-finding fashion, the series was nominally set in Bedfordshire, near Renwick's home town of Luton, but the exterior shooting mostly took place in Dorset, with the Meldrews' house actually being in Tresilian Way, Walkford, near Christchurch.

> VICTOR
>
> Oh God, my leg's started twitching now. I wondered when that was going to happen. Shaking about like a Morris dancer. All I need to do is put a couple of bells on the end of it. I can't stop it. It's always the same when my muscles get tense.

> MARGARET
>
> Here we go. The Ministry of Silly Walks.

> VICTOR
>
> It's no laughing matter if you had to put up with it.

> MARGARET
>
> You don't take enough exercise. That's your problem. Too much sitting around all day. Sitting around fretting about everything under the sun. No wonder you end up all on edge.

VICTOR goes to the lavatory.

> MARGARET
>
> You can't so much as suck a Polo without crunching it.

VICTOR returns.

> VICTOR
>
> Who can't?

> MARGARET
>
> You go right through the entire packet like a beaver in one of those old cartoons.

VICTOR returns to bed, groaning.

                    VICTOR
        Now, I think if I stick it in the air, don't
        stretch it and stop the trembling. Ah, that's
        better.

VICTOR and MARGARET finally get off to sleep, but are woken
by the car alarm going off again.

                    VICTOR
        Bloody thing again. What the hell's going on?

                    MARGARET
        It's that cat sitting on the front. Go away, shoo,
        go away, go on.

                    VICTOR
        I can't switch it off. What's wrong with this
        bloody thing? The battery's gone.

                    MARGARET
        You can't leave it like that.

                    VICTOR
        I'll go and switch it off with the key under the
        bonnet. Where are my slippers?

                    MARGARET
        Here.

VICTOR leaves, switches off alarm, then returns.

                    VICTOR
        I'll have a word with that garage tomorrow, you
        see if I don't. You leave your car there for three
        days, and they do nothing. Probably using it to go
        about joyriding in. I swear I could smell seaweed
        from that air filter.

                    MARGARET
        Victor, what on earth is that you've got on your
        foot?

MARGARET turns on bedside light.

                    MARGARET
        Oh-arrggghhhh, you've got your foot in a rotting
        hedgehog.

VICTOR

Good God, it must have been when my slipper came
off. I thought it was a bit soggy. I thought it was
just perspiration. Steady, steady, there it is.

Picking it up with a stick and going to throw it out of the
window.

Ruddy thing, where do they come from?

Throws it out the window, a cat yowls.

Serves you right for sitting on my car.

MARGARET

Come here. Oh look, you've got all his little
needles stuck in your foot.

VICTOR

I've had it for one night, Margaret. I have,
straight, I was just getting off then, as well.
Just going to sleep and dreaming. Dreaming this
really strange dream. They'd emptied all the
water out of Loch Ness to see if there were any
monsters. And when the lake was completely empty,
there lying in the mud was this giant sixty-foot
teaspoon.

# *Last of the Summer Wine* (1991)

## 'Give Us a Lift'

## Roy Clarke

**Series:** *Last of the Summer Wine* (BBC1, 296 shows over one *Comedy Playhouse* pilot, 31 series 27 specials and one *Funny Side of Christmas* segment, 1973–2010), series 13, show 2.

**Original transmission:** BBC1, Friday 25 October 1991, 8 p.m.

**Cast in excerpt:** Brian Wilde (Foggy Dewhurst), Kathy Staff (Nora Batty), Stephen Lewis (Smiler), Bill Owen (Compo Simmonite), Juliette Kaplan (Pearl), Robert Fyfe (Howard), Peter Sallis (Norman Clegg), Jane Freeman (Ivy).

**Producer/director:** Alan J.W. Bell.

The impetus for the world's longest-running situation comedy came from BBC Television's head of comedy Duncan Wood – former producer of both *Hancock's Half Hour* and *Steptoe and Son* – who knew he wanted a sitcom about a trio of geriatrics. He also knew that he wanted Roy Clarke – who had just experienced some success with *The Misfit* for ATV, starring Ronald Fraser – to write it. Clarke was initially unsure of the comic value of three northern pensioners at a loose end, but he felt he had something to build on when he hit on the idea of them just being 'feckless adolescents in their own way', as he described them to *The Guardian* in 1973.

Initially, the trio consisted of: Cyril Blamire, a childish know-all whose military bearing belied his rank of corporal in the Royal Signals; Norman Clegg, a relatively sensible widower; and William 'Compo' Simmonite, a scruffy, lazy, lecherous little man, with designs on Nora Batty, the temptress with the wrinkled stockings. The three men wandered the hills and dales around Holmfirth, musing on life, the universe and everything, usually reaching whimsical and surreal conclusions. Often, Compo or Blamire would come up with a hare-brained scheme, on which Clegg would sound a note of caution, but go on to help them with it anyway.

Bates left the show in 1975, resulting in the arrival of Brian Wilde as Walter 'Foggy' Dewhurst, who liked reminding his companions of his wartime exploits. The trio of Compo,

Foggy and Clegg would come to define the series, even when Wilde left for a four-year sabbatical between 1986 and 1990. In the eyes of many, *Last of the Summer Wine* was cosy, unthreatening TV, but rebellion and subversion were never far from the surface. The women are sarcastic, the men just want to be left alone (apart from when it comes to Compo and Nora) and Clarke's dialogue sparkles. There was so much more to the *Last of the Summer Wine* than three old blokes rolling downhill in a bathtub.

★ ☆ ★

EXT. COUNTRYSIDE – DAY

A linesman is working up a telegraph pole. FOGGY aims his walking stick at the linesman, as if it were a rifle. The linesman notices him.

> FOGGY
> It brings back wartime memories. Burma, 1943. You know, snipers up trees. You've just reminded me. I wish I had a fiver for every sniper I've shot out of a tree. At least I think they were snipers. Come to think of it, I suppose they could have been employees of the Burmese telephone system.

NORA Batty is standing on a set of steps, looking down on SMILER, while COMPO watches from a nearby window.

> NORA
> Come on, show yourself. You want a sack of good King Edwards. Make sure he opens the sack and lets you see they're all right. Don't come back here with any rubbish. And you want a sack of Brussels sprouts. Them tiny nutty ones. I don't want them that look as though they belong in someone's buttonhole. Well, what are you hanging about for? Off you go.

> SMILER
> I'm going, I'm going.

                                    COMPO
              Has she got you on a chain gang, then, Smiler?

                                    SMILER
              You're not kidding.

                                    NORA
              Running a few errands won't hurt him. You'd be
              better off with something to do.

                                    COMPO
              Make me an offer.

                                    NORA
              Get off inside.

                                    COMPO
              Don't let that nasty expression fool you, Smiler.
              She just puts that on in public to hide the fact
              that when I'm near, her heart skips a beat.

                                    NORA
              Skips a beat? It skips half a dozen when you're
              wandering around in your underwear.

NORA goes indoors.

                                    COMPO
              See that? She's gone inside for a quick tremble.
              Well, you've either got it or you haven't. The
              old sexual magnetism, son. Woo hoo. What's it like
              being Nora Batty's lodger?

                                    SMILER
              It's like being married.

Educated at Gainsborough Grammar School, Clarke's pre-writing career
included stints as a tailor's assistant, a policeman, a teacher and a 'packie' –
the person who lumbered a door-to-door salesman's suitcase around for him.

                    COMPO
It can't be too much like being married.

                    SMILER
It's like being in the army again. You're always
on jankers.

                    COMPO
Well, I don't mind as long as I don't start
enjoying it.

COMPO retreats from the window.

CLEGG and HOWARD are on their knees, looking closely at the
ground. PEARL comes out of the house in high dudgeon.

                    PEARL
What the dickens are you doing?

                    HOWARD
Cleggy was just showing me his beetle.

                    CLEGG
Well, it's not actually my beetle.

                    PEARL
Beetle?

                    HOWARD
He's only a little beetle.

                    PEARL
Well, I'm relieved to hear that.

                    HOWARD
I've never seen one like it before.

                    PEARL
Well, it's looking at you two. It's probably
thinking something very similar.

                    CLEGG
It occurred to me that it might be an unusual
beetle. A discovery of genuine scientific
interest. Do you realize that I could have a
beetle named after me?

                              PEARL
        Norman? A beetle called Norman?

                              CLEGG
        No, not Norman. Clegg's beetle. I was just
        checking with Howard if he'd ever seen one like it
        before.

                              HOWARD
        I haven't. It's a very unusual beetle.

PEARL walks away, clearly thinking that CLEGG and HOWARD have
gone mad.

                              HOWARD
        They never get really excited about things like
        beetles.

                              CLEGG
                          [Looks down]

        It's gone. It's gone. We've been standing here.

                          [Agitated]

        Lift your feet up.

INT. CAFE - DAY

COMPO, FOGGY and CLEGG walk in. COMPO bangs on the counter to
get IVY's attention.

                              COMPO
        Here, Clegg's found a beetle.

                              IVY
        Not in here, he hasn't.

                              COMPO
        No, not in here.

                              IVY
        Well, I wish he'd make that perfectly clear. I
        don't want my customers thinking I permit creepy-
        crawlies in here.

Two customers lurking by the door leave suddenly, thinking
they must be the 'creepy-crawlies'.

FOGGY

Your average Anglo-Saxon beetle is very small
as beetles go. You should have seen them in the
jungle. Ye gods. A whirr of wings, an angry
buzzing and they'd fly off with your steel helmet.

COMPO

He does talk some fanny.

CLEGG

It was only about that big. A handsome little
fella. He was a sort of shiny bottle green.

COMPO

I wish you'd kept it.

CLEGG

Ah, well, it slipped away while Pearl was talking
to us.

FOGGY

Howard has the same instinct.

IVY

Do you lot want serving, or are you just going to
stand there, talking beetles?

CLEGG

I'll just have one of these.

He steps forward to grab a rock cake, but IVY slaps his hand.

IVY

Not with your beetle hands, you'll not.

She picks it up with tongs and places it on a plate with a
thud.

EXT. COUNTRYSIDE – DAY

COMPO, FOGGY and CLEGG are walking.

CLEGG

Either these hills are getting steeper or
gravity's getting heavier.

FOGGY

Oh, nonsense. A spot of vigorous exercise.

At the time of the original *Comedy Playhouse* pilot, the location of Holmfirth was fresh in the mind of BBC comedy bosses, having featured in a 1972 documentary on entertainment called *Having a Lovely Time*, in which Barry Took visited the town's working men's club and interviewed the owner of Bamforth's, the Holmfirth-based company that specializes in risqué seaside postcards.

CLEGG

It's a lot like being really ill, is vigorous exercise. Have you noticed the similarities? Your ears are ringing, you've spots before your eyes, you're liable to be sick. Ah yes, vigorous exercise is quite a lot like being really ill.

FOGGY

Just be grateful that you're not going uphill, wearing full equipment, and carrying rifle and bayonet.

COMPO

Oh, I wish I was. The first twit who'd get a prod would be thee, and I wouldn't fancy sitting down for a while either.

FOGGY

Ah, very well, we'll take a breather.

CLEGG

Breather? I gave up doing that half a mile ago.

# The Smell of Reeves and Mortimer (1993)

## 'Noel's Addicts'

### Jim Moir and Bob Mortimer

When *Vic Reeves Big Night Out* began on Channel 4 in 1990, it was clear to most viewers that Bob Mortimer was just as much the show's star as the man with his name in the title. When the pair moved to BBC2 in 1993, the balance was redressed. Leeds-born, Darlington-raised, art school-trained surrealist Jim Moir had moved to London in the mid-80s and combined a day job as a factory inspector with evenings performing on the comedy circuit in various character guises. The most popular proved to be Vic Reeves, a self-styled 'light entertainer' given to bellowing Smiths songs in cheesy showbiz arrangements. At one 'Vic Reeves' Big Night Out' show in a south London pub, a member of the audience began to join in. Soon, Middlesbrough-born trainee solicitor Bob Mortimer was a regular part of the show.

The original *Big Night Out* TV series was very much in the spirit of those pub shows, with its bare set, its homemade props and costumes, and absence of location filming. Fortunately, the ramshackle nature of the venture made the most of the tiny budget. When the pair moved to the BBC, more money was available. Location work was in and director John Birkin, who had served his apprenticeship as a production manager on BBC variety and comedy shows, gave 'Britain's top light entertainer and singer' the shiny-floor habitat he deserved. As well as introducing new characters like Le Corbussier et Papin – a pair of Frenchmen with

**Series:** *The Smell of Reeves and Mortimer* (BBC2, thirteen shows over two series and one *Fry and Laurie Host a Christmas Night with the Stars* segment, 1993–5), series 1, show 4.

**Original transmission:** BBC2, Tuesday 12 October 1993, 9 p.m.

**Cast in excerpt:** Vic Reeves (Ken Taylor, Dave Arrowsmith, Chris Bell, Bruce Forsyth, Dave Lee Travis), Bob Mortimer (Noel Edmonds, Pat Wright).

**Producer/director:** John Birkin.

digestive problems, and the psychotic folk singers Mulligan and O'Hare (who bear a disturbing resemblance to, Terry Wogan and James Galway, respectively), *The Smell of Reeves and Mortimer* was notable for its deranged parodies of mainstream TV shows, including *MasterChef, Food and Drink* and *Antiques Roadshow.*

One of the other spoofs in series one was this burlesque of a relatively obscure early evening filler programme hosted by Noel Edmonds, now remembered primarily, if not exclusively, for inspiring this sketch. Only the host's name remains the same, along with the vaguest outline of the original format. Everything else is a product of the unique brain-wiring of Jim Moir and Bob Mortimer. Incidentally, NTV was a segment of Edmonds' big Saturday-night show *Noel's House Party.*

The version printed here reinstates sections cut on original transmission, and includes some of Reeves' and Mortimer's painstakingly detailed instructions in quote marks.

★ ☆ ★

INT. STUDIO – DAY

VIC and BOB are going through the channels on a 1950s-style TV set, trying to find something to watch.

                              BOB
          Ah, that's better.

On the screen is BOB in a false beard and wig, looking like NOEL EDMONDS, with three doughnuts revolving around his head. CUT to a studio with 'NOEL'S ADDICTS' logo painted on the floor. PAN to opening at the rear of the set, where BOB stands, in an Edmonds wig and beard, dressed in an enormous fat suit, in which various bottles and packages appear to be stuffed randomly.

                         VOICE-OVER
          It's No-No-No-No-No-Noe-Noe-Noel's Addicts.

Every participant in this show is holding a vinegar bottle where possible.

NOEL (BOB)

Welcome to the wonderful world of addiction-n-n
[holds up a bottle of cider], boy scouts. Now
everyone loves drinking strong cider.

[Pulls 'wacky' face]

I know I do, but with a bra in it? Everything will
become a lot clearer when I introduce you to my
first guest, Ken Taylor, who's got a collection of
things suspended in bottles of cider. Let's go and
greet Ken.

NOEL walks over to KEN (VIC). There is a table with three
bottles of cider, a half-eaten salami and a Brie French
baguette sandwich and an old axe. Next to the table is KEN
who is sitting on a wooden school chair in the same style
as the table. He is eating chocolate cake on a white paper
plate. KEN is very obese, with a false rubber set of double
chins.

NOEL

Hello, Ken, nice to meet you. Ken Taylor! He's
addicted! Hello, Ken.

[Shaking hands]

Nice to meet you.

KEN

I won't get up. I can't.

[Wheezes hideously]

NOEL

So, Ken, you suspend things in cider.

KEN

That's right, Noel. Always have done.

NOEL

[Puts on half-Cockney, half-Mummerset accent]

That's an unusual 'obby. What does your wife think
of thaaat?

                         KEN
        She don't mind. I've been putting things in cider
        since we first met.

                         NOEL
        Haaaaaaa.

[An exhale from the lung, not so much a laugh as a sharp
blast of noisy moist air … it stops very abruptly]

                         KEN
        Did I say something funny, Noel?

                         NOEL
        What was the first thing you ever put in cider?

                         KEN
        First thing I ever put in cider were a bread bin.
        Did I say something funny, Noel?

NOEL

Haaaaaaaa. Now, Ken, if there was one thing
[Adopts Cockney accent] above all else, that you
could put in cider what would that be?

KEN

Well, me and the wife are both keen musicians,
Noel, so I'd love to put my organ in cider.

NOEL

Haaaaaa. Ken Taylor, you're one of my all-time
favourite addicts. Thank you.

KEN

Did I say something funny, Noel?

Applause. NOEL walks away from KEN's set back to the main set
as KEN starts attacking the table with the axe.

NOEL

Poor wife. Really. Careful everyone, we're about
to go live, NTV, and it could be your room. Let's
go.

CUT to a shot of an empty sofa.

NOEL

It's not a cock-up, is it? I hate them. Oh no.

CUT back to sofa, now containing two Geordie men, PAT WRIGHT
and DAVE ARROWSMITH.

NOEL

Thank God you're there, lads. I thought for a
terrible moment that you'd just popped out.

PAT (BOB)

What are you saying, like? There's no danger of
us popping out of these bras. Dave, look at this
joker.

DAVE (VIC)

Pat, who are you talking to?

PAT

I'm talking to this joker. Says our bras aren't up
to the job.

DAVE
Pat, there's no one there.

PAT
Ah, Dave, man, you're useless. Hey, fella, these
are top-quality brassieres, and you can stick your
camera too.

[Gets up and disconnects camera]

There you go, I've sorted him out for you, Dave,
no worries.

NOEL
Where do we get them from? I don't know!

Every week we get literally thousands of letters
from people who have collections of animals or
nuts. This week, I'm going to introduce you to a
fellow who's cleverly combined the two. Mr Chris
Bell.

'NOEL arrives at CHRIS' set. This consists of a large white
screen six foot square with the name "Chris Bell" on it, a
large school dining table and a school chair. On the table
are twelve to fifteen pottery horses, each of which is
drawing (i.e. via a harness) a different type of nut, for
example: walnut, cob, peanut, brazil, doughnut, coconut,
almond, pecan, cashew, macadamia, hazelnut, Clive James
nut, chestnut, wingnut, tigernut, monkeynut, pistachio,
winegaurdnut [sic]. NB During the following piece Chris Bell
is going to make a number of puns based on nuts and horses.
These have been helpfully placed in quotation marks. Each
time one is said a scorekeeper on the screen (i.e. like the
one that keeps tag of the number of score draws when the
football results are coming through on Saturday Grandstand)
clicks over to record the pun. This scorekeeper reads 'Score
Draws'. Also after each pun a reception bell rings to log the
pun audibly.'

NOEL
So Chris, what exactly is it that you collect?

CHRIS (VIC)
Let me tell you, Noel. What I do is I collect
horse-drawn nuts …

                        NOEL
      That's amazing. Let's have a 'pecan' at them.

                        CHRIS
      Hey, nice one, Noel. Nice touch. You're on top
      form tonight. Right Noel, I'll tell you about
      them, right, what I do is I collect these and
      I'm absolutely 'nuts' about them.  I could talk
      about them till I'm 'horse' in the mouth. I got
      'saddled' with this little lot when my Aunt
      'Hazel' who lived in 'Brazil' died in the 'reign'
      of Louis-Philippe the 'pear'-shaped king.

A klaxon sounds. CUT to VIC as BRUCE Forsyth, wearing a false
chin shaped like a pair of bum cheeks.

                        BRUCE
      You get nothing for a pear. Not in this game. Heh-
      bib-bib-bib …

            [Caricature Brucie noises]

                        CHRIS
            [Looking out of shot as if to BRUCE]

      What's your problem? What's the problem with a
      pear, then?

                        NOEL
      This is fascinating … So what's this one – a
      'cashew'?

                        CHRIS
      Bless, you, Noel. Haaaah! I'm as good as you,
      ain't I? Noel, you like looking at my nuts, didn't
      ya?

                        NOEL
      Haaaaaaa [very forced]. Chris Bell, fantastic
      addict.

Applause, with camera remaining on NOEL to follow him back to
main set.

                        NOEL
            [As he walks back to the main set]

> And now, ladies and gentlemen, we've all been
> waiting for … Yes, it's time to present this
> week's wobbly melon award.

Applause as NOEL mounts himself behind a podium which has
a drawing of Noel Edmonds (provided by VIC) with the words
'Noel Edmonds' below and on the top has a nice watermelon
(eight inches high).

> NOEL
> And now the moment you've all been waiting for.
> Yes, it's the Wobbly Melon Award.

> [Activates melon wobbling facility]

> To receive the Melon award this week, you'll know
> him as Clement Attlee. Ladies and gentlemen,
> Clement Attlee!

Applause. Enter DAVE LEE TRAVIS (VIC) carrying a framed
picture of Noel Edmonds from his DJ years (i.e. with big
shirt collars, etc).

> NOEL
> Oh no, not you [pathetically acting as if
> surprised], it's my good friend DLT.

> DLT
> [Waving picture around]

> Boing!

> NOEL
> What a surprise! What's that you've got there?

> DLT
> Noel, it's an old picture of you, when you looked
> slightly different.

> NOEL
> [Takes picture from DLT, places hand over mouth in fake
> shock]

> It's a picture of me when I looked slightly
> different! Terrible!

CUT to a man in a green bodystocking with comic bloodshot
eyes and a proboscis on his forehead, alongside two women in
curly wigs dressed as pieces of soft fruit.

> NOEL
> Oh no, it's Mr Stamen and the retarded Philips
> sisters from Kent. It's all going crazy.

> DLT
> It's crazy ding-dong, nick-nack, zing-zang.

> NOEL
> Let's get out of here my good chum, DLT. It's a
> madhouse.

Everyone dances around. NOEL and DLT start fighting. Credits
roll: 'Written by Mustard Gas. Script Associate Town Gas.
Cameraman Mr Mix Up. Tilting provided by Bongo Jim and his
Peppery Penguin. Union Jacks supplied by Grumpies Magic
Vinegar Pot. Producer Crab with Bronze Hand. Director Arse
Magic. A Terrys Chocolate Orange Production.'

# The Day Today (1994)

## 'War'

## Christopher Morris, Armando Iannucci and the cast

**Series:** *The Day Today* (BBC2, six shows, 1994), show 5.

**Original transmission:** BBC2, Wednesday 16 February 1994, 9 p.m.

**Cast in excerpt:** Chris Morris (Anchorman), Steve Coogan (Alan Partridge), Patrick Marber (Dônnnald Bethl'hem), Andrew Burt (Martin Craste), Doon Mackichan (Suzanna Gekkaloys), Steve Coogan (Douglas Trox), David Schneider (Sylvester Stewart and Man with glasses), Robert Putt (Man menaced by Hugh Scully), John Thomson (Hawtrey).

**Producers:** Christopher Morris/Armando Iannucci.

**Director:** Andrew Gillman.

Spoofing the style and substance of news broadcasting has always been a rich seam of comedy, and *The Day Today* – developed from the BBC Radio 4 news satire *On the Hour* – is the high watermark of the genre. Where it triumphed was to nail the form of current affairs programming perfectly, in terms of the graphics, music and vernacular, and then to fill each half-hour with nonsense.

The nonsense was not without purpose. It served to highlight the absurdities of the style and presentation of news on the television. Chris Morris's deranged anchorman apart, the star of the show was Alan Partridge, Steve Coogan's sports reporter character whose self-belief greatly outstripped his intelligence or abilities. Although *The Day Today* ran for just one perfect series, Partridge has gone on, through chat shows and a mock-documentary sitcom about his life, almost existing in parallel to the real Coogan.

In this extract, the news media's demand for excitement and events is taken to its logical extreme by having anchorman Morris provoke a war between Australia and Hong Kong. Far-fetched? In its day, *The Day Today* was a heightened, demented version of the way news is reported. Viewed now, it seems more like a sober reflection.

INT. TV NEWS STUDIO - DAY

> MORRIS
>
> Today's historic trade agreement between Australia
> and Hong Kong marks a new season of hope for
> the future of world trade. The two countries
> have been at each other's throats for years, but
> now the hatchet's been buried by a treaty which
> allows unrestricted trading between all parties
> at all levels. I'm joined now by Martin Craste,
> the British minister with responsibility for the
> Commonwealth, and Gavin Hawtrey, the Australian
> foreign secretary in Canberra. Gentlemen, this
> is pretty historic stuff, well done. A future of
> unbridled harmony then? Australia?

> HAWTREY
>
> Yeah, I think that Martin Craste and I can be
> pretty satisfied. It's a good day.

> MORRIS
> [To CRASTE]
>
> If, as in the past, Australia exceed their
> agreement, what will you do about it?

> CRASTE
>
> This is a pretty satisfactory treaty which I am
> sure will work well. Naturally, if the limits were
> exceeded this would be met with a firm line, but I
> can't see this being necessary.

> MORRIS
>
> Mr Hawtrey, he's knocking a firm line in your
> direction. What are you  going to do about that?

The reason for Chris Morris looking significantly different in some sections
of the transmitted version of this sketch is that some of the material was re-
used from the non-broadcast pilot.

HAWTREY

Well, in that case we'd just reimpose sanctions as
we did last year—

MORRIS

Sanctions!

[To CRASTE]

Hang on a second, they've only just swallowed their
sanctions and now they're burping them back up in
your face.

CRASTE

I think sanctions is rather premature talk.
Certainly if sanctions were imposed we would have to
retaliate with appropriate measures. But I can't—

MORRIS

I think 'appropriate measures' is a euphemism, Mr
Hawtrey - you know what it means, what are you going
to do about that?

HAWTREY

Well, I'd just have to go back to Cabinet.

MORRIS

And ask them about what?

HAWTREY

I dunno, maybe it's a matter for the military—

MORRIS

The military!

CRASTE

I think military measures is an entirely
inappropriate reaction, and I think this is way, way
over the top.

MORRIS
[To HAWTREY]

Sounds like you're being inappropriate! Are you?

HAWTREY

Course I'm not being inappropriate! Martin Craste
knows that full well.

CRASTE

This is the sort of misunderstanding that I thought
we'd laid to rest during our negotiating period.

MORRIS

Misunderstanding it certainly is, it's certainly
not a treaty, is it? You're both at each other's
throats, you're backing yourselves up with arms –
what are you going to do about it? Mr Hawtrey, let
me give you a hint. Bang!

HAWTREY

What're you asking me to say?

MORRIS

You know damn well what I want you to say! You're
putting yourself in a situation of armed conflict –
what are you plunging yourself into?

HAWTREY

You'd like me to say it?

MORRIS

I want you to say it, yes!

HAWTREY

You want the word?

MORRIS

The word!

HAWTREY

I will not flinch …

MORRIS

You will not flinch from …?

HAWTREY

War.

MORRIS

War!

[He's delighted]

Gentlemen, I'll put you on hold – if fighting
did break out, it would probably take place
in Eastmantown in the Upper Cataracts on the

Australio-Hong Kong border. Our reporter Dônnnald Bethl'hem is there now - Dônnnald, what's the atmosphere like?

                    BETHL'HEM
Tension here is very high, Chris - the stretched twig of peace is at melting point. People here are literally bursting with war. This is very much a country that's going to blow up in its face.

                    MORRIS
Well, gentlemen, it seems we have little option now but to declare war immediately!

                    CRASTE
This is quite impossible, I couldn't possibly take such a decision without referring to my superior, Chris Patten, and he's in Hong Kong!

                    MORRIS
Good, because he's on the line now via satellite. Mr Patten - what do you think of the idea of a war now?

PATTEN nods his head absently.

                    MORRIS
I'll take that as a yes!

                    CRASTE
Very well, it's war!

                    HAWTREY
War it is!

Behind BETHL'HEM, a shell explodes.

                    BETHL'HEM
That's it, Chris - it's war! War has broken out - this is a war!

                    MORRIS
           [Looking far too pleased with himself]

That's it! Yes - it's war!

The normal blue studio lighting changes to blood red. A wall of huge letters spelling 'WAR' is illuminated. Technicians pour in and start turning the studio into a media command centre. CRASTE and his desk are hurriedly wheeled away.

                MORRIS
From now on, *The Day Today* will be providing the most immediate coverage of any war ever fought. On the front line and in your face, Dônnnald Bethl'hem.

           MAN WITH GLASSES
Standing by, Douglas Hurd.

                MORRIS
*The Day Today* smart bombs have nose-mounted cameras, this is smart bomb Steven [goes to a monitor showing in-flight cruise missile footage], and that is Suzanna Gekkaloys.

              GEKKALOYS
I'll be reporting from inside the fight!

          [She races off]

                MORRIS
Like some crazy Trojan! And keeping an eye on everything that's going on out there, at *The Day Today* news pipe, Douglas Trox!

                 TROX
Chris!

                MORRIS
But first, the weather from Sylvester Stewart.

STEWART is wearing a large cardboard collar with the British Isles drawn on it, which he rotates for each region.

               STEWART
And now the weather, starting in the south-east, where the sun should plop through after a dull start, a bit like having your hand sewn back on after a farming accident. Let's revolve the weather collar now seventy degrees to the Midlands, where I was first bereaved. And there'll be a large cack of heavy cloud covering the area, but it should stay dry enough for you to dance outside until our lord Beelzebub calls upon us.

Now, if we rotate the throat circle back to the West Country, and you can see there'll be several gits of bad weather across most of the sky. Some rain, but no more severe than soft porn. In summary then, and that's all the weather.

MORRIS
Back to the war, and in the front line at Eastmanstown, our reporter Dônnnald Bethl'hem. Donald, what's the latest?

BETHL'HEM
As I swilled the last traces of toothpaste from my mouth this morning a soldier's head flew past the window, shouting the word 'victory'.

MORRIS
Seems to be a lot of action behind you there – have you seen any fighting yourself?

BETHL'HEM
Today I saw the body of an old woman on the ground – she was lying in a pool of her own tomatoes.

There is an explosion behind him – he gets shrapnel in his back and collapses, twitching.

MORRIS
Thank you, Dônnnald. Earlier today, I've been down among the fighting  myself. This is my report.

Assorted shots from Bosnia etc. appear.

MORRIS
There's something about the way these people move that tells you they are a nation at war. Look into their eyes, and you can read the words 'I have a  reservation at the restaurant of death'. It's a messy bistro, with a bad name for soiling its customers' clothes. We've seen only one napkin in four days. [Someone waves a white flag from a window] People here are confused, spending  most of their time running about like idiots. Earlier today, we met a family who thanks to this war now have no home. A war which they feel anyway has nothing to do with them.

A CHILD and his mother speak. MORRIS translates.

> MORRIS (AS CHILD)
> This is not our war. We are being forced to swallow
> the rotten egg of an angry political goose.

> MORRIS
> That boy is now a war orphan. One more victim of
> what they call here the 'desert confetti'. I have a
> child about his age myself. When I phoned him ten
> minutes ago, I told him to move out of the house to
> make room for his new brother.

Back in the studio, MORRIS strides about purposefully, lit by
red lights.

> MORRIS
> Back live now, progress on *The Day Today* smart bomb
> - Jonathan! Get rid of Hurd! Thanks!

Hurd vanishes from a monitor, replaced by a bomb's eye view of
the war zone.

> MAN WITH GLASSES
> Well, Chris, as you can see there's the missile,
> cruising at around 2000 per second trying to locate
> the target the soldier it's aimed at - there's the
> soldier, it goes in through the mouth, down through
> the oesophagus, into the stomach and there's the
> explosion.

The camera enters the gob of a surprised trooper before the
picture turns to static.

> MORRIS
> Absolutely bang! That's *The Day Today* bringing you
> another tear on the face of the world's mother!
> Alan! Sport!

> PARTRIDGE
> Thanks, Chris. And now some late-night soccer
> results. I'm Alan Partridge - this is division two.
> Hull Paragraph 5, Portsmouth Bubblejet 1. Sheffield
> Hysterical 3, Chunky Norwich 1. Richmond Arithmetic
> versus Nottingham Marjorie match postponed due to
> bent pitch. Good night.

Graphic: the word 'WAR' on a radar screen.

> MORRIS
> Suzanna Gekkaloys has broken through to the front
> line – this is her contribution to history.

> GEKKALOYS
> This is the very heart of the conflict – the men
> here have been fighting non-stop for three days.
> We drove in at night, straight into the middle
> of a rocket battle. The air now is thick with
> what they call here the 'electric  cornflakes'.
> We're under strict instructions not to leave the
> vehicle, but to drive on through.

GEKKALOYS immediately stops her Jeep and jumps out.

> GEKKALOYS
> [Voice-over]

> With no cover, we ran across open space to a
> nearby house.

GEKKALOYS kicks the door down, races inside and shoots one of
the occupants.

> GEKKALOYS
> [Voice-over]

> We found an injured man, we did our best.

> [Shoots man]

> There are always casualties in war. There was
> a family sheltering in the back room. We had
> no tongue in common, but through the universal
> language of mutual need [GEKKALOYS yells at a
> terrified woman who is trying to force her out] I
> knew she was saying 'Come, set your equipment up
> in our refuge, the world must see this mess'.

> GEKKALOYS
> These brave people are now sleeping, but they know
> that tomorrow, our aerials and transmitters could
> make this house a prime target. Chris.

MORRIS, with a different haircut, is somehow in the studio
and on the battlefield at the same time.

>MORRIS

Back to the war now, and in the noise and heat of
what they call here the 'flying scissorbeams',
there is no optimism — or at least wasn't until
just two minutes ago, when we received these
pictures of a miracle from the front line, less
than a mile from where I'm standing.

A flaming body hurtles across the frame behind him.

>MORRIS
>[Voice-over]

This was the scented rose in the bumgut of Satan,
for here at 7.13 precisely, the fighting stopped.
Soldiers, who moments earlier had been shooting
each other's teeth out, suddenly put down their
guns and joined in peaceful commune. Some played
games, or like these men, planned a musical.
The reason for this calm lay inside a shed, for
here, the massed forces of two world powers were
unified by nothing more than the distress of a
cat stuck on a high shelf. No one knows how it
got there, but these brave fighting men, moved by
the simplicity of the animal's plight, decided to
forget their differences and try to get it down.

Various soldiers rescue the cat and cuddle it.

But even as the men celebrated, their heads were
blown clean off, for somebody, nobody knows who,
had filled the cat with nitro-glycerine.

>VOICE-OVER
>*The Day Today* – news from telly to belly!

>MORRIS

Just time for a quick look at tomorrow's headlines
– 'Plastic surgeon arrested with stash of
stolen mouths', that's in the *Express*, the *Hull
Aphrodite*, 'Police chief crushes lizard with
whistle', there he is looking wretched, the *Daily
Mail*, 'Child made of paint wins by-election', the

Murdoch papers tomorrow, 'Crazed wolves in store a bad mistake admits Mothercare', and there's the same story in the *Sun*, and the *Daily Mirror* have a special pull-out note for the milkman, 'five pints please', they'll be doing three, two and four later in the week. That's it, that's *The Day Today* on the day a man on this programme told how he was menaced by Hugh Scully.

MAN
He just came in and went [pulls a face, which is morphed into something ridiculous] and went out.

MORRIS
That's it - good night.

MORRIS gets up as the credits roll and walks around the studio. The other people congratulate him. Clips from the show appear with accompanying music.

ANNOUNCER
Available from now on commercial video, *The Day Today: This is our war*! Featuring the men and women who've sacrificed themselves at the altar of fact - and the beat of over a thousand pop classics!

Tunes playing include: 'Jet' by Paul McCartney and Wings (stock footage of fighter jets in action), 'Get Down On It' by Kool And The Gang (various shots of soldiers and reporters ducking for cover, including Kate Adie, with a crew member exclaiming 'fucking hell' as she does so), 'Dreadlock Holiday' by 10cc (soldiers in camouflage helmets), 'The Clapping Song' by the Belle Stars (Iraqi prisoners clapping), 'Sorry I'm a Lady' by Baccara (a picture of a woman in combat gear), 'You Really Got Me' by The Kinks (footage of people who've been shot, including BBC reporter Martin Bell being carried away on a stretcher), 'Stop Your Sobbing' by The Pretenders (people weeping), 'I'm Wishing on a Star' by Rose Royce (flares lighting up battlefields at night), 'Disco Inferno' by The Trammps (explosions and burning people), 'Oops Upside Your Head' by the Gap Band (Iraqis surrendering), 'Hands Up (Give Me Your Heart)' by Ottawan (even more surrendering Iraqis).

ANNOUNCER
*The Day Today: This is our war*. Bang after bang after bang after bang!

# *The Fast Show* (1996)

## 'That's Amazing'

Simon Day

We have Harry Enfield to thank for *The Fast Show*.
Whenever Enfield rejected a character or situation
offered by his writers Charlie Higson and Paul
Whitehouse, they kept it to one side with the idea of
pitching their own show. Their unique selling point
came when they saw an edited compilation of quickie
highlights from the Enfield series. Both realized that
a show where sketches didn't hang about, some being
reduced to nothing more than a punchline, could be a
goer. They offered the concept to ITV, who disagreed,
but BBC2 controller Michael Jackson went for it. The
result was one of the most influential sketch comedy
shows ever broadcast. Although many of the sketches
were over in a flash, even the shortest were rich in
detail, meaning and characterization.

Although it was nominally Higson and the endlessly versatile
Whitehouse's show, the principal cast – Caroline Aherne,
Arabella Weir, John Thomson, Simon Day, Mark Williams
and Paul Shearer – were all seasoned writer-performers,
contributing their own specialities. In particular, Day brought
a lot to the show, not least his stand-up comedy character,
music hall nostalgist Tommy Cockles. In this extract,
however, he is an Australian survivalist with a TV show of
his own.

**Series:** *The Fast Show*
(BBC2, twenty-five shows
over four series and one
special, 1994–2000),
series 2, show 2.

**Original transmission:**
BBC2, Friday 23 February
1996, 9 p.m.

**Cast in excerpt:** Simon
Day (Carl Hooper),
John Thomson (Dick
Wellington).

**Producers:** Paul
Whitehouse and Charlie
Higson.

**Directors:** Sid Roberson
and Mark Mylod.

HOOPER

G'day, an' welcome to *That's Amazing* with me, Carl
Hooper. What would you do, if you were walkin'
down the road one night, an' ya came face to
face with a monster? That's right – a terrifying
monster. Well, Dick Wellington here did just that.
He came face to face with his wife.

HOOPER laughs. WELLINGTON looks none too amused.

HOOPER

No! No, he didn't. So, tell us about your monster
dick. I mean … tell us about your monster, Dick …
Your shout, mate.

WELLINGTON

Well, alright. Well, Carl, I live in Adamland – in
Northern Australia – it's, er, an area held sacred
by the local aborigines. It's a mystical area, and
some even say it might be haunted, y'know?

The first edition of *The Fast Show* contained twenty-seven different sketches in its twenty-eight minutes and fifty-eight seconds. The shortest item was just twelve seconds long.

HOOPER
Shaddup, mate! Just tell us about yer monster, will ya?

WELLINGTON
Yes, alright. Well, one night I was walkin' back from the pub, an' there it was, blockin' my path. I recognized it instantly – it was the byu-byu-gwai-gwai. Which is an aboriginal half-spirit, half-snake, half-man bird.

HOOPER
Right. Did it have huge fangs?

WELLINGTON
Yeah!

HOOPER
And big claws?

WELLINGTON
Yeah!

HOOPER
An' what colour was it, mate?

WELLINGTON
Ah, that's hard to say – it was invisible.

HOOPER
Invisible?

WELLINGTON
Mmm.

HOOPER
But you just said it had huge fangs and claws.

WELLINGTON
Yeah, that was a guess.

HOOPER

So, how'd you know it was there?

WELLINGTON

Oh, by the unearthly sound.

HOOPER

Like a terrifying roar?

WELLINGTON

Nah - a terrifying silence.

HOOPER

So, you saw an' heard an invisible and silent
monster.

WELLINGTON

Yeah, that was - that's right. It was abs-
absolutely terrifyin'. I've been on medication
ever since.

HOOPER

So, let me get this straight. How'd you know it
was there? Did it leave a huge imprint in the
ground?

WELLINGTON

No, mate. No, no imprint - it was hovering.

HOOPER

Mate, do me a favour.

WELLINGTON

What's that, mate?

HOOPER

Git off me show.

When shown in the USA, the series was retitled *Brilliant!*, using
the catchphrase of one of Paul Whitehouse's characters, an easily
impressed teenager.

Johnny Depp is a massive fan of the series, and was rewarded with a cameo role in the final run, as a customer of Ken and Kenneth, the camp, overly familiar 'Suit you, sir' tailors, played by Whitehouse and Williams.

<pre>
                    WELLINGTON
        Now?

                     HOOPER
        Now.

                    WELLINGTON
        Oh. I've taken a picture. It's really spooky. You
        can't see a damn thing. Look!

WELLINGTON holds up a completely black Polaroid as proof.

                     HOOPER
        I bet you can't. Will you get off my show, please?
        Like, now.

Pause as WELLINGTON moves to door. HOOPER sighs disgustedly.

                     HOOPER
        Next week on the show, we've got a—

                    WELLINGTON
        I've got a recording! You can't see a damn thing!

                     HOOPER
        GET OFF MY SHOW!

                    WELLINGTON
        They exist! They're out there! There's over a—

                     HOOPER
        GO!

HOOPER starts to approach WELLINGTON.

                    WELLINGTON
        Oooh!
</pre>

# Brass Eye (1997)

## 'Animals'

## Chris Morris, Peter Baynham, Graham Linehan and Arthur Mathews

**Series:** *Brass Eye* (Channel 4, seven shows over one series and one special, 1997–2001), show 1.

**Original transmission:** Channel 4, Wednesday 29 January 1997, 9.30 p.m.

**Cast in excerpt:** Chris Morris (Host/Foster Pann/ Bernard Lerring/Da Fronk).

**Producers:** Christopher Morris and Caroline Leddy.

**Director:** Michael Cumming.

After the success of *The Day Today*, Chris Morris began work on a solo project, initially titled *Torque TV*. The idea was to combine the growing tendency to make emotive, judgmental programmes about issues of the day, and the willingness of celebrities to pass comment on those issues, no matter how ill-informed they were. Morris had developed his celebrity-bothering skills during his six-month run on BBC Radio 1 in 1994, most notably when he persuaded The Jam's bass player Bruce Foxton to provide a tribute for Michael Heseltine's obituary tape. Allied to this was his love of surreal wordplay and an acute appreciation of the clichéd mangling of the English language sometimes perpetrated by radio and television journalists. The result was *Brass Eye*, a many-layered send-up of current affairs television.

It was a risky venture. A pilot was made at the BBC, but the Corporation passed on the option of the series. Channel 4 took the idea on, but, with the work completed and the series scheduled, a last-minute decision was taken by Channel 4 chief Michael Grade to delay transmission until all of the legal concerns had been ironed out. The series finally made it to air in late January 1997, with several cuts. One item that had been dropped involved a musical about the Yorkshire Ripper. Morris got his revenge for the delay by slipping a flash-frame into the final show of the series, declaring 'Grade is a cunt'. The series was finally shown uncut in 2001, along with a new edition covering paedophilia and media reactions to it. It proved even more controversial than the original series, with Morris forced to go, briefly, into hiding. After a quiet few years, Morris re-emerged with the feature film *Four Lions*, about a team of clueless suicide bombers, showing his commitment to avoiding easy topics is as strong as ever.

★ ☆ ★

INT. TV NEWS STUDIO - DAY

> MORRIS
> Over the centuries, man's relationship with animals has been complex. In ancient Egypt, felines were worshipped because the Egyptians thought they were funny. Many of today's familiar relics are cat monuments. These vast cat heads were built underground, and seen by no one.

Graphic shows two pyramids, a cat's head superimposed underneath the ground shows them to be ears.

> MORRIS
> Europe too has its animal traditions - in Zaradosa, the streets still get crazy with the annual running of the wasp.

Stock footage of a Spanish bull run.

> MORRIS
> In Britain in the last century, it was quite acceptable for a young gentleman to lose his virginity to one of London's many whoredogs. Dickens and Prince Albert both boasted of their experience.

CUT to black and white footage of a dog walking around in a dress, captioned '(c) British Dog Archive'.

> MORRIS
> Today, animals are used more discreetly - as a vital lubricant in the wheels of government.

One of the hoaxes that didn't make the final cut involved Reggie Kray, on the telephone from Maidstone Prison, lending his support to a non-existent animal welfare campaign. Despite covering their tracks and hiring vacant offices to lend the campaign credibility, the spoof was traced back to the production company, Talkback, and one member of the team fielded a threatening visit from a henchman of the twins.

> FOSTER PANN
> It was my job for seventeen years to procure wild beasts for the, er, Houses of Parliament and to get bats, gibbons …

> MORRIS
> Ex-civil servant Foster Pann purchased over a thousand animals to work in Westminster.

Caption: 'Foster Pann, Perm. Sec. for Beast Procurement 77-95'.

> FOSTER PANN
> Michael Heseltine finds it very useful, erm, if he's angry to have an ape to slap. Kenneth Clarke has a baby moose in a cupboard.

> MORRIS
> The most common use of animals are zebras – hurrying between offices with documents pinned to their bodies.

> FOSTER PANN
> Tony Benn had a tapir in the seventies that used to send messages on round Whitehall … Rude messages to the Lords, ha ha, I always remember he used to pin to the head of the tapir, ha ha ha. Most of it was great fun, I enjoyed the job, the only difficulty I had was, er, trying to haul a basking shark up the Thames for Jack Ashley. It didn't really work out, it died after about three days of being tethered to the terrace. Jack was quite unpopular after that for a while.

CUT TO EXT. LONDON STREET - DAY

MORRIS is walking down the street. A pub is in shot.

> MORRIS
> So much for the fat brass of Westminster, but this
> east London boozer knows all about animal abuse.

MORRIS hits door, a dog barks.

> MORRIS
> Because here, every week, beer-users gather to watch
> large men fight with weasels.

CUT to hidden camera footage of weasel fighting.

> BERNARD LERRING
> There's normally about forty, forty men in a room,
> standing round in a ring, and a bag above your head.
> Somebody pulls a string, the weasels cascade out
> onto you, and you've got as short a time as possible
> to, er, dispatch them all. I've seen men die weasel
> fighting.

Caption: 'Bernard Lerring, Former Weasel Fighter'.

> LERRING
> When you're fighting a weasel it's bigger than a man.
> And there is money in it, if you're good there's
> other perks as well. The women; they fancy you if
> they see you kicking the shit out of a weasel.

> MORRIS
> After thirteen years in which he pulped over four
> thousand weasels, Bernard Lerring suffered a compound
> nervous breakdown.

Morris rather more successfully spoofed 'Mad' Frankie Fraser, a member of the rival Richardson gang, in *Brass Eye*, asking him to categorize how annoyed certain scenarios got him by way of the 'Frankie Fraser Madometer'. The scale on the device ran: low miff, narked/narky, lightly bonkers, massive huff, and mad as a lorry.

> LERRING
> I lost it, and, er, I just picked up a living
> doing otters, which are very easy, are very docile
> animals, and, erm, even when they pump them full
> of rat hormones which they do – you could kill an
> otter in about a second … just kick its face off.

CUT TO EXT. FOX HUNT – DAY

> MORRIS
> There are many legal sports that kill animals too.

Caption: 'Patrick Da Fronk, Master of Hounds, Blesney Hunt'.

> DA FRONK
> I think the thing that, that people get fussed
> about is that a fox is, is a small brown furry
> animal very much like a dog, erm, I don't think
> they'd be nearly so worried if it was a little
> four-legged car, full of chips.

A graphic appears, showing the 'Man vs Animal evil continuum
paradox'.

CUT TO STUDIO

> MORRIS
> The evil in our relationship remains a paradox. If
> you plot 'number of animals abused' against 'what
> makes people cruel' versus 'intelligence of either
> party', the pattern is so unreadable, you might as
> well draw in a chain of fox-heads on sticks. And
> if you do that, an interesting thing happens – the
> word 'cruel' starts flashing. So, are we cruel to
> hunt foxes?

CUT TO FOX HUNT

> DA FRONK
> The fox feels nothing. It's made of … string.

CUT TO EXT. BUS ON DESERT ROAD – DAY

> MORRIS
> Or are we too nice? This is a bus-load of flies
> that are being sent on holiday to Africa. They'll
> enjoy Somalia – but should they?

CUT TO INT. LABORATORY - DAY

                  MORRIS
    Can it possibly be right for gene-men to play with
    DNA?

A scientist cradles a cat/chicken hybrid.

                 SCIENTIST
    This one, erm, survived a couple of days then just
    keeled over and died.

CUT TO EXT. MAN CHASING CHICKEN DOWN ROAD - DAY

                  MORRIS
    Is this wrong?

CUT TO EXT. FARM - DAY

                  MORRIS
    How on earth can you justify this?

A balaclava-clad man machine-guns pigs, out of frame.

                  MORRIS
    And has anybody ever come up with a reasonable
    argument for this?

CUT TO EXT. RESIDENTIAL STREET - DAY

MORRIS knocks on a door. A man answers, with a bird peeping
out from his trousers.

*Brass Eye* benefited hugely from complex and over-the-top graphic sequences,
again by Russell Hilliard and Richard Norley, the ex-ITN graphic designers
who had done the same for *The Day Today*. Similarly overblown was the
theme music, composed by Morris himself, and Jonathan Whitehead.

# *I'm Alan Partridge* (1997)

## 'Watership Alan'

## Steve Coogan, Armando Iannucci and Peter Baynham

**Series:** *I'm Alan Partridge* (Talkback for BBC2, twelve shows over two series, 1997–2002), series 1, show 3.

**Original transmission:** BBC2, Monday 17 November 1997, 10 p.m.

**Cast in excerpt:** Steve Coogan (Alan Partridge), Chris Morris (Peter Baxendale-Thomas), Felicity Montagu (Lynn).

**Producer:** Armando Iannucci.

**Director:** Dominic Brigstocke.

Having introduced Alan Partridge to the viewing public as a sports reporter in *The Day Today*, and then taken him into the netherworld of chat with *Knowing Me, Knowing You*, Steve Coogan and Armando Iannucci gave Partridge fans an insight into the Norwich-born king of all media's daily life with *I'm Alan Partridge*. It would be a mistake to view the series as a situation comedy. It was more a series of documentaries, shot at BBC Television Centre in front of a live studio audience.

During the first series, Partridge was in limbo. Awaiting a call from the BBC to do a second series of *Knowing Me, Knowing You*, presenting the graveyard shift on Radio Norwich and living in a motel equidistant between London and the capital of Norfolk. Viewed with contempt by the staff of the Linton Travel Tavern, with the exception of brutal Geordie handyman Michael, the series was a tragi-comic portrait of a man in despair. In the second series, five years later, it emerged that this despair had resulted in a morbidly obese Partridge driving barefoot to Dundee, gorging on Toblerones. Viewed as a whole, *I'm Alan Partridge* is a cautionary tale about fame.

INT. INTERVIEW STUDIO – DAY

ALAN is interviewing a ruddy-faced gentleman.

                    JINGLE
         Radio Norwich: Up with the Partridge.

                    ALAN
         You're joining me, Alan Partridge, and Peter
         Baxendale-Thomas of the Norfolk Farmers' Union.
         Now, yesterday I, sort of, trod in a rather large
         farmer's pat when I made some comments about
         intensive farming. Where did I go wrong?

                    PETER
         Well, I think your comments were ill founded. They
         were deeply ignorant, they showed a complete lack
         of understanding of modern agricultural methods,
         and simply served to highlight the sort of intense
         stupidity that farmers encounter from armchair
         pundits who forget to think before they open their
         mouths. But with a full and frank apology that
         you're about to give us this morning I'm sure you
         can dig yourself out of this rather ugly hole.

ALAN forces a smile through his irritation.

                    ALAN
         Yeah. Erm, sorry. Er, do you have any requests,
         anybody you want to say hello to, or …?

                    PETER
         Look, I'm just trying to say that when you make
         ignorant comments like you did the other day, you
         serve simply to alarm the public and inflame the
         farmers, which is exactly what you've done. Why
         don't you just apologize and make it nice and
         simple—

ALAN interrupts PETER with a loud moo.

                    ALAN
         Thought that'd fool you. You could talk the
         hind legs off a donkey. But your donkeys are
         probably born without hind legs because of all the
         chemicals you put in their … chips.

PETER

Alan, I don't have donkeys. And even if I did I wouldn't feed them chips. This is exactly the sort of rubbish you came up with the other day when you talked about putting a spine in a bap.

ALAN

I admit that was a mistake. I shouldn't have said bap.

PETER

Well, good. Well, that's a start.

ALAN

Well, no, I should have said baguette. Because a spinal column would fit in a baguette.

PETER

Listen, you've upset half the farmers in this community. You seem to alienate everybody you come across, including, I gather, your wife, which is why you end up living like some bloody tramp in a lay-by.

ALAN

It's a travel tavern.

PETER

I don't care what you call your sordid little grief-hole. It makes no difference to me. The fact is that an awful lot of my colleagues are—

ALAN
[Interrupting]

Are farmyard animals, yes.

The show from which this excerpt is taken was recorded in the week between the death of Princess Diana and her funeral. At the end of the recording, Coogan thanked the audience profusely for turning up at all, let alone laughing as lustily as they had.

PETER
You're talking about my friends, here.

ALAN
I've probably got more friends than you've got
cows.

PETER
This is ridiculous.

ALAN
How many cows have you got?

PETER
I've got a hundred cattle.

ALAN
Yeah, I've got a hundred and four friends.

PETER
I don't see what this is going to gain you. Why
don't you just issue a frank and full retraction
of what you said, and you'll get yourself out of a
lot of silly bother.

                    ALAN
Yeah, you are a big posh sod with plums in your
mouth.

                    PETER
I don't think it's got anything to do with class—

                    ALAN
And the plums have mutated and they've got beaks.

                    PETER
Beaks?

                    ALAN
Yes, beaks.

                    PETER
Have you got any more of this, or do you want to
stop at quacking plums?

                    ALAN
No, no. You make pigs smoke.

                    PETER
I want to know where you think you earned the
right to go swanning off on these ludicrous
flights of—

                    ALAN
Ah, swans. You feed beefburgers to swans.

                    PETER
Do I?

                    ALAN
Yes, you do.

                    PETER
Alright, well, perhaps you can tell me what's
wrong with feeding beefburgers to swans?

                    ALAN
What?

                    PETER
Well, if you fill a swan's stomach up with
beefburgers it's full of fat and it'll float
better. That's why we do it.

                    ALAN
Really?

                    PETER
No, you complete cretin. I'm just contributing
to this total farce. What else are you going to
accuse me of?

                    ALAN
I'll tell you what. You farmers, you don't like
outsiders, do you? You like to stick to your own.

                    PETER
What do you mean by that?

                    ALAN
I've seen the big-eared boys on farms.

                    PETER
Oh, for goodness' sake.

                    ALAN
If you see a lovely field with a family having a
picnic, and there's a nice pond in it, you fill
in the pond with concrete, you plough the family
into the field, you blow up the tree, and use the
leaves to make a dress for your wife who's also
your brother.

                    PETER
Look, have I got anything else to say here or
shall I go?

The reception area and restaurant sets were visible to the studio audience.
The other interiors were enclosed sets built behind this front area, visible
to the audience only on the studio monitors. The series attracted misplaced
criticism from some quarters for use of 'canned laughter'. In fact, all interior
scenes were shot in the presence of a live audience.

ALAN

Well, listen, I'll tell you what the point is. You
have big sheds, but nobody's allowed in, and inside
these big sheds are twenty-foot-high chickens.
Because of all the chemicals you put in them.

While ALAN talks, PETER shakes his head, gathers his stuff
together, and goes to leave.

ALAN

And these chickens are scared. They don't know why
they're so big. They go 'oh why am I so massive?'
And they're looking down on all the other little
chickens, and they think they're in an aeroplane
because all the other chickens are so small … do you
deny that?

[Peter has left]

No. His silence, I think, speaks volumes.

ALAN's personal assistant LYNN enters the room. ALAN gestures
furiously at her to take PETER's seat.

ALAN

And … and basically, do you agree that everything
I've said thus far is completely correct?

LYNN

Yes.

ALAN mouthes 'lower', and gestures.

LYNN
[In a deep voice]

Yes.

ALAN

And do you also run over badgers in your tractor,
for fun?

LYNN

Yes.

ALAN

Thank you, Peter Baxendale-Thomas. This is T'Pau.

# Men Behaving Badly (1997)

## 'Stag Night'

Simon Nye

*Men Behaving Badly* was one of the great sitcom successes of the 1990s, but it nearly disappeared from our screens after its second series, a victim of the 1990 Broadcasting Act that had resulted in Thames Television losing the London ITV franchise. In a then-unprecedented move, it was picked up by BBC1, at the behest of the new head of entertainment David Liddiment, resuming its run in July 1994. It sat well with what the media declared to be lad culture, but was in fact a deceptively enlightened series. The show's leading women – Dorothy and Deborah – were far smarter than Gary or Tony. Tony was a well-meaning sexist without much of a brain, while Gary was a bright chap whose immaturity and cowardice usually got in the way of any good intentions he might have. In this excerpt from the first episode of the penultimate series, the preparations are beginning for Gary and Dorothy's wedding, an event put off many times, about which neither seemed truly convinced until in the final Christmas special, they were on the brink of parenthood.

**Series:** *Men Behaving Badly* (Hartswood Films for Thames/BBC TV, forty-two shows over six series and two specials, 1992–8), series 6, show 1.

**Original transmission:** BBC1, Thursday 6 November 1997, 9.30 p.m.

**Cast in excerpt:** Martin Clunes (Gary), Neil Morrissey (Tony), Leslie Ash (Deborah), Caroline Quentin (Dorothy), Race Davies (Sally-Anne).

**Producer:** Beryl Vertue.

**Director:** Martin Dennis.

INT. COMMUNAL HALL - NIGHT

DEBORAH emerges from her flat, dressed elegantly. She checks herself in the hall mirror while she waits.

> DEBORAH
> [Shouting upstairs]

Dorothy!

TONY and GARY come out of their flat. They are dressed for a real lads-on-the-town night out, TONY in a shirt open to the navel etc. DEBORAH gazes at them.

> GARY

What?

> DEBORAH

Just a wild guess, but are you off on your stag night?

> GARY
> [Attempting to be suave]

Just a few quiet drinks.

> DEBORAH
> [To Tony]

I hear you took the job Dorothy told you about.

> TONY

Yeah, after what you said about stretching my mind.

> DEBORAH

That's good, because I think you've got this potential, you know.

The original series came about after producer Beryl Vertue read Simon Nye's debut novel and persuaded him to adapt it. In the first series, Gary's flatmate was Dermot, played by Harry Enfield.

                              TONY
Yeah, because the mind's like a loaf of bread,
isn't it, it needs the yeast of experience in
order to rise.

                              GARY
Excuse me, excuse me, can we not be sensitive on
my stag night, please?

                              TONY
Sorry, mate.

                            DEBORAH
I've got a friend who's interested in one of those
pools. Here, I'll give you her number.

She gets a pen out of her bag and writes a telephone number
on TONY's hand. He watches with his usual blind adoration.

                              TONY
Do you want to come with us?

                              GARY
No! No girls!

                              TONY
Sorry, mate.

                            DEBORAH
I can't anyway. It's Dorothy's hen night.

DOROTHY finally arrives, also elegantly dressed. She looks at
the men.

                            DOROTHY
Where are you two off to, Las Vegas?

                              GARY
                          [Very macho]

Listen, I'm not apologizing, on my last proper
night of freedom, for doing what men do. This is
my stag night. I shall be acting like a stag.

GARY makes antlers with his hands and emits a hideous noise
somewhere between a rutting stag, a foghorn and someone being
violently sick.

                          DOROTHY
                      [Affectionately]

            Yeah, well, don't overdo it, love.

                           GARY
                      [Suddenly meek]

             Alright, love.

They kiss and then GARY and TONY leave, making stag noises.

FADE TO INT. LIVING ROOM - NEXT DAY

GARY is waking up on the sofa. He looks hungover and has
a smear of gaudy lipstick on his face. He struggles to an
upright position.

                       SALLY-ANNE
      I don't understand why we couldn't use your bed.

GARY realizes there is a half-dressed woman sitting on the
other end of the sofa, who appears to be a prostitute. GARY
looks confused and afraid.

                       SALLY-ANNE
           Which is your bathroom?

GARY

It's the quite small room with the bath in it.

SALLY-ANNE gives him a blank look and gets up to find it
herself.

GARY

I'm Gary.

SALLY-ANNE

Hi Gary.

GARY

Listen, it's only fair to warn you that I'm
getting married in a few days.

SALLY-ANNE

Oh dear.

GARY

What I'm trying to say is, you're lovely, from
what I remember, but we probably haven't got a
very long-term future.

SALLY-ANNE
[Dryly]

Well, that's my life in ruins.

She heads for the bathroom.

GARY
[After her]

Only fair to warn you.

A review of the first episode described it as 'superficially … a lot hipper than a
Jim Davidson show, since these are gags with sociology degrees, but it's still
the old sex-war stuff'.

                    [To himself]

    Oh.

GARY stands, his blanket draped round him, and heads for
the kitchen, wading through empty lager cans and remnants of
takeaway food. In the kitchen, GARY finds TONY face down on
the floor, asleep in last night's clothes.

                         GARY
    Tony, Tony, Tony.

GARY nudges TONY with his foot and stands there, looking
apprehensive. TONY starts to stir.

                         GARY
    I think I've just slept with a woman. I know I
    did.

TONY gets up. He looks down at his utterly crumpled trousers
and shirt.

                         TONY
    Do I look creased in this?

                         GARY
    Promise you won't tell Dorothy?

                         TONY
    Oh, why?

                         GARY
    Because it's not very nice! How would you like it?

                         TONY
    Well, it would have been great but I could only
    afford one woman.

                         GARY
    Do you mean you paid for her to sleep with me?!

                         TONY
    Well, to be fair, mate, why do you think she was
    here when we got back?

                         GARY
    I thought she'd seen me and followed me home, in a
    nice way.

> TONY
> Why would she do that?

> GARY
> Because she liked me!

> TONY
> Sorry, mate.

An awkward silence. TONY looks contrite.

> TONY
> Hey, what was it like?

> GARY
> I can't really remember that much of it. She
> didn't seem very involved.

> TONY
> When I rang round I tried to find someone you'd
> like. Her parents come from the West Country, same
> as yours.

> GARY
> Cheers, mate.

> TONY
> Dorothy said she didn't want to know what you were
> up to.

> GARY
> Believe me, she'll want to know if I spent
> the night with some tart … I understand you're
> familiar with Central Somerset.

SALLY-ANNE has emerged from the bathroom, ready to leave.
GARY is all polite smiles.

Simon Nye later collaborated with David Nobbs on an updated version of *The
Fall and Rise of Reginald Perrin*, starring Martin Clunes from *Men Behaving
Badly* as the new Reggie.

                    SALLY-ANNE
    Well, more Devon really.

                    GARY
    Well, thanks, that was great! I wonder if I could
    ask you to leave quite quietly …

He ushers her towards the hall, then stops. From Deborah and
Dorothy's flat we hear a noise, like a footstep or a creaky
floorboard.

                    GARY
    In fact, don't take me wrong, but would you mind
    leaving under a blanket?

                    SALLY-ANNE
    Yes, I would.

                    GARY
    I could get you a nice one.

                    SALLY-ANNE
    I'm going now.

                    GARY
    We've been having a little bit of trouble with a
    sticky front door. We've been coming and going
    through the front window. It slides up and down
    quite easily.

                    SALLY-ANNE
    Bye.

                    GARY
    Bye.

GARY goes over to the half-drawn curtains and peeks out.
As SALLY-ANNE leaves, so does a man, having come from the
upstairs flat. He blows a kiss up at the window.

# *Father Ted* (1998)

## 'Are You Right There, Father Ted?'

### Graham Linehan and Arthur Mathews

Graham Linehan and Arthur Mathews had met in the 1980s as writers for the Dublin music paper *Hot Press*. When not working as music journalists, the pair did musical comedy (with Mark Woodfull) as U2 parody act The Joshua Trio. One of the Trio's routines involved a priest, and this was the basis for what was to become Father Ted Crilly. Later, after working on *The Day Today* and writing *Paris*, an unsuccessful, but well-regarded situation comedy for Alexei Sayle, the chance came to develop this priest character further. At Hat Trick Productions, Geoffrey Perkins, original radio producer of *The Hitch-hiker's Guide to the Galaxy* and later BBC Television's head of comedy, nurtured the idea to fruition, and *Father Ted* became a Friday night favourite on Channel 4.

Ted was worldly, banished to exile on Craggy Island following an incident that he claims to have been a misunderstanding, but which appears to have been simple embezzlement ('The money was just resting in my account'). For his sins, he has to live with two other priests, a young simpleton called Dougal and an old alcoholic called Jack, along with their obsessive-compulsive charlady Mrs Doyle. Dermot Morgan, who played Ted, was well known in his native Ireland for playing a priest on the satirical RTE radio show *Scrap Saturday*, and had always been in Linehan and Mathews' mind for the role when writing it. Sadly, he collapsed and died on the same night as recording the final show.

**Series:** *Father Ted* (Hat Trick Productions for Channel 4, twenty-five shows over three series and one special), 1995–8, series 3, show 1.

**Original transmission:** Channel 4, Friday 13 March 1998, 9 p.m.

**Cast in excerpt:** Dermot Morgan (Father Ted Crilly), Ardal O'Hanlon (Father Dougal Maguire), Frank Kelly (Father Jack Hackett), Pauline McLynn (Mrs Doyle), Patrick Kavanagh (Father Seamus Fitzpatrick), Ozzie Yue (Sean Yin), Vernon Dobtcheff (Old Nazi), Peter Sakon Lee (Yin son), Ann Callanan (Mrs Carberry), Eamon Rohan (Colm).

**Producer:** Lissa Evans.

**Director:** Declan Lowney.

INT. FATHER FITZPATRICK'S LIVING ROOM – DAY

FATHER TED and FATHER FITZPATRICK are in front of a bookcase.
FATHER FITZPATRICK is looking through the books.

> FATHER FITZPATRICK
> Let's see now, *Humanae Vitae*, you know sometimes I
> leaf through this to see just how far we've come.
> *Celebration of the Christian Mysteries*, *Daeus
> Canida*, *Benthro Mepilo*; ah, Stephen King's *The
> Shining*.

> TED
> Well, thanks for the tea, Father. See you the next
> time we, emm … we, emm … Sorry about this, Father,
> I hope you don't mind me asking but, em, what
> have you got a padlock on that door for? Is there
> something top secret in there?

> FATHER FITZPATRICK
> My collection.

> TED
> Oh yes, that's right, what is this you collect?
> It's war memorabilia.

> FATHER FITZPATRICK
> That's right, would you like to have a look?

> TED
> Oh, I'd love to.

FATHER FITZPATRICK and TED enter the padlocked room and start
looking at a display.

> FATHER FITZPATRICK
> Taken from the German advance on Russia, you can
> see where the hammer hits the shell casing.

> TED
> Gosh, that's very interesting.

> FATHER FITZPATRICK
> These are helmets, mostly infantry.

> TED
> Yes, these would be German as well, wouldn't they?

FATHER FITZPATRICK

That's right.

TED

You don't have anything from the Allied side?

FATHER FITZPATRICK

No, no. That sort of thing wouldn't interest me at all, I'm afraid.

PAN out to the rest of the room, decorated with Nazi banners, pictures of Hitler and lit candles. An old man sits in the corner.

TED

That's my curiosity satisfied.

FATHER FITZPATRICK

And this is the last photograph taken of Herr Hitler. He's signing a few death warrants there.

TED

Funny, how you get more right wing as you get older! Right, well, great. This is all wonderful stuff.

FATHER FITZPATRICK

You know some people when they see it, they're not too sure but you seem genuinely interested.

TED

Oh, I am genuinely interested.

The old man in the corner starts shouting in German. He has a Nazi tapestry on his lap.

FATHER FITZPATRICK

What are you doing here? I told you no sleeping here. This is an old friend of mine, Ted.

The old Nazi starts singing, 'Deutschland, Deutschland'.

INT. TED'S HOUSE - DAY

TED is walking down the hallway. He looks at the grandfather clock and then at his watch. He fixes the grandfather clock to the right time - three o' clock. Instead of the three hourly chimes, Father Jack's voice comes from the clock, 'feck, arse, drink'. TED opens the clock door to see Father Jack's face inside. He closes the door and proceeds to the front room. DOUGAL is sitting on the sofa.

> DOUGAL
> Ted, look at the table. It's so dirty I can write me name in it!

> TED
> There's a 'G' in Dougal.

> DOUGAL
> Where?

> TED
> Right, that's it, I'm fed up living in filth. We're just going to have to get this place clean, Dougal. And look at you. Look at that hole in your tank top. What if the parishioners saw that?

> DOUGAL
> Where? Ah God, would you look at that!

DOUGAL probes a small hole in the top of his tank top. He then stands up, turns around and displays a large gaping hole in the tank top covering his entire back.

> TED
> And this here, look. A perfectly square bit of black dirt on the window. I mean how could you get a perfectly square bit of black dirt on a window? I would have thought that was practically impossible.

> DOUGAL
> It's just Mrs Doyle can't do any cleaning. Her back is very bad since she fell off the roof.

Once again, MRS DOYLE falls past the window screaming.

> DOUGAL
> See, she can't keep her balance at all.

> TED
> That's it then, I'm just going to come out and say it. We're going to have to clean this place ourselves.

DOUGAL

What?

TED

You heard me, Dougal. Are you with me?

DOUGAL

Well, yeah.

TED

[Shouting]

Right, then let's go, let's clean this mother.

DOUGAL

Yeeeeaaaah.

TED takes an old drinks can from the table and slowly drops it into the bin.

DOUGAL

Ted, what about that bit of the lamp that came off? I could pick that up!

TED

Good idea.

DOUGAL

[Picking up the lampshade]

Wow.

TED

I'm bored now.

DOUGAL

Yeah.

TED

Dougal, look.

TED takes the lampshade off DOUGAL, puts it on his head and starts to impersonate a Chinese man.

TED

I am Chinese if you ple-ease. Come on Dougal, lighten up!

TED turns around to look out the window where he sees three Chinese people standing. He takes the lampshade off his head and turns to DOUGAL.

                         TED
                    [Frantically]

Wha … Who … Wha … ? Dougal, there were Chinese people there.

                       DOUGAL
Oh, right, yeah.

                         TED
I mean what is … I mean …

                       DOUGAL
That's the Yin family. They're living over there in that whole Chinatown area.

                         TED
Chinatown area? There's a Chinatown on Craggy Island? Dougal, I wouldn't have done a Chinaman impression if I'd known there was going to be a Chinaman there to see me do a Chinaman impression.

                       DOUGAL
Why not, Ted?

                         TED
Because. Because it's racist. They'll think I'm a racist. I'm going to have to catch up with them and explain I'm not a racist.

TED runs outside to the Chinese people who are in their car. TED stands beside the car to try and explain himself. The Chinese family beep their horn and rev their engine.

                         TED
And basically if I don't stretch my eyes like that from time to time I get this thing the doctor calls 'Fat Eyes'.

The car speeds away spraying TED with mud.

                         TED
                 [Waving at the car]

I hope you wouldn't think it'd be anything of a
racial nature. Thanks for being so understanding,
see you again, bye.

CUT TO TED'S HOUSE

TED has just come off the telephone.

                    TED
Right, that's that.

                    DOUGAL
Oh-ho. That's that, all right. What's that?

                    TED
I ordered some new stuff for the house. Get rid
of this old tat. Dougal, you don't think I upset
those Chinese people earlier?

                    DOUGAL
I dunno, Ted. It was like that time we put on
that variety show and you did that impression of
Stephen Hawking.

                    TED
He was the last person you'd expect to turn up.
That was a million to one shot. God, he can fairly
move in that wheelchair when he's angry!

                    DOUGAL
But don't worry about it, Ted. Anyway who did you
phone, Habitat?

Although many thought *Father Ted* was an Irish-made sitcom, Hat Trick was
and is an English company, and all studio work was undertaken at the London
Studios on the South Bank of the River Thames in London. Most
of the location work was done in County Clare in the Republic of Ireland.
The third series was always intended to be the final run, as Dermot Morgan
feared typecasting.

> TED

No. Habithat. Like Habitat it sells soft
furnishings but also priests' clothes.

> DOUGAL

Does it not get confused with Habitat though?

> TED

No, that's never happened before except just
there, when you did it.

> DOUGAL

Anyway, what else did you order?

> TED

Priest socks. Really black ones.

> DOUGAL

I read somewhere, I think it was in an article
about priest socks that priest socks are blacker
than any other type of socks.

> TED

That's right, Dougal. Sometimes you see lay people
wear what look like black socks but if you look
closely you'll see they're very, very, very, very,
very, very, very dark blue.

> DOUGAL

Actually, that's true. I thought my uncle Tommy
was wearing black socks but when I looked at them
closely they were just very, very, very, very,
very, very, VERY, very, very, very dark blue.

> TED

Never buy black socks in a normal shop. They'll
shaft you every time!

<u>EXT. DAY</u>

TED goes outside for a walk.

> COLM

Hello there, Father.

> TED

Ah, hello, Colm.

[Laughing]

Out and about?

                    COLM
Ah, same as yourself.

                    TED
Good, good.

                    COLM
I hear you're a racist now, Father.

                    TED
Wha … What?

                    COLM
How did you get interested in that type of thing?

                    TED
Who said I'm a racist?

                    COLM
Everyone's sayin' it, Father. Should we all be
racist now? What's the official line the church is
takin' on this?

                    TED
No, no.

                    COLM
Only the farm takes up most of the day and at
night I just like a cup of tea. I mightn't be able
to devote meself to the ol' racism.

MRS CARBERRY - an old woman with lots of shopping bags -
comes over.

                MRS CARBERRY
Good for you, Father.

                    TED
What? Oh, Mrs Carberry!

                MRS CARBERRY
Good for you, Father. Well someone had the guts to
stand up to them at last. Comin' over here, takin'
our jobs and our women and actin' like they own

the feckin' place. Well done, Father. Good for you. Good for you. I'd like to feckin …

MRS CARBERRY is swinging her shopping bags in a deranged fashion.

> MRS CARBERRY
> Feckin' Greeks.

> COLM
> It isn't the Greeks, it's the Chinese he's after.

> TED
> [Panicking]

I'm not after the Chinese.

> MRS CARBERRY
> I don't care who he gets so long as I can have a go at the Greeks. They invented gayness!

> TED
> Look, we are not having a go at anybody. I am not a racist, alright. God!

> MRS CARBERRY
> Feckin' Greeks!

TED leaves and COLM walks over to Mrs Carberry.

> COLM
> How's Mary?

> MRS CARBERRY
> She's fine. She got that job after all.

> COLM
> Great!

CUT TO EXT. OUTSIDE A SMALL TRADITIONAL PUB – DAY

A Chinese voice shouts 'racist' and eggs are thrown at TED. He goes into the pub.

INT. PUB – DAY

The music suddenly stops. TED looks around him to see that

everyone in the pub is Chinese, including the small Irish
music band in the corner.

CUT TO INT. MR YIN'S HOUSE - DAY

The phone is ringing.

                    MR YIN
        Hello.

                    TED
        Hello, is that the Yin dynasty? Family, is that
        the Yin family?

                    MR YIN
        Yes, this is Sean Yin.

                    TED
        Hello, it's Father Ted Crilly here. I think I owe
        you an apology.

CUT TO TED'S HOUSE

There is the sound of a bell and brakes screeching. DOUGAL
comes over and picks up the hamster on his bicycle.

                    TED
        Right then, see you in a while. Ha ha, Dougal,
        that's everything cleared up. They're coming
        straight around. I'll just be very nice to them
        and people will stop saying that I'm a racist.
        It's great. Nothing can go wrong.

                    DOUGAL
        Fantastic. So the story is you're not a racist.

                    TED
        What? No. It's not a story. I am not a racist.

MRS DOYLE enters from the kitchen. Her shoulder is hunched
to one side and she is pushing a tray of tea along the floor
using the side of her foot.

                    MRS DOYLE
        Tea everyone? Father Crilly, I hear you're a
        racist.

                    DOUGAL
     No, Mrs Doyle, he's not a racist.

DOUGAL winks at MRS DOYLE.

                    TED
     I am not. I am not a racist. Mrs Doyle, we're going
     to have to do something for your back. You can't go
     on like this. I'm just going to try something.

                    MRS DOYLE
                    [Nervously]

     No!

                    TED
     Don't worry, Mrs Doyle.

                    MRS DOYLE
     Oh no, no, no, no-ho.

                    TED
     Just relax.

                    MRS DOYLE
     No. Argh! [As TED grabs hold of MRS DOYLE's chin
     and snaps her into place]

                    MRS DOYLE
     Oh. Oh yes. That's much better.

                    TED
     Are you sure? You look …

                    MRS DOYLE
     Oh yes, yes, yes. This is great. I'll be fine now,
     Father.

TED moves to twist MRS DOYLE's head again.

                    MRS DOYLE
     Noooo! Seriously, Father. I feel twenty years
     younger.

MRS DOYLE hobbles out of the room.

                    DOUGAL
     Ted, the Chinese are comin'.

                              TED
        Oh, right. Where are they? Oh feck it, this big
        mark is still in the window. Ha, never mind!

TED starts to wave at MR YIN and his son through the window
with the perfectly square bit of black dirt.

                         MR YIN'S SON
        I don't know why we have to talk to this fascist.

                            MR YIN
        Come on now, it may have just been …

The Yins look up to see Father TED waving at them through the
window. The square bit of dirt is positioned under TED's nose
so that he resembles Hitler. MR YIN'S SON storms away.

                              TED
        Where are they going? I invite them round and they
        don't even let me tell them my side of the story.

TED's arms are flailing out of control. MR YIN looks at TED
once again from the outside. TED now resembles an angry
Hitler.

CUT TO INT. TED AND DOUGAL'S BEDROOM

TED is sitting up in bed talking to DOUGAL.

                              TED
        This is terrible. People think I'm, I'm some sort
        of Nazi racist; and I'm not. What can I do?

                           DOUGAL
        Ted, here's an idea right off the top of me head.
        Now I haven't thought it through so it's probably
        not brilliant but what the hell, sure I'll just
        talk and see what comes out. Anyway, how about
        some sort of special event, eh, celebrating all
        the different cultures on Craggy Island and then
        people will think you're a fantastic man instead
        of a big racist.

                              TED
        My God!

What?

TED

That's a good idea!

DOUGAL

No, it isn't.

TED

It is, Dougal, it is!

DOUGAL

No, Ted there's probably something wrong with it.
You just haven't thought it through.

TED

No, no, Dougal, you've had a brilliant idea. Hah!
But break it down for me a bit more. What would an
event celebrating all the different cultures in
Craggy Island actually be like?

DOUGAL

What?

TED

What would it involve? I mean, celebration, yes,
but what form could it take?

DOUGAL

Ted, I want out.

TED

What do you mean?

DOUGAL

I went too far too soon. I didn't know what I was
gettin' into Ted. I didn't know you had to follow
a good idea with loads more little good ideas. I'm
sorry, Ted. I'm going to sleep in the spare room.

TED

Dougal.

DOUGAL

I'm sorry.

# The Royle Family (1998)

## 'Bills, Bills, Bills'

## Caroline Aherne, Craig Cash and Henry Normal

*The Royle Family* is a sitcom about a family sitting watching the television. Put like that, it sounds fairly unpromising, but the words put into the characters' mouths by Caroline Aherne, Craig Cash and Henry Normal helped make it one of the most successful shows of the last twenty years. Obviously the performances helped too. Wythenshawe-raised Aherne first emerged as a comedian on the Manchester scene in the late 1980s and early 1990s, performing as a country and western singer called Mitzi Goldberg, a nun by the name of Sister Mary Immaculate and a well-meaning old dear called Mrs Merton. At the time, Granada was still producing comedy programmes for regional consumption, including a one-off chat show called *That Nice Mrs Merton* and a sketch show called *The Dead Good Show*, featuring Aherne with Steve Coogan and John Thomson. Thomson and Aherne then went on to become part of *The Fast Show* team, and it was this that established them in the eyes of the national audience.

With *The Royle Family*, Aherne flew in the face of sitcom orthodoxy, insisting to the BBC that it had to be on film, without an audience, at a time when laugh tracks on sitcoms were still the norm. Having been influenced in her teens by Mike Leigh, she knew what she was after, and she was right. An audience would have killed the slow-burning nature of much of the comedy. In addition, the way it was lit for film suited the cigarette smoke haze of the Royles' slightly dingy

**Series:** *The Royle Family* (Granada for BBC2, twenty-four shows over three series and six specials, 1998–2010), series 1, show 1.

**Original transmission:** BBC2, Monday 14 September 1998, 10 p.m.

**Cast in excerpt:** Caroline Aherne (Denise Royle), Sue Johnston (Barbara Royle), Ricky Tomlinson (Jim Royle), Ralf Little (Antony Royle), Doreen Keogh (Mary).

**Producer:** Glenn Wilhide.

**Director:** Mark Mylod.

front room perfectly. Moreover, most of the episodes appear to take place in real time, with the audience eavesdropping on the Royles for that half-hour.

★ ☆ ★

INT. ROYLES' LIVING ROOM – DAY

JIM

Ninety-eight quid? Eh? Ninety-eight quid. It's good to talk, my arse. 9-2-9 1-2-4-6, whose number's that?

BARBARA

Mary.

JIM

What? You've been ringing bloody Mary next door? If you'd have shouted, she could hear you.

DENISE

She can hear you.

BARBARA

Give it a rest, the pair of you.

JIM

Rest, my arse. It's two pound fifty phoning next door. She's in and out of here all bloody day like a yo-yo. I'll put you a serving hatch in.

DENISE

You're as tight as a crab's arse, you are, dad.

JIM

Crab's arse, my arse, it's two pound fifty. It's a good job she's cured her stutter.

DENISE

The phone's there to be used.

JIM

The phone's there for emergencies. How many times do you see me ringing anyone?

The Royle Family became the basis for a running sketch in *Alistair McGowan's Big Impression*, where members of the Royal Family inhabited an identical living room. Jim Royle was replaced by the Duke of Edinburgh and Barbara was replaced by the Queen, while Alistair McGowan and Ronni Ancona played Prince Charles and Camilla Parker-Bowles with the voices and mannerisms of Craig Cash's character Dave and Aherne's character Denise.

                    DENISE
     Who are you going to ring? You've got no mates.

               [Nudges BARBARA. They laugh.]

A voice is heard from the hallway.

                    MARY
          Oooooh. Only me.

                    BARBARA
          Hello, Mary.

                    MARY
          Everyone alright?

                    DENISE
          Hey, Mary, is your Sheryl in?

                    MARY
          Yes, she is.

                    DENISE
     Will you ask her to bring us round the catalogue?

                    MARY
               [Standing, plumping cushions]

          Yes, I will.

                    DENISE
          Ta.

                    BARBARA
          Come on, love.

MARY sits down.

> MARY
> 
> I've just come round to wish you all the best in your
> new career, Barbara.

> JIM
> 
> Career, my arse. She's going to work part-time in the
> bakery, but why don't you go home, then she can ring
> you up and tell you all about it.

> BARBARA
> 
> Eh, I've had our Denise testing me on prices, and
> I've got it off by heart down to pastries. Test us,
> Mary.

> MARY
> 
> Vanilla slice?

> BARBARA
> 
> 38p.

> MARY
> 
> I'll have two.

They both laugh.

> JIM
> 
> How much is a cup of tea in your bakery?

> BARBARA
> 
> They don't do tea.

> JIM
> 
> Ah, same as here, then. No chance of drowning.

> BARBARA
> 
> Are you stopping for a brew, Mary?

> MARY
> 
> No, I've got a pile of ironing, and it won't do
> itself now, will it?

MARY leaves.

> JIM
> 
> She's hilarious, her. How does she come up with them?

                    BARBARA
Oh, come on, Denise, test us some more.

                    DENISE
Crusty cob.

                      JIM
Here, who's been ringing Aberdeen?

                    BARBARA
14p.

                    DENISE
Meat and potato pie.

                    BARBARA
67p.

                    DENISE
No.

                    BARBARA
68p.

                    DENISE
No.

                    BARBARA
69p.

DENISE

No.

BARBARA
[Grabbing price list]

Shite.

DENISE

Hey, might be they do wedding cakes?

BARBARA

Oooh yeah. Hey, I'll be able to get you a discount.

DENISE

Oooh, how much will one cost?

BARBARA

About two hundred pounds.

JIM

How much?

BARBARA

Two hundred pounds.

DENISE

How many tiers is that?

JIM

There'll be plenty of bloody tears if it's two hundred pounds. Is his dad paying out towards this wedding lark or what?

DENISE

I've told you, dad. He's on a disability allowance.

JIM

So, he's paying bugger all and he'll get a better parking space.

Front door opens and closes, in walks ANTONY.

ANTONY

Any tea going, mum?

> BARBARA
>
> Yeah, your tea's in the oven.

> ANTONY
>
> What is it?

> BARBARA
>
> Egg and chips.

ANTONY walks through to the kitchen.

> JIM
>
> Antony, who do you know in Aberdeen?

> ANTONY
>
> Aw, mam, they're all soggy.

> JIM
>
> Get them ate, they all go to make a turd.

> BARBARA
>
> You'll all have to get used to making your own.

> JIM
>
> Yes, your mother's a career woman now. Antony,
> which room are you in now? This room or that room?

> ANTONY
>
> This room.

> JIM
>
> What's the light on in that room for?

ANTONY goes to turn the kitchen light off.

> JIM
>
> Who do you think I am? Rockefeller?

The TV screen is in view. They are watching a trailer for
*Birds of a Feather*.

> ANTONY
>
> It's that Lesley Joseph, innit? Ain't there owt on
> the other side?

> JIM
>
> She's got a mouth like a horse, that one, hasn't
> she? See her, she wants a good swipe of shite.

# The League of Gentlemen (1999)

## 'The Road to Royston Vasey'

### Reece Shearsmith, Mark Gatiss, Steve Pemberton and Jeremy Dyson

**Series:** *The League of Gentlemen* (nineteen shows over three series and one special, 1999–2002), series 1, show 2.

**Original transmission:** BBC2, Monday 18 January 1999, 9.30 p.m.

**Cast in excerpt:** Steve Pemberton (Pauline), Mark Gatiss (Mickey), Reece Shearsmith (Ross), Edward McCracken (Colin).

**Producer:** Sarah Smith.

**Director:** Steve Bendelack.

The performing arts world owes the now-defunct Bretton Hall College near Wakefield in West Yorkshire a great deal. Its alumni include playwright John Godber, comedian and activist Mark Thomas and TV dramatist Kay Mellor; to say nothing of Mark Gatiss, Steve Pemberton and Reece Shearsmith, three-quarters of the League of Gentlemen. The fourth, non-performing, member of the League, Jeremy Dyson, studied at nearby Leeds University. Sharing a love of the macabre and grotesque, the quartet created a live show that relied more on Sellotape than make-up to create the look of the characters. A Perrier win for their Edinburgh show in 1997 led to Radio 4's *On the Town with the League of Gentlemen*, set in the fictional northern town of Spent.

After the live and radio success, the League transferred to television, changing the location from Spent to Royston Vasey. One character who didn't make the move from the radio series was midget shopkeeper Mr Ingleby, but his replacements became arguably the best-known characters in the League's whole repertory, namely, Edward and Tubbs Tattsyrup, proprietors of a 'local shop for local people', which harbours a dark secret in the attic. However, the extract chosen here concerns the miserable employment prospects in Royston Vasey, made immeasurably grimmer by the pen-obsessed control freak in charge of the jobseekers' restart sessions at the local Job Centre.

EXT. OUTSIDE THE JOB CENTRE – DAY

Dr Chinnery, the vet, cycles past at great speed, dragging a whimpering dog (obviously fake) behind him on a lead.

INT. JOB CENTRE – DAY

                    PAULINE
    Hokey cokey, pig in a pokey. Good morning,
    jobseekers. Now before I begin, I know one of the
    best pens has gone missing. Can I have it back,
    please?

A pen is thrown at PAULINE from the mass of jobseekers.

                    PAULINE
    Thank you. Now, as you're aware, today we're going
    to be looking at your career options. Some of
    you, like Ross here, will want to follow in your
    father's footsteps, but you can't sign on forever.
    So, instead, we're going to be looking at sales
    jobs, namely, how to sell this. *The Big Issue*.
    Now, for those of you not in the know, *The Big
    Issue* is a magazine. It's a bit like *Bunty*, but
    written by tramps. Inside, it's got stories and
    poems and, look, Mickey love, pictures.

                    MICKEY
    Yeah.

                    PAULINE
    And you, jobseekers …

                    ROSS
    Pauline, *The Big Issue* is for homeless people.

                    PAULINE
    Mmmm?

                    COLIN
    We're unemployed.

                    PAULINE
    That's right, Colin. And you can earn a little bit
    of money for yourselves by getting out there and
    selling this to real people.

Royston Vasey is the real name of blue comedian Roy 'Chubby' Brown, and he appeared in a cameo role in the series, playing the town's potty-mouthed mayor. The Derbyshire village of Hadfield was the main centre of the location shooting for the series, with studio work being undertaken at Yorkshire Television's studios in Leeds.

ROSS

Oh, come off it. Just because we're on the dole, doesn't mean we're stupid.

PAULINE

Mickey, love. What is the capital of France?

MICKEY

[Thinks for a couple of seconds]

Wine.

PAULINE

Come on, Ross, on your feet. I need you for this exercise. Now then, jobseekers, I want you all to imagine, if you can, that we're standing on a very busy high street. I'm an attractive young housewife …

They all laugh derisively.

PAULINE

… and I want Ross here to sell me this. In your own time.

PAULINE walks off singing.

ROSS

*Big Issue*.

PAULINE

Pathetic.

[Mimicking him in a childish voice]

*Big Issue*. Come on, Ross.

[Clicking fingers]

I want to see you try.

                    ROSS
*Big Issue*. Help the homeless.


                  PAULINE
Ah, better, see, now he's got my interest.

                    ROSS
Hclp the homeless. It's only a pound.

                  PAULINE
Good. Watch how I'm starting to pity him.

                    ROSS
Do you want a copy then?

                  PAULINE
Ask me nicely.

                    ROSS
Do you want a copy, madam?

                  PAULINE
Ask me more nicely.

                    ROSS
There's no such thing as more nicely.

She walks off.

                    ROSS
Oh, all right please, will you buy *The Big Issue*?
It's for a good cause.

                  PAULINE
            [With her back to ROSS]

Beg me.

                    ROSS
What?

                  PAULINE
You heard, Ross. Beg me. Come on, you need the
money, I don't. Make me feel superior.

ROSS

That's no reason to buy it.

PAULINE

Beg me, Ross. Be a good little doggie and beg me.

ROSS

Your job is to—

PAULINE

Come on, sing for your supper. Beg, doggie, beg.

ROSS

This has got nothing to do with your job.

PAULINE

Beg, doggie, beg.

ROSS

Your job is to—

PAULINE

Beg me, Ross.

ROSS
[Shouts]

No. No, I won't.

PAULINE

What?

ROSS

I won't beg you, Pauline.

PAULINE

I see.

PAULINE holds out her hand for the magazine. He slaps it down.

PAULINE

Sit down, please, Ross.

Walks over to where ROSS is sitting and hits him around the side of the head with the magazine.

Since the last TV series of *The League of Gentlemen*, Mark Gatiss has written extensively for television, including some episodes of *Doctor Who*. Shearsmith and Pemberton collaborated on the BBC2 series *Psychoville*. Jeremy Dyson has written several books and worked as script editor on *The Armstrong and Miller Show* and the Simon Amstell sitcom *Grandma's House*.

PAULINE

Well, piss off, then. Do you want to have a go, Mickey love?

MICKEY

No.

PAULINE

Come on, course you do. Remember, we're in a high street, I'm a housewife.

MICKEY
[Scared]

*Big Issue.*

PAULINE

*Big Issue*? How much is it?

MICKEY

A pound.

PAULINE

A pound? Here, have a fiver. See, Ross? Do you see how easy it is? It's as simple as Mickey. Ooooh, you're nothing. You're worthless. Less than the shit on my shoes. I'm extending your Restart by a month, and then I'm sending you on a whole series of meaningless courses, and then you're going to come back here, and I'm going to re-Restart you.

PAULINE starts walking threateningly through the other jobseekers.

And the rest of you, buck your ideas up. Knuckle down. And give me those pens back.

# *Phoenix Nights* (2001)

## 'Psykick'

## Peter Kay, Dave Spikey and Neil Fitzmaurice

**Series:** *Phoenix Nights* (Goodnight Vienna Productions for Channel 4, twelve shows over two series, 2001–2), series 1, show 3.

**Original transmission:** Channel 4, Sunday 28 January 2001, 9.30 p.m.

**Cast in excerpt:** Peter Kay (Brian Potter and Max), Alex Lowe (Clinton Baptiste), Dave Spikey (Jerry St Clair), Patrick McGuinness (Paddy).

**Producers:** Mark Herbert and John Rushton.

**Director:** Jonny Campbell.

In the 1970s, television made comedy from northern clubland by using it as the basis for a variety show, *The Wheeltappers and Shunters Social Club.* A quarter of a century later, Bolton-born comic Peter Kay returned to the theme for a situation comedy. The Phoenix Club was run by Brian Potter, a miser with delusions of grandeur, and staffed by grotesques and misfits, yet the depiction of these people was warm and affectionate – for all their faults, they were trying their best to bring a bit of the London Palladium to a Lancashire Nissen hut.

Between them, Kay and his co-writers, Dave Spikey and Neil Fitzmaurice, created a world that was heightened and absurd, yet instantly recognizable to anyone with any experience of working men's clubs and similar institutions. In this extract, the audience at the Phoenix is faced with the worst act they're ever likely to see, recommended to St Clair by Potter's nemesis, rival club owner Den Perry.

INT. PHOENIX CLUB - NIGHT

The sound of thunder is heard over the PA. The audience
applauds politely.

                    VOICE-OVER
                    [Deep voice]

    Hundreds of years ago, when man walked the planet,
    he had no real means of communication. In time,
    man developed a phenomenon which has never been
    fully understood by the psychic community. This
    phenomenon is … Clinton Baptiste.

More thunder. BAPTISTE enters.

                    BAPTISTE
                  [Weedy voice]

    Y'alright?

                  [Applause]

    Now … I'm getting a voice. The spirit's very
    strong tonight. Very strong. Hey … Oh. I'm gettin'
    the name … I'm hearing the name … John. Is there a
    John in the audience?

                  SEVERAL MEN
    Yes!

EXT. PHOENIX CLUB ENTRANCE - NIGHT

MAX and PADDY are on the door.

                      MAX
    How's that Piagra?

                    PADDY
    'S'alright. Shit for bubbles.

                      MAX
        [Looking at his glow in the dark watch]

    Oh. Hey? Great, these. What flavour did you get?

                    PADDY
    Aniseed.

Before becoming a stand-up comedian, Dave Spikey was a biomedical scientist in the haematology department at Bolton General Hospital. He made his television debut as part of a double act in the 1986 revival of the ITV talent show *New Faces*.

                         MAX
        Has it kicked in yet?

                         PADDY
        Can't tell.

                         MAX
        Should've got a diver's watch. Look at this.

                         PADDY
        It's not the kind of diving I'll be doing.
        Evenin', girls. Want to have a look into me
        crystal balls?

                         MAX
                  [Showing off his watch]

        See where you're goin'?

                         FIRST GIRL
        What's that smell? What are you chewing?

                         PADDY
        In you go.

                         FIRST GIRL
        It stinks!

                         PADDY
        Yeah. Get in.

                         MAX
        See where you're goin'. It's half six in Japan.

INSIDE THE CLUB

BAPTISTE is continuing with his act.

> BAPTISTE

Your mother, John. She were quite young when she died. Am I right?

> JOHN

Ninety-three.

> BAPTISTE

But she were young in herself? Young at heart. And she seemed to slow down a lot towards the end. Am I right?

> JOHN

Yeah.

> BAPTISTE

This is your partner, correct?

Both JOHN and PARTNER nod.

> BAPTISTE

Now, I think there's something you want to tell her, am I right?

> JOHN

No.

> BAPTISTE

I think there is. Something you wanted to get off your chest, you're maybe a bit ashamed of? Don't you think you should tell her, John? Before you both get hurt?

> JOHN

Nothin', there's nothin'!

BAPTISTE does a showbizzy point at JOHN.

> JOHN'S PARTNER

What is it?

> JOHN
> [To BAPTISTE]

Hey, mouth!

<u>ON THE DOOR</u>

MAX is still looking at his watch. PADDY reads a porn magazine.

> PADDY
> Dave likes to see me holding what?

> MAX
> Anything?

> PADDY
> Nothing. Not a pulse.
>
> [Looks down at crotch]
>
> Come on, son, let's have you.

<u>INSIDE THE CLUB</u>

BAPTISTE has made an old lady cry.

> BAPTISTE
> Don't worry, love. you'll still be able to visit.

Crowd gasps.

> BAPTISTE
> Now, I'm feelin' it very strongly … over here. What's your name, love? Don't tell me … It's Se … So …

> SONIA
> Sonia.

> BAPTISTE
> Sonia. Sonia. Now, Sonia, love, you've not been very well, have you love? Am I right?

> SONIA
> [Indicating friend sitting next to her]
>
> No, Debbie's been ill.

> BAPTISTE
> [Swinging round to DEBBIE]
>
> Debbie. You have, haven't you, love? You've been very poorly, and it's not been easy, has it?

```
                    DEBBIE
                    No.

                   BAPTISTE
        And it is terminal, isn't it?

                    DEBBIE
         No, no.

Crowd gasps. BAPTISTE looks at DEBBIE as if to suggest she's
lying or in denial.

                   BAPTISTE
        Right, hands up who can't have children.

Audience gasps again.

ON THE DOOR

                     MAX
                [Watch beeping]

        Shit, I'm out of oxygen!

Door bursts open, to reveal JOHN and his PARTNER leaving.

                 JOHN'S PARTNER
        I know there's something goin' on. Tell me what's
        goin' on!

                     JOHN
        Nothing!

                [To MAX and PADDY]

        It's wrong what he's doing in there. He's just
        offending people!

                 JOHN'S PARTNER
        Tell me what's goin' on!
```

The club used in the series to represent the Phoenix is St Gregory's Social
Club in Farnworth, Greater Manchester.

MAX

Whoa, stay back, Paddy. Domestic. Don't get involved, son.

INSIDE THE CLUB

BAPTISTE has offended yet another punter.

BAPTISTE

You've gotta be cruel to be kind. Hey, don't shoot the messenger! I'm only telling you what the spirits are telling me.

BAPTISTE approaches a burly member of the audience.

BAPTISTE

Now, I'm gettin' the word …

BAPTISTE pauses for effect.

BAPTISTE

… 'nonce'.

                              AUDIENCE
        Ooh!

The punter picks BAPTISTE up by his jacket and carries him
out of shot. There is a shattering sound.

CUT TO CLUB DOOR - NIGHT

POTTER and JERRY watch people leaving at the end of the
evening.

                              POTTER
        Thank you very much. Good night, God bless.

                              JERRY
        Night, Bill.

                              BILL
        We're not comin' here again.

                              POTTER
                             [To JERRY]

        Where the bloody hell did you get him from?

                              JERRY
        Came highly recommended.

                              POTTER
        By who?

                              JERRY
        Den Perry.

      The series had a spot of bother following the appearance of fire safety
   officer Keith Lard (played by Kay), who, it was alleged, had an unnatural
   attachment to dogs. Real-life Bolton fire safety officer Keith Laird took legal
   action, with the result that all subsequent repeats and DVD releases have
   had to include a disclaimer explaining that there is no actual connection
                          between Lard and Laird.

> POTTER

Den Perry? Jerry, Jerry, Perry? Jerry, Perry, Perry! He wants us shut down, man!

BAPTISTE is leaving, with a bloody nose.

> POTTER

Oh! Thank you. Thank you, good buddy. Thank you for upsetting my customers. Customers I've just had to refund!

> BAPTISTE

How long did I do?

> POTTER

Too long.

> JERRY

Fifteen minutes.

> BAPTISTE

Really? I don't usually last longer than ten. It's them. They can't handle the truth!

> POTTER

You. Some bloody psychic.

> [Points to nose]

You didn't see that coming, did you?

> BAPTISTE

Can I have me money?

> POTTER

Can I have … can you have? Can you read minds? Can you read minds? Read this.

[Puts fingers to temples as if transmitting a thought]

Hey?

> BAPTISTE

You can walk.

> POTTER

Get out of it. Get out. Get off!

# *The Office* (2002)

## 'Appraisals'

### Ricky Gervais and Stephen Merchant

When Ricky Gervais made his television debut on
Channel 4's *11 O'Clock Show*, playing an oafish character
called Ricky Gervais, few could have expected him to co-
write one of the most popular sitcoms of the first decade
of the twenty-first century. *The Office* began, like *The
Likely Lads*, with an exercise on a BBC directors' course
which Gervais's friend Stephen Merchant attended.
Shot in the style of a mockumentary, albeit with no
narration, it followed in the footsteps of John Morton's
clever, subtle *People Like Us*, but achieved a far greater
level of success.

Concerning the day-to-day running of the Slough office of
paper merchants Wernham Hogg, Gervais himself played
boss David Brent, a risible, oleaginous figure respected only
by the idiotic would-be office politician Gareth Keenan, played
by Mackenzie Crook. The bitter-sweet love story between
sales representative Tim and receptionist Dawn was one of
the highlights, as was the intransigence of accountant Keith,
displayed fully in this extract.

**Series:** *The Office*
(fourteen shows over two
series and two specials,
2001–3), series 2, show 2.

**Original transmission:**
BBC2, Monday 7 October
2002, 10pm.

**Cast in excerpt:** Ricky
Gervais (David Brent),
Mackenzie Crook (Gareth
Keenan), Ewen Macintosh
(Keith Bishop).

**Producer:** Ash Atalla.

**Directors:** Ricky Gervais
and Stephen Merchant.

INT. OPEN-PLAN OFFICE - DAY

> BRENT
> I'm doing our staff appraisals, and some people
> can get a little bit nervous about that. They
> think they're walking the long mile to put their
> head on the block, which is wrong. They fill out a
> form in advance.

GARETH holds up the form.

> BRENT
> They don't only sort of list their strengths and
> weaknesses, but also mine as a boss, so it's a
> chance for them to tell me where we're going
> wrong. It's very much an opportunity to …

> GARETH
> … separate the wheat from the chaff.

> BRENT
> No, that sounds bad. It's not a witch hunt. We're
> not trying to find out who the worst people are.

> GARETH
> We know who they are already. I've written them on
> my form.

> BRENT
> You shouldn't have written them on your form.

> GARETH
> [Handing BRENT the form]

> I've underlined the worst ones.

> BRENT
> You're missing the point.

Shot of people working outside in the office.

CUT TO BRENT'S OFFICE

KEITH is chewing gum and staring at BRENT during his
appraisal.

> BRENT
> Under strengths, you've just put accounts.

Before the David Brent character had a name, he was referred to as
'Seedy Boss' in the script.

                    KEITH
    Yeah.

                    BRENT
    That's your job. That's just …

                    KEITH
    Mmm.

                    BRENT
    No, Keith, I'm looking for your skills, within
    your job. Is there anything else you could have
    put there?

                    KEITH
                [Throws up hands]

    No.

                    BRENT
    OK. Under weaknesses, you've put eczema.

Another shot of the outer office.

                    BRENT
    You've left this section completely blank, Keith.
    You haven't done the Q and A.

                    KEITH
    I thought that you filled that in.

                    BRENT
    No, no, no, no. This is aimed at you. Look. 'To
    what extent do you believe you have the skills and
    knowledge to perform your job effectively?' Then
    you tick one of the boxes. 'Not at all', 'To some
    extent', 'Very much so', 'Don't know'. What would
    you tick?

                          KEITH

'Don't know'.

                          BRENT

OK. Number two. 'Do you feel you've received
adequate training to use your computer
effectively?'

KEITH chews gum.

                          KEITH

What are the options?

                          BRENT

Same as … they're always the same, always the
same. 'Not at all', 'To some extent', 'Very much
so', 'Don't know'.

                          KEITH

'Don't know'.

                          BRENT

'Don't know' again. OK. 'Do you feel you are given
the flexibility to decide how best to accomplish
your goals?'

KEITH keeps chewing.

                          BRENT

Do you want the options again?

                              KEITH
        Yeah.

                              BRENT
        'Not at all', 'To some extent', always the same,
        'Very much so', 'Don't know'.

                              KEITH
        'Don't know'.

                              BRENT
        If 'Don't know' wasn't there, what would you put?

KEITH keeps chewing and staring.

                              KEITH
        What are the options?

                              BRENT
                        [Clearly rattled]

        'Not at all', 'To some extent', 'Very much so',
        'Don't know'.

                              KEITH
        'Very much so'.

                              BRENT
        Do you know what the question was?

                              KEITH
        No.

                              BRENT
        OK. Do you, let's … we're going to leave that
        there.

As well as being sold to eighty countries, *The Office* has been remade in
several different languages for different markets, including French, German,
Quebecois, Chilean and Israeli versions. There has also been a highly
successful US version, with Steve Carell playing the manager character.

# Bremner, Bird and Fortune (2007)

## 'Financial Adviser'

### John Bird and John Fortune

**Series:** *Bremner, Bird and Fortune* (Vera for Channel 4, eighty-five shows over sixteen series and eight specials, 1999–2010), series 12, show 1.

**Original transmission:** Channel 4, Sunday 30 September 2007, 7 p.m.

**Cast in excerpt:** John Fortune (Interviewer), John Bird (George Parr).

**Producer:** Geoff Atkinson.

**Directors:** Steve Connelly and Chris Fox.

When Rory Bremner began featuring John Bird and John Fortune on his BBC2 show in 1991, it was a meeting of the satirical generations. Bird and Fortune had been Cambridge contemporaries of Peter Cook during the late the 1950s and early 1960s, and had gone on to work with Cook at his club in Soho, The Establishment. Bird had been the first choice to host *That Was The Week That Was*, and made a pilot, but was unavailable for the series. From the 1960s to the 1980s, both Bird and Fortune worked extensively in theatre and continued writing and performing for television, sometimes with John Wells.

The dialogues that were to bring them to a new audience via Rory Bremner's show had their roots in The Establishment days. Either Bird or Fortune would take the mantle of an authority figure called George Parr, while the other would attempt to interview him. The comedy lay in the mixture of evasions, delusions and uncomfortable truths that spewed from the vain, pompous, deceitful, greedy, incompetent Parr's mouth. From week to week, Parr could be anything that needed deflating: a politician, a military commander, a banker. The template seems to fit with the worst examples of all of these characters.

INT. TV STUDIO - DAY

>INTERVIEWER
George Parr, you are an investment banker?

>PARR
[Smugly]

Yes, I am. Yes.

>INTERVIEWER
And of course we've just had an extremely serious banking crisis.

>PARR

Mmm hmm.

>INTERVIEWER
And there are lots of people in the City, like yourself, who earn millions in salaries and bonuses.

PARR looks even smugger.

>INTERVIEWER
So, shouldn't you have seen this coming?

>PARR
Well, it is true that we didn't actually foresee it in the strict sense of the word.

>INTERVIEWER
Or in any sense of the word.

>PARR
Or in any sense of the word. No, no. We didn't foresee it, but when it happened, we did notice it, which is almost as good, isn't it?

>INTERVIEWER
[Incredulous]

We've just had the first run on a bank in this country for 140 years. You're a banker, what is your reaction?

Bird had begun working with Bremner in 1989, after Bremner had decided his show was veering too much towards light entertainment. Bringing in Bird and scriptwriter John Langdon had helped to make 'it into a more politically literate kind of show, trying to recover the integrity that had been lost', he told the *Guardian* in 1991.

PARR

Well of course, everybody in banking, we all felt deeply embarrassed.

INTERVIEWER

Embarrassed?

PARR

Embarrassed, yes. I hardly dared take my Ferrari in for its service, yesterday.

INTERVIEWER

What are you going do about it?

PARR

What can I do about it? Bloody thing needs a service. I've only got two Ferraris.

INTERVIEWER

Yes, but what was the cause of this?

PARR

Oh, it was about the banking crisis? Of course, it wasn't my fault, it wasn't banking's fault. It was entirely the fault of Mervyn King.

INTERVIEWER

But he's just put ten billion pounds into the banking system. Wasn't that what you were asking for?

PARR

Yes, but he's done it far too late, you see, and nobody wants it anymore. He should have done it much earlier, because it was obvious that Northern

Rock was getting into difficulties. It was obvious
that most people in the City were borrowing too
much and lending too riskily.

INTERVIEWER

Including you.

PARR

Well, I was just doing what everybody else was
doing. That's how we operate in the City. What I
want to know is why didn't he do it earlier? Why
wait until the entire banking sector looked as
stupid as it actually was.

INTERVIEWER

So, what you're saying is that although Mervyn King might not have been able to prevent the crisis, he could have prevented the spectacle of people queuing up in the high street to get their money out?

PARR

Exactly, exactly.

INTERVIEWER

People were queuing at two o'clock in the morning.

PARR

Yes, two o'clock in the morning. The British people have only ever done that for Tim Henman, and look how badly that always turned out.

INTERVIEWER

But these scenes must have been humiliating for the banking industry?

PARR

We don't like to see it. It makes us look silly.

INTERVIEWER

Silly? What about the banks falling over themselves to pick up these packages of dodgy mortgages. They have very little idea how much they're worth, if they're worth anything at all?

PARR

That's not silly, that's a sophisticated market in operation.

INTERVIEWER

So, you don't think there's anything fundamentally wrong with the banking system?

PARR

No, there are some very, very clever men in the City. Just as an example, the fact that the Alliance and Leicester lost a third of its value in a day, and the very next day got a third of its value back, that shows that the system is fundamentally sound and rational.

The George Parr interviews are largely improvised on set, running to ten or twelve minutes in their original form before being edited down for transmission. In 1995, Channel 4 began running some of the improvisations in full, under the title *The Long Johns*.

INTERVIEWER

Yes, well. Can you explain why, at the beginning of the Northern Rock crisis, the government made an offer which didn't reassure the public? The Chancellor of the Exchequer himself said people shouldn't worry, because their money was perfectly safe.

PARR

Well, that's very simple. The public are used to the government telling them lies.

INTERVIEWER

You mean if the government is prepared to tell lies about the reason for invading another country, they wouldn't be too bothered about lying about people's money?

PARR

About people's money, no, exactly. What Alastair Darling should have done was say to everybody, 'Go down to Northern Rock now, take every last penny out'. You see? People would have said, 'Well, there must be some reason why the government's telling me to take my money out, I'm going to leave it where it is'.

INTERVIEWER

And then the whole thing might have just faded away?

PARR

Blown over. Well, it should never have happened in the first place. It was only because some bright spark asked, 'How much do you think these American houses are actually worth?' and of course, as soon as they asked that question, we all panicked.

> INTERVIEWER
> Because you found out?

> PARR
> No, we didn't find out. We still haven't found out how much they're worth, if anything.

> INTERVIEWER
> Despite what you call a very, very sophisticated market?

> PARR
> Look, we went on the assumption that property values always go up.

> INTERVIEWER
> Well, that's not very sophisticated, is it?

> PARR
> It's as sophisticated as we ever get.

> INTERVIEWER
> Yes, but why if this is the case, and that's what happened, every time you sell someone a financial product, you put a big warning on it saying 'Your investments may go down as well as go up'?

> PARR
> Yes, well, we have to do that, it's one of the pettifogging regulations, but it's only meant for ignorant punters.

> INTERVIEWER
> So it doesn't apply to you?

> PARR
> Certainly not, and of course the punters themselves are now reassured because the government has guaranteed their deposits.

> INTERVIEWER
> Yes, and also put ten billion pounds into the banking sector. Was that absolutely necessary?

PARR

It was necessary as a symbolic gesture, because
what the market needs is confidence.

INTERVIEWER

Whose confidence?

PARR

My confidence. The confidence that I have a 35-
room house to go to with six cars in the garage,
and a private helicopter, and that I'll earn
enough from my Christmas bonus to pay my Filipino
staff twelve pounds a month.

INTERVIEWER

These are huge sums that we're talking about here.
Where in the end is all this money going to come
from?

PARR

Well, I don't know. Wherever governments get their
money. Taxation, I suppose. I don't know anything
about tax, I never pay any.

INTERVIEWER

Don't you think it's wrong that extremely rich
people, I don't know, people who run private
equity funds, and people like you hardly pay any
tax at all?

PARR

There's absolutely nothing wrong with that. The
City is far too valuable to the British economy.
And in any case, if you tax us, we'll go abroad.
And that's not just an idle threat. We can go and
wreck somebody else's financial system.

INTERVIEWER

Finally, can we talk about moral hazard?

PARR
[Leans forward]

About what? Sorry?

INTERVIEWER

Moral hazard?

PARR

No, sorry, I know what hazard means. What's the
other word?

INTERVIEWER

Oh, never mind. The point about moral hazard is
that the thought is that executives like yourself
will go on making more and more stupid and more
and more risky loans to prop up the value of their
bank because when everything goes wrong, the Bank
of England is going to come along and bail them
out.

PARR

Well, I certainly hope so. I'm looking forward to
it.

INTERVIEWER

Look, I don't want to be insulting, but it does
seem to me that you haven't learned anything from
this whole episode.

PARR

On the contrary. I've learned one very important
lesson.

INTERVIEWER

And what is that?

PARR

And that is if you're going to make a cock-up,
make sure it's an absolutely enormous cock-up
because then the government will bail you out.

INTERVIEWER

George Parr, thank you very much.

PARR

Pleasure.

# *The Thick of It* (2009)

## 'Nicola meets Malcolm'

### Simon Blackwell, Jesse Armstrong, Roger Drew, Will Smith, Sean Gray, Armando Iannucci, Ian Martin and Tony Roche

When BBC2 searched for *Britain's Best Sitcom* in 2004, Armando Iannucci advocated *Yes Minister* as the show most worthy of the garland. It had, he said, 'made the driest subject possible – the minutiae of politics – into sparkling comedy'. Little more than a year later, Iannucci, along with a distinguished team of co-writers, a dream cast and a minuscule BBC4 budget, was achieving the same comic alchemy with *The Thick of It*. The new show reflected the triumph of presentation over policy in the modern political world. The minister for social affairs and citizenship, Hugh Abbot, played by Chris Langham, dealt less with civil servants and more with the prime minister's director of communications, Malcolm Tucker, played by Peter Capaldi, an eloquently foul-mouthed spin doctor, determined to keep bad coverage at bay whatever the cost.

The minister has the dubious benefit of a trio of advisers. Glenn Cullen and Ollie Reeder are party political animals, while DoSaC director of communications Terri Coverley is a civil servant. Cullen and Reeder form an unlikely double act, the latter frequently abusing the former for nothing more heinous than being middle-aged. Cullen is a fundamentally decent and loyal man, while Reeder is attempting to climb the greasy pole of politics, hampered by his own arrogance and ineptitude.

**Series:** *The Thick of It* (BBC4 and BBC2, twenty-two shows over four series and two specials, 2005–2012), series 3, show 1.

**Original transmission:** BBC2, Saturday 24 October 2009, 9.25 p.m.

**Cast in excerpt:** Rebecca Front (Nicola Murray), James Smith (Glenn Cullen), Chris Addison (Ollie Reeder), Peter Capaldi (Malcolm Tucker).

**Producer:** Adam Tandy.

**Director:** Armando Iannucci.

Much of *The Thick of It* concerns the politicians' attempts to second-guess the media and avoid public humiliation. Following Langham's well-publicized troubles, the lead role was recast, with Rebecca Front's Nicola Murray taking over as minister. The following extract is Murray's first encounter with Tucker.

★ ☆ ★

INT. NICOLA MURRAY'S OFFICE - DAY

                    NICOLA
So, Malcolm Tucker, Malcolm Tucker, [sings]
Malcolm Tucker, Malcolm. I'm not nervous.

                    GLENN
Are you?

                    NICOLA
It's just Malcolm's one of those things that I'm
aware of without ever having really come into
contact with. Like a rat.

                    OLLIE
No, he'd hate that. He thinks of himself more as a
thin white Mugabe.

                    GLENN
Because if you are worried about Malcolm, you
know, we have amassed a few tips over the years.

                    OLLIE
We have worked out when he's going to give you a
verbal colonic, and some avoidance manoeuvres.

                    GLENN
        [Doing awkward martial arts moves]
Tae-kwon-spin.

TUCKER walks in.

                    MALCOLM
Is this the Number One Ladies' Detective Agency?

                         NICOLA
          Malcolm Tucker. The real deal.

NICOLA steps forward to shake MALCOLM's hand.

                         MALCOLM
          The real deal. You're looking great.

                   [Turns to OLLIE and GLENN]

          Alright, Hinge and Bracket. Time to go and hang
          up your lady cocks. Nicola Murray, here you are,
          Secretary of State for the Department of Social
          Affairs and Citizenship.

CUT away briefly to OLLIE in the outer office, mocking GLENN
with a rubbish martial arts move. CUT back to NICOLA's
office.

                         NICOLA
          Yes, I now have one of the longest job titles in
          western politics. Thank God I don't have to wear a
          lapel badge.

                         MALCOLM
          It's a pity we couldn't just make an abbreviation
          of it, like PFI. Which I think stands for 'pretty
          fucking embarrassing', if you're a bit sloppy
          about the details, which clearly your fucking
          husband is.

                         NICOLA
          James works for Albany, fine. He wasn't even
          working there when the contract was awarded.

                         MALCOLM
          Don't worry. That was just me. That's the sort of
          thing the press will throw at you. You step out of
          line, they'll be all over you, like a pigeon on a
          chip. Is that your chair?

                         NICOLA
          Yes, it's cool, isn't it? It's got lumbar support.

                         MALCOLM
          Bin it. People don't like their politicians to be
          comfortable. They don't like you having expenses.

They don't like you being paid. They'd rather you lived in a fucking cave.

> NICOLA
> OK, fine. So what should I be sitting on? Shall I just get an upturned KFC bucket?

> MALCOLM
> A fucking normal chair. Right? Not a fucking massive vibrating throne.

CUT TO OUTER OFFICE

> GLENN
> Malcolm must be hating this. All these bright fresh new ministers to blood in and to plan a by-election.

> OLLIE
> If it's any consolation to you, a little bit of you will always be in this department, because she's nabbed your chair, hasn't she? She's got your chair, and, in fact, your dandruff, which she doesn't know.

> GLENN
> Ha ha. If I go, that chair is coming with me.

> OLLIE
> You know those old men who go to the park to read the paper? That'll be you. You can go on your chair. They'll make you king of all the tramps.

CUT BACK TO NICOLA'S OFFICE

> MALCOLM
> So, er, you've got three kids, yeah?

> NICOLA
> I've got four. Katie's sixteen, she's the eldest. She's just left school.

> MALCOLM
> Not going to college, university or anything?

> NICOLA
> She's a bit of a rebel.

After early work with Spike Milligan and Ken Campbell, Chris Langham became one of the writing team for *The Muppet Show*. He had to stand in as a guest on the show when the booked star, Richard Pryor, was unable to make it. He was also part of the original *Not the Nine O'Clock News* team, but left after the first series.

MALCOLM
What sort of a rebel? I mean, look, what are we talking here? A pierced navel or holidays at a Pakistani training camp?

NICOLA
It's chiefly heroin. Although she has cut down since getting pregnant by that Nigerian people-smuggler, because the track marks would have affected her porn career.

TERRI enters.

TERRI
Sorry to disturb. Morning, Malcolm. Just wanted to give you a few things here. That's change from the fruit salad, this is this morning's papers. Please excuse me.

TERRI leaves.

NICOLA
I'm surprised that you hadn't vetted me. I thought you'd know about the kids?

MALCOLM
It's just that you were a sort of late-ish kind of appointment, that didn't give me enough time to fuck the Is and fist the Ts, as Robert Robinson might say.

CUT TO OUTER OFFICE

                          GLENN
Sounds to me like she's only bringing in one other
person, so I wonder whether she might keep one of
us on permanently.

                          TERRI
Thank God I'm safe.

                          GLENN
Jeez, we know you're safe, Terri. How do we know
you're safe? We know you're safe because you keep
using the word 'safe' like bloody Jim Bowen.

Many of Tucker's baroque insults are the work of the series' 'swearing consultant', Ian Martin. When not concocting fresh profanity, he writes for *Architect's Journal*, having previously spent sixteen years writing for *Building Design*.

OLLIE
[Jim Bowen impersonation]

You've got DoSaC, that's safe. Do you want to go for the Treasury, young lady?

CUT BACK TO NICOLA'S OFFICE

MALCOLM
OK, Mrs Walton. What about these other kids? What ages are they?

NICOLA
Eleven, nine and five.

MALCOLM
Eleven? So that's secondary school?

NICOLA
No, she's still at primary. State primary. Lovely little school with terrible SATS results, but you know, a really good broad demographic. A steel band.

MALCOLM
She'll be going to secondary school, what, in September?

NICOLA
Yeah. I can see where this is going. It's not an issue.

MALCOLM
Great. If it's not an issue, I'll just fucking toddle off. I'll go and have a nice relaxing wee sleep under a duvet. I probably won't even have

to tug myself off, because I'm so fucking relaxed about that, because I know that there is no fucking issue here, right.

NICOLA

She's not going to the comprehensive, Malcolm, she's going to a local independent school.

MALCOLM

Jesus H. fucking Corbett. Do you honestly, do you honestly believe that, as a minister, you can get away with that? You are saying that all your local state schools, all the schools that this government has drastically improved, are knife-addled rape sheds. And that's not a big story? For fuck's sake. Sort it or abort it.

NICOLA

Let's get this clear. My family is off limits. This job is not going to get anywhere near my husband and my kids. It just doesn't.

MALCOLM

Of course it fucking does, as per the wee barcode and the serial number under your right armpit, you are now built and owned by the state, and you are under the spotlight twenty-four hours a day, darling. You know what you are? You're a fucking human dartboard, and Eric fucking Bristow's on the oche flinging a million darts made of human shit right at you. Can you take that? Can you?

NICOLA

OK, look, you, the all-swearing eye. You didn't know how many kids I had. You had to ask me. So who on earth in the press is going to even know or care?

MALCOLM

Do you remember *The Big Breakfast*? Do you remember that programme?

NICOLA
[Exasperated]

Yes.

MALCOLM

Do you remember when Chris Evans started that,
you know it was a big success. Then they had that
guy Johnny Vaughan. Remember him? Everybody loved
him. Fuck knows why, but they loved him. Do you
know what this is here? This here is series ten
of *The Big Breakfast*, and do you know what you
are? You're the fucking dinner lady that they have
asked to come and present the show. The reason I
didn't know about you and your children is that
you were so low down on the list of candidates for
this job, I didn't even have the chance to look
into you. So low. Way way way way way down. You
are now being scrutinized for what you wear, what
you say, for your hair, your shoes, your fucking
earrings, your fucking cleavage and your dress,
which by the way is way too loud.

NICOLA

Too loud?

MALCOLM

Yeah. I'm getting fucking tinnitus here. Look,
your crooked husband I can make go away, but your
crooked husband combined with you being worried
about your underage daughter coming home up the
duff from some truanting bastard, I cannot. She
goes to the comp. OK?

The departmental scenes in the first six episodes of *The Thick of It* were shot
in disused offices at the former Guinness brewery in Park Royal, London. For
the specials, the location moved to the BBC Media Centre at White City. For
the third series, the DoSaC scenes were shot in a disused office block near
Watford, while other scenes made use of the Media Centre's atrium.

# *Outnumbered* (2011)

## 'The Cold Caller'

## Andy Hamilton and Guy Jenkin

**Series:** *Outnumbered* (Hat Trick Productions for BBC1, thirty-two shows over four series, two specials, two *Comic Relief* segments, two *Sport Relief* segments and a *Children in Need* segment, 2007–2011), series 4, show 5.

**Original transmission:** BBC1, Thursday 29 September 2011, 9 p.m.

**Cast in excerpt:** Hugh Dennis (Pete Brockman), Claire Skinner (Sue Brockman), Ramona Marquez (Karen), Daniel Roche (Ben), Tyger Drew-Honey (Jake), Samantha Bond (Angela), Pip Torrens (Armitage – cold caller).

**Producers/directors:** Andy Hamilton and Guy Jenkin.

Andy Hamilton and Guy Jenkin have traditionally been thought of as satirical writers, having been the creators of the long-running newsroom sitcom *Drop the Dead Donkey*. However, in recent years, their take on family life and the anxieties that come with being the parents of three bright, independent-minded children has proved to be one of the great delights of modern TV comedy. Often when adults write lines for children, there is a temptation to make them wise-crackers beyond their years. Hamilton and Jenkin sidestepped this by giving the child actors the outlines of the scenes they were in and letting them create their own lines within that framework. The result was brilliantly natural and very funny.

That's not to dismiss the performances of the adults, with both Hugh Dennis and Claire Skinner capturing a certain type of exasperation beautifully, a feeling resulting from a desire to set out ground rules, while acknowledging the constant need to compromise without appearing to climb down and let the child think they've won.

INT. BROCKMAN'S HALL - DAY

PETE and SUE meet by the stairs.

> PETE
>
> Sue … Sue.

> SUE
>
> Jake is going out with a nineteen-year-old girl.

> PETE
>
> Angela's here.

> SUE
>
> What? You let her in?

> PETE
>
> Nineteen? … One nine …?

> SUE
>
> She can't stay.

> PETE
>
> I told her she could stay the night. How do you
> know he's … going out with a nineteen-year-old?

> SUE
>
> I nearly managed to con my way on to his Facebook
> page. What the bloody hell is Angela doing here?

> PETE
>
> She's written a book … Nineteen? This girl is—

> SUE
>
> A book?

> PETE
>
> … four years older than him.

> SUE
>
> What kind of book?

BEN appears.

> BEN
>
> Hey, did you hear about the cowboy who had brown
> paper trousers and a brown paper shirt and a brown
> paper hat? He was found guilty of rustling.

                              PETE
        Not now, Ben.

                               BEN
        What's rustling?

                              PETE
        Ben … Go!

BEN goes.

                              PETE
        He's going to be a comedian.

                               SUE
        A comedian?

                              PETE
        Nineteen!

                               SUE
        Angela!

JAKE comes out of the living room and squeezes past them and
up the stairs.

                              JAKE
        No violence now, Mum.

PETE watches him go, looking shocked and a little impressed.

                              PETE
                          [Quietly]

        Nineteen …

The child actors in *Outnumbered* come with excellent pedigrees. Ramona
Marquez is the daughter of *Hotel Babylon* actor Martin Marquez, while Tyger
Drew-Honey is the son of porn star Simon Lindsay Honey (better known as
Ben Dover) and former *Penthouse* editor Linzi Drew.

                          SUE
         Can you stop saying that?

                    ANGELA (OUT OF VIEW)
         Hi Sue! … Aren't you going to come in and say
         hello to your sister?

SUE and PETE steel themselves to greet ANGELA. MIX to
exterior of house.

INT. KITCHEN - DAY

ANGELA, PETE and SUE sit awkwardly.

                          SUE
         So, let me get this straight, you're giving advice
         on families to other people.

                        ANGELA
                   [A little snappy]

         Yes. I am.

                          PETE
         She finally understood her pain was a gift.

The doorbell rings.

                          SUE
         Karen! Door!

                    KAREN (OUT OF VIEW)
         OK.

BEN runs in.

                          BEN
         I've got this really good joke off Twitter. It's a
         Frankie Boyle joke …

                          PETE
         I'm going to stop you right there.

                          BEN
         I've already told it to Misty.

                          PETE
         Did she laugh?

She made some noises. I wouldn't really call it
laughing as such.

KAREN (OUT OF VIEW)
Ben! It's for you!

BEN runs out.

SUE
So, does this book draw on our family?

ANGELA
A tiny bit, but enough of me and my writing. I
hear you've got some secretarial work …

SUE looks at PETE.

PETE
I never said secretarial

SUE
I run the office at a Multi Media Interconnect
Company.

ANGELA
And what's that?

SUE
They provide connectivity solutions for different
kinds of media.

ANGELA
But what exactly—

SUE
Look, I don't know, I run the office. I don't
know. OK!

ANGELA
And how's everything with Jake? Has he got a
girlfriend yet?

PETE and SUE look at each other.

PETE
Well … um …

SUE
Well, yes, there are rumours.

ANGELA
But you haven't had the big day, when you meet her for
the first time?

SUE
No, but that big day will be coming soon.

PETE
Will it?

                          SUE
                        [Quick]

        Yes, yes it will.

BEN comes in carrying a battered and slightly scary
ventriloquist dummy.

                          PETE
        What the f—

                          BEN
              [Speaking as the Dummy]

        That was Ibrahim at the door. He's given me to Ben.
        I was in his attic and they didn't want me, and his
        grandmother said I was the work of the devil.

                          SUE
        Ben … He's horrible.

                          BEN
        [As Ben] No I'm not.

        [As Dummy] Yes he is.

        [As Ben] No I'm not.

        [As Dummy] Oh yes you are.

FADE as the group watch BEN bond with his Dummy, with SUE and
PETE trying to clam him up.

INT. KITCHEN - DAY

Lowered voices.

                          PETE
        I just don't think we should rush up to him
        and say, 'So you've got a nineteen-year-old
        girlfriend'.

                          SUE
        Every time you say 'nineteen-year-old girlfriend',
        you've got a bit of a grin on your face.

                          PETE
        I don't have a—

                    SUE
It's illegal.

                    PETE
Technically.

                    SUE
No, not technically …

                    PETE
Well only if they're … y'know … actually—

                    SUE
You think he's got a nineteen-year-old girlfriend
and they're … reading poetry to each other, you're
doing the grin.

                    PETE
I am not, I—

                    SUE
You are.

                    PETE
Look, my face at rest just happens to look a bit
like a grin, I—

                    SUE
You admire him, don't you?

                    PETE
No, I—

                    SUE
Because he's doing something you could only dream
of as a teenager.

                    PETE
OK, well, let's not forget you had a boyfriend, a
steady boyfriend, at fourteen … which is like the
equivalent of about eight now.

                    SUE
He was fourteen, the same age as me.

                    PETE
I've seen the photograph, he—

                                    SUE
How would you feel if Karen was fifteen and had a
nineteen-year-old boyfriend?

                                    PETE
Well.

                                    SUE
Oh, you're not grinning now.

                                    PETE
Well, that would be different.

                                    SUE
Why?

                                    PETE
Because … because …

                                    SUE
Because she's a girl?

                                    PETE
I haven't said that.

                                    SUE
You haven't said anything yet. Why is that
different?

                                    PETE
Because …

                                    SUE
Yes?

                                    PETE
We'll have a word with Jake.

# Acknowledgements

First of all, I must thank all of the writers and agents who said yes. I must also give special thanks to Rebecca Parkinson, managing director of Vera Productions, who took the time to help me with some hard to find information with regard to the Bird and Fortune sketch included here.

Also, several hats are doffed in the direction of Barry Cryer, who put me in touch with Neil Shand at a point when we thought we'd have to give up on the *Q6* sketch.

Over at Atlantic Books, this project was the idea of Richard Milbank, a comedy fan and a publishing pro. It was a delight to sit with him in the initial meetings about the project, trading lines from long-forgotten sketches. Thanks also to Sarah Norman, Nicole Muir and James Nightingale, who saw the project through to publication, and to Toby Mundy, as ever, the all-seeing eye.

At the AM Heath literary agency, my co-conspirator Euan Thorneycroft haggled expertly with Milbank and Mundy to ensure that I was doing this both for love and money.

At large in the community, numerous friends helped with suggestions of items for inclusion and information about the material. Martin Fenton, Gavin Sutherland, Simon Harries, Ian Greaves, John Williams, Shaun Butcher and Steve Arnold spring immediately to mind, but there were many others. Thanks also to my longest-serving/suffering friend, Stephen Gilchrist, with whom I watched the likes of *Alexei Sayle's Stuff* and *A Bit of Fry and Laurie* on original transmission.

For programme information, I am indebted to Mark Lewisohn's *Radio Times Guide to TV Comedy* and the *Kaleidoscope British TV Comedy Research Guide 1936–2011*.

Both are the standard works in the field, and anybody attempting to research British TV comedy without them needs to have a word with themselves.

At home, my wife Susannah and my daughter Primrose coped admirably with teetering piles of DVDs and my dominance of the living-room TV. As usual, my half-Cavalier, half-Jack Russell research assistant Lyttelton bears full responsibility for any cock-ups.

Lowestoft, July 2012

# Credits

*The author and publisher wish to thank the following
for permission to use copyright material:*

*The Fall and Rise of Reginald Perrin*, 'Jimmy's Offer' © David Nobbs, 1977

*Fawlty Towers*, 'Communication Problems' © John Cleese and Connie Booth, 1979

*Butterflies*, 'Leaving' © Carla Lane, 1979

*End of Part One*, 'Nationtrite' © Andrew Marshall and David Renwick, 1980

*Not the Nine O'Clock News*, 'Constable Savage' © Not the Nine O'Clock News Ltd, 1980

*Yes Minister*, 'The Compassionate Society' © Antony Jay and Jonathan Lynn, 1981

*Only Fools and Horses*, 'A Touch of Glass' © John Sullivan, 1982

*The Les Dawson Show*, 'Cissie and Ada' © Terry Ravenscroft, 1983

*Chance in a Million*, 'Stuff of Dreams' © Richard Fegen and Andrew Norriss, 1984

*Victoria Wood: As Seen on TV*, 'Acorn Antiques' © Victoria Wood, 1986

*Blackadder the Third*, 'Dish and Dishonesty' © Rowan Atkinson, John Lloyd, Richard Curtis and Ben Elton, 1987

*A Bit of Fry and Laurie*, 'Cocoa' © Stephen Fry and Hugh Laurie, 1989

*Alexei Sayle's Stuff*, 'Democracy' © Alexei Sayle, Andrew Marshall and David Renwick, 1989

*Absolutely*, 'Stoneybridge Olympic bid' © Absolutely Productions Ltd, 1990

*French and Saunders*, 'Womanly World' © French and Saunders Productions Ltd, 1990

*One Foot in the Grave*, 'Timeless Time' © David Renwick, 1990

*Last of the Summer Wine*, 'Give Us a Lift' © Roy Clarke, 1991

*The Smell of Reeves and Mortimer*, 'Noel's Addicts' © Jim Moir and Bob Mortimer, 1993

*The Day Today*, 'War' © Christopher Morris, Armando Iannucci and the cast, 1994

*The Fast Show*, 'That's Amazing' © Simon Day, 1996

*Brass Eye*, 'Animals' © Chris Morris, Peter Baynham, Graham Linehan and Arthur Mathews, 1997

*I'm Alan Partridge*, 'Watership Alan' © Steve Coogan, Armando Iannucci and Peter Baynham, 1997

*Men Behaving Badly*, 'Stag Night' © Simon Nye, 1997

*Father Ted*, 'Are You Right There, Father Ted?' © Graham Linehan and Arthur Mathews, 1998

*The Royle Family*, 'Bills, Bills, Bills' © Caroline Aherne, Craig Cash and Henry Normal, 1998

*The League of Gentlemen*, 'The Road to Royston Vasey' © Reece Shearsmith, Mark Gatiss, Steve Pemberton and Jeremy Dyson, 1999

*Phoenix Nights*, 'Psykick' © Peter Kay, Dave Spikey and Neil Fitzmaurice, 2001

*The Office*, 'Appraisals' © Ricky Gervais and Stephen Merchant, 2002

*Bremner, Bird and Fortune*, 'Financial Adviser' © John Bird and John Fortune, 2007

*The Thick of It*, 'Nicola meets Malcolm' © Armando Iannucci and Tony Roche, 2009

*Outnumbered*, 'The Cold Caller' © Andy Hamilton & Guy Jenkin, 2011

# Illustrations